Testimonies

"It is from personal experience that I understand what this world and culture has in mind for young women today. The standard is mediocrity, powerlessness as a women and dimness in purpose. Laura's Bible study is the perfect, most needed antidote that I can think of. Her study inspires me as a woman to take bold, thrilling risks for God, to seek purpose in my existence and to pursue ambition with a brave heart! Her study is radically unique and refreshing in a day and age where women are daily placed by the media in roles that foster disrespect and depleted standards. Why is her study valuable? It is through the investigation of 1 Samuel that her readers begin to understand that they are placed on Earth for a purpose. There is no mistaking it. Their creator has a plan for them and with every ounce of His strength He will pursue and love them. This is a message that is rarely, if ever, taught to women my age. This study is intellectual, organized, action-oriented and intent in growing a generation to a place of significance and worth in the eyes of the Lord."
Carly Decker

"I think the most remarkable thing about Laura's study is that anyone can gain from it. Laura has mastered a nice balance in her approach to 1 Samuel. A new believer or immature Christian could benefit and be challenged by doing the study, and it is written clearly so that she can understand it. However, as a seminary student who has studied the Old Testament from many points of view, I still gained much from the study and was challenged in my walk with Christ. Furthermore, Laura is intensely personal with the study. She relates the Scriptures to her life through personal stories and anecdotes. God Almighty is an intensely personal God and he created us to relate to each other personally. Laura's study allows us to experience this aspect of God. I have told several of my friends, both at seminary and in other circles about this study, and many of them are interested in working through it."
Melanie Coffman
Denver Seminary student

"After reviewing this study, I found it to be profoundly insightful and encouraging. Many of the personal examples are very relevant for today's women, and the reader is certainly able to connect on an intimate level with the feelings and experiences of the author. There is a real need in Christian circles today for women to connect with one another in love and for women to understand that God is real and really interested in their lives. We are constantly bombarded by our society to believe that God doesn't care about us or our needs; that He is a distant and unknowable God. This study helps to combat this pervasive world view with many practical applications and anecdotes that touch the very heart of a woman. I believe that this study would be a wonderful tool for individual women, women's Bible studies, and church resources to reach out to women on a level that all women can relate to and that it will truly impact the world for Messiah. I know that it will be a true blessing to all the women who are fortunate enough to walk through the journey that it reveals."
Christina Frei
Director of J.O.T. homeschool cooperative
Children's Director

"This Bible study offers a refreshingly intimate experience with God, Jesus, and the Holy Spirit. It has been a blessing to do this study. Beholding Him has many assets, but one of the most important ones is that it presents the truth in a way that is easy to grasp."
Karin Kallendar
Sunday school teacher.

"During the course of my nine years with Campus Crusade, I have met few women with the influence that Laura has with women. She is a leader of leaders, and that comes from a deep, personal relationship with the Lord."
Jennifer Grant
Editor and Writer

"Laura Krokos has succeeded in writing a study that causes the reader to interact with the Word of God-and beyond a superficial level!-and to be motivated to change. Laura is passionate about God and His Word, and passionate about people and helping them grow."
Elizabeth Smith
Bear Valley Church adult Sunday school teacher.

"Laura Krokos is a spiritually gifted teacher who has the wisdom and insight to speak straight to the heart of women. This study will play a great role in many people's spiritual goals to hear God personally as it did for me this summer. It's dynamically presented and practically structured to speak to women at all spiritual levels so anyone will learn and grow. This encourages you to look to God to see your unique gifts and also to prayerfully and purposefully put those gifts into action in your everyday life."
Jackie Jones
Youth group leader and Sunday school teacher.

"Laura has been a huge influence in my life. She discipled me one summer of six weeks, and those six weeks changed my life forever. She truly loves and follows the Lord with everything that she is. She seeks him in every area of her life, encourages others to do so, shares Christ's love with every person she comes in contact with and has an amazing passion for the Lord's goal through this world"
Brittany Ralston
Campus Crusade for Christ staff member

"The study is well organized and provides great opportunities for growth even for mature Christians. Beholding Him is not a fleeting, feel good study, but rather a study with depth and with the intent of true transformation…I would strongly recommend it"
Dusti Austin
Bear Valley Church women's ministry leader.

"I have reviewed the Bible study written by Laura Krokos called Beholding Him, Becoming Missional. I see it as a valuable tool to be used in turning the hearts of believers toward their Savior through the study of His Word… Laura creatively asks questions and recommends activities that involved her readers in the study and challenges them to learn and apply the Truth of the Word to their lives-a much needed pursuit among all believers."
Judy Lemon
Grace Bible Church women's ministry leader.

"Laura brings great perspective on how this book applies to our lives today and shares illustrations of how God has moved in her own life. As I was working through the study, I found myself anticipating the next lesson and the next day."
Sandy Peterson
Grace Fellowship women's ministry leader
Colorado Christian University Benefits specialist

Beholding Him, Becoming Missional

Awakening to the Mission through the Study of 1 Samuel

Laura Krokos

All Scripture taken from the New Living Translation unless otherwise noted.
Library of Congress Control Number: 2010936108
Printed in the United States of America

To Asher, Uriah and Eden, may God grow you into passionate lovers of Him who give your all to know Him and make Him known. I pray that you will use your incredible stories and unique gifts to glorify Him and be examples of Daniel 11:32, "Those who know their God will display strength and take action."

Acknowledgments

I want to thank my husband Austin who is the man I respect most in life, who loves God with everything he has and is willing to risk his all for God's glory, my dad for telling me often that he loves me and is proud of me, my step dad for teaching me to do hard things, Carly Decker and Hannah Buckman for their encouragement which always came at a much needed time, Mary Ann Jeffreys and Kerry Bleikamp for helping me shape my words, Elizabeth Smith for helping me pull ideas together, Lois Hasselblad and Rocky Mountain Bible Church for providing a place to get away and write and Kaylee Sewell for using her gifts to film and edit the videos on the website.

But to my mom I owe my greatest thanks. Her entire life she has made sacrifices for me, encouraged me beyond description, inspired me, prayed for me and been generous toward me with everything she had. Without her encouragement and enablement, I would not have started writing or been able to finish. I am humbled to have received the benefits of being my mother's daughter.

Table of Contents

Introduction

"And all of us have had that veil removed so that we can be mirrors that brightly reflect the glory of the Lord. And as the Spirit of the Lord works within us, we become more and more like him and reflect his glory even more" (2 Corinthians 3:18). Just as the moon reflects the sun affecting the earth in life altering ways, we too reflect what our heart is set on; what we are gazing at. I love the scene in *Runaway Bride* where Julia Roberts playing Maggie Carpenter, is being coached by her ex-fiancé, Bob, on keeping her eyes fixed on Richard Gere, playing Graham, as she walks down the isle. As she walks down the isle with her eyes fixed on her latest fiancé, she is able to keep moving forward through her fear, step by step. A camera flashes, distracting her. She takes her eyes off Graham and then her fears overtake her, and once again she runs. What a great picture of us as we have our eyes fixed on Christ, the Author and Perfecter of our faith. When our hearts are fixed on Him, we are able to confidently move forward in what He has called us to, even if it is small steps. But the minute we take our eyes of Him, we get distracted and end up running from what He desires for us, which also happens to be the very best thing for us.

First Samuel is packed full of stories of people who will encourage you to bravely take steps of faith for God's glory. My deep hope for this study is that Your intimacy with the Lord will grow as a result of beholding Him, and as you know Him more, you will be moved to action as Daniel 11:32 describes "those who know their God will display strength and take action."

A friend of mine is leading a team of college students on a mission's trip in India as I type this. I got an email from her yesterday sharing an experience they had that I would love to share with you. The adventure of taking risks for God is a beautiful gift from Him, that not only blesses us by seeing Him come through for us, but also blesses others by getting to hear the story of God showing Himself to be great and mighty. Because of Emily's willingness to go and take students to a very poor, dirty and despised country, to tell people about Jesus, we get the benefit of hearing how God has already shown Himself as Redeemer. In one day this is the glimpse of God they got.

> This afternoon we went to see some old friends of mine at the Aruna Project in the red-light district of Mumbai. The Aruna Project continues to amaze me! The work they are doing is incredible! This particular red-light district has over 40,000 sex-slaves and the Aruna staff go everyday into the brothels to tell the women, the pimps, and the madams about Jesus and help rescue the women out of this trade! Many of the staff are former prostitutes themselves--many of them HIV positive--two of the staff I mentioned after my trip in December, are a mother and her son. Mom was a prostitute and she raised her son in the brothels. As he got older he eventually became a pimp and pimped out his own mother. Both mom and son have given their lives to Christ and go back into the brothels every day to help others come out of this work.

> While half of the group prayer-walked this part of the red-light district, the other half of our group visited another part. They split into pairs and each pair went with one Aruna staff on visitations to all different brothels where the women haven't been completely "broken" enough by the pimps to be allowed to stand on the streets. Instead they are held captive inside these places. It's amazing that the Aruna staff are even allowed inside to visit and pray with the prostitutes. They walked into these dark buildings, up and down dark staircases, brushing past men who are either customers or working to keep the women

Captive inside the brothels. They visited with the prostitutes, met their children, talked with them, and prayed with them.

Emily shared with the students an excerpt from Shattered Dreams by Larry Crabb which related to what God was teaching her so far on the trip. "How then shall we live? What can we do? How are we to find hope when God's kindness hurts, when bad things happen that God could have prevented? …As we prepare to answer these questions, we must lay down a beginning principle: If we are to discover a hope that continues through shattered dreams, that hope must be available to sick people, poor people, lonely people, unnoticed people. And it must be the same hope we offer to healthy, rich people with lots of friends and talent. We must discover a hope that thrives when dreams shatter, when sickness advances and poverty worsens and loneliness deepens and obscurity continues, the same hope that anchors us to God when dreams do come true."

She told them that she feels "that in the States it is so easy for me to twist in my mind who God is, what His goodness is like, and what hoping in Him means. I've perverted the Gospel to mean what I want it to mean. But this god I've created in my head does not hold up, when so many "dreams shatter" of what life is like and how broken this world really is. I have to figure out who God really is and the true hope that He offers us, each street kid, amputee, and prostitute."

I pray this study will be used by the Holy Spirit in your life to remove your false and low thought of Him and replace them with the beautiful and glorious truth of who He is and what He is like and as a result make you women that displays strength and takes action! Oh, that we would be women as John Piper describes as coronary Christians, "Oh for coronary Christians! Christians committed to great causes, not great comforts. I plead with you to dream a dream that is bigger than you and your families and your churches. Un-deify the American family, and say boldly that our children are not our cause; they are given to us to train for a cause."[1]

A few tips as you go through this study:

1. There are many uncommon and even hard to pronounce names in First Samuel. Don't let this shake you. You are not required to be a specialist in Hebrew name pronouncing. You have freedom to pronounce the names however you would like and keep reading.

2. The website **www.BeholdingHimBecomingMissional.com** will be referred to a lot. You do not have to go to the website when directed to, but my hope is that it will enhance the study for you.

3. There are group discussion questions at the back of the study on page 234. If you are an internal processor, it may help to glance at these so you can be prepared to share your thoughts, feelings and insights with the group.

4. This will be a challenging study. If a week comes and you are not able to get to all the verses, show yourself grace. Do what you can and that is great!

5. And finally, you will get the most internal change from this study when you put your heart out there and be vulnerable with your group. The most growth will take place when you share hard things with the group and see that the women in the group still accept and love you. This study is not intended to be an intellectual assent, but a tool used to help hearts connect and be moved to action.

Excited to be on this journey with you,

Laura

---

1   Piper, John (2004). *Life is a Vapor*. Sisters, Oregon: Multnomah Publishers.

Pursuing

Week 1

Day 1

Page Jumpers

Read 1 Samuel 1:1-28

List things that jump off the page (verses, ideas or thoughts that stand out to you):

- the Lord is in controll of Hannah's womb
- "pouring out my soul"
-

Cloud of Witnesses

During World War II, Corrie and Betsie Ten Boom were arrested and shuffled from one prison to the next for hiding Jews in their home. They ended up at Ravensbruck, one of the worst concentration camps in Nazi Germany. The 35,000 women at this work camp were daily brutalized at the hands of the guards. In the book, *The Hiding Place*, Corrie vividly describes her and Betsie's arrival at Ravensbruck. When they first walked into what would become their living quarters, they immediately were overcome by the smell of backed-up sewers and soiled bedding. As they walked through the room piled with platforms of bedding stacked to the ceiling, they came to a small platform where they would sleep, crowded next to many other women. As they climbed over the platforms to get to their own, they began to feel pinching on their legs. The bunk house was infested with fleas. Horrified at the conditions they would have to endure, Corrie looked at her sister and asked "Betsie, how can we live in such a place?" Betsie turned to the Lord with that question. She remembered a verse in 1 Thessalonians and excitedly explained to Corrie that the Lord had given them the answer: "To give thanks in all circumstances for this is God's will." Obedient, they thanked God for everything, even the fleas. As the days passed, Betsie and Corrie read the Bible to a growing group of women in their barracks twice a day, and many came to know Christ personally. Later they discovered the reason for this amazing opportunity: the guards would not enter the barracks for fear of the fleas.

Betsie went to be with the Lord at the age of 49, one week before Corrie was released and permitted to return home. In 1959, Corrie discovered her release was due to a clerical error. One week after her release, all the women her age were killed. Like Hannah in the Old Testament, Betsie Ten

Boom is an example of an incredible woman who was authentic in her relationship with God, who believed what the Scriptures said about Him was true, and who gave thanks in all circumstances.

This week I pray that through God's Holy Spirit we are able to take our whole hearts before God in prayer, believing and acting on what we know is true about Him even though we may not see or feel it, and learn to give thanks in all circumstances.

Here Am I

Spend some time writing out a prayer asking God to speak to you this week as we look at how Hannah took her whole heart to the Lord, was honest about who she really was, believing and acting on what was true about God and was an example of living with an attitude of thankfulness.

Pursuing

Week 1

Day 2

Jehovah, the self-existent living One, the One Who will always be personal and absolute: we want to relate to You more honestly and more deeply. Please enable us to hear from You, and to respond appropriately and whole-heartedly.

Eyes to See

Read 1 Samuel 1:1-28 again.

> *How often would the family travel to Shiloh and why did they go there?

> *How would you describe the journey to Shiloh? (How far away, who went... Try to picture it and think of what the atmosphere would be like emotionally, physically, mentally...)

> *Describe what would happen with Hannah and Peninnah at Shiloh.

> ***Shiloh**-Fifteen miles from Ramah, a two-day journey for a family. Bible Background Commentary 282*
>
> ***Feast of Tabernacles**- The law called for three annual pilgrimages. The Feast of Tabernacles was one of them, also known as Feast of Booths or Feast of Ingathering. It celebrated God's protection and guidance in the wilderness (the Exodus) and was a renewing of commitment to God and trust in His guidance and protection. It involved the whole family and taught family members of all ages about God's nature and what He had done for them. NASB Life Application Study Bible Pg. 205*
>
> ***Barrenness**- In Hannah's day being barren was viewed as punishment from God. A woman who was barren was often ostracized or given lower status and often felt embarrassed and ashamed. Bible Background Commentary Pg. 281*

*What is Elkanah like and what leads you to think this?

*What are some characteristics you would use to describe Hannah?

*Does Peninnah remind you of anyone you know? (They can remain nameless.) How would you describe Peninnah?

Ears to Hear

Hannah turned to the Lord and took her whole heart to Him, being honest about what she really thought and felt.

Chapter 1 gives us a good framework to help us understand what Hannah may have been facing and feeling. Imagine if you were in Hannah's situation, wanting something year after year and not experiencing even a glimmer of hope of your situation ever changing. Envision having someone you live with continually get what you want and then rubbing it in your face. Picture not just once in a while, but daily seeing another have and perhaps take advantage of the gift they have been given. Imagine facing the continual thoughts and comments that you don't measure up or fit into the social circles, facing thoughts that you have no value, purpose or anything to contribute to the world. Could she also have experienced the well-meaning but hurtful advice of others? Could she have felt that God was punishing her or was mad at her? Maybe she felt confusion and self-pity, perhaps questioning why her husband still loved her even though she couldn't give him a living legacy but instead caused him embarrassment in the community. Did she wonder why he even stuck with her when all the other men divorced their wives that were barren? Why did he remain lovingly devoted and even give her special treatment despite what others thought? On top of all of this, when she went to the temple, her spiritual authority totally misunderstood her, assuming things about her and her heart that were not true.

I would imagine most of us have experienced some of these feelings at one point. But what did we do with our thoughts and feelings? Did we suppress them and hope they would go away? Did we spend our thought life complaining about them? Did we become bitter and hopeless? Did we end up with a critical outlook on life? Or did we turn to the Lord like Hannah? Did we bring our deepest desires to God and let Him give us rest?

Having a heart like Hannah's is not easy. She was vulnerable in telling God and others what her real desires were. As I was growing up and my mom and I went shopping I would see something I wanted and would think *how cute*. Then when I looked at the price tag and knew I couldn't have it, jokingly I would say, "Oh, that is ugly, I don't want that anyway." God showed me that I naturally can do this with Him, too. As an example, my husband Austin and I tried to have a baby for three years. During this time I went to God saying, "Please give us kids," but I wouldn't continue asking just in case He said no. This way I would have a way out, having the attitude, "I didn't really want that anyway." I would "ask" and maybe step out and take some action to "seek" by praying a little bit more and trying to learn how to really get pregnant. But I would never "knock". I would never persist, just in case He didn't open the door. I would intellectually approach God but leave my real desires securely hidden. I was so afraid to take my heart and desires to God for fear that He would let me down. I was fearful that I would be crushed and abandoned by my God. I was afraid that instead of experiencing His love for me, I would see Him ignore me and brush me off. As God revealed this to me I began to "knock," to really persist in prayer and take steps of faith in new directions. God did come through with miracle after miracle to provide us with our son, Asher Steven Krokos. His first name means "happy," his middle name is my father's name, and his initials are a reminder that we ASKed and God provided.

How beautiful that when the disciples asked Jesus to teach them to pray, He emphasized persistence, coming to Him completely, not just nonchalantly. God's desire is to have all of our desires, passions, hopes, and expectations taken to Him, to connect with Him on the most real level of who we are.

Heart to Understand

"Then Jesus left Galilee and went north to the region of Tyre and Sidon. A Gentile woman who lived there came to Him, pleading, 'Have mercy on me, O Lord, Son of David! For my daughter is possessed by a demon that torments her severely.' But Jesus gave her no reply, not even a word. Then His disciples urged Him to send her away. 'Tell her to go away,' they said. 'She is bothering us with all her begging.' Then Jesus said to the woman, 'I was sent only to help God's lost sheep-the people of Israel.' But she came and worshiped Him, pleading again, 'Lord, help me!' Jesus responded, 'It isn't right to take food from the children and throw it to the dogs.' She replied, 'That's true, Lord, but even dogs are allowed to eat the scraps that fall beneath their masters' table.' 'Dear woman,' Jesus said to her, 'your faith is great. Your request is granted.' And her daughter was instantly healed" (Matthew 15:21-28).

Here we see a beautiful picture of how Jesus provoked this woman to share her heart with Him. He does so in some very unusual ways. He pretends to ignore her, but she persists. He tells his disciples so she could overhear how He was sent to the Jews, but she persists even more bowing herself before Him. Jesus continues this dance of drawing her to pursue Him. She follows, withholding nothing of her heart (in front of many intimidating people no less). He continues this process and finally ends by praising her for her faith! I just keep thinking of kids where the boy likes the girl and tries to woo her into chasing him. This is God's heart for us: a passionate love that doesn't settle for mediocrity.

*If you were this woman, how far would you (showing from your past experiences) persevere in letting Jesus know your heart?

5

*In your prayer life, to what extent do you share your heart with our Lord? Think of some specific examples. The last time you spent time with the Lord, what did you talk about?

*What are some of your deep hopes and desires? Have you talked to God about them? Was it with your whole heart or did you hold back at all?

*What fears produce resistance to letting Jesus know your deep longings?

*In considering your specific fears, find 1-3 related verses in Scripture that remind you of what is true about God.

-

-

-

*In seeing more of your tendency to hide your heart from God, how does this affect your view of Jesus and what He did on the cross?

*How is God leading you to respond to Him? Take some time to act on it.

"May we have no higher goal than to see someone think more highly of our Father, our King." Max Lucado

Pursuing

Week 1

Day 3

Jehovah-Rapha, God Who heals, our hearts are so far from being totally open and vulnerable with You. We desire intimacy with You and need You to heal our broken hearts that are sometimes reluctant in turning to You. Through Your Spirit empower us to be willing to be real with You.

It seems that Hannah really knows the Lord. She went to Him in her distress as we observed on day 2, knowing His concern and care for her and His ability to take her distress away. She called Him, "Lord of Hosts," which emphasized not only His supreme personal power but also His power over everything in the material and spiritual universe. She knew that He could still hear her even though she didn't speak out loud, and she *continued* praying.

Eyes to See

Read 1 Samuel 1:1-28 again.

*When Hannah took her heart to the Lord, what happened?

*What does this help you understand about God's work in individual lives?

*Why was Hannah no longer anxious?

*What does Psalm 73 show us about changes in our perspective? Is this similar to Hannah in anyway? Why or why not?

As we take all we are to God, delighting in Who He is, He brings our true desires to surface. "He gives us the desire of our hearts" (Psalm 37:4). Hannah entered the sanctuary of God, pouring out her whole heart to Him, and as she did her emotions and thoughts were moved to dedicate her answer to prayer baby to Him.

Ears to Hear
When Hannah believed what was true about God and acted on that truth, her emotions followed.

Our feelings are a gift from God though it may not always feel like it. Our emotions allow us to know God more. They give us expression and experience of our God. They allow us to understand a little more of what Jesus must have felt, being rejected by those He ministered to and being betrayed by a friend. But He also experienced the joy of seeing new life born and sharing great affection with close friends. As with many things in life it is very easy to make emotions the center of our existence and to live in such a way that we experience never-ending good emotions and never bad. How easy it is to idolize our emotions and make it our purpose in life to be happy, to let them be the ultimate authority of what we do with our time and attitude. If Hannah had been idolizing her emotions, her attitude would not have been that of pouring out her heart to the Lord and leaving with a face that was no longer sad but rather thankful. Instead she would have been critical, blaming and bitter.

In contrast to relying on our emotions as the authority in life, believing what is true about God is like gazing at His glory and being transformed to look more like what we see (see 2 Corinthians 3:18). This requires repeatedly reminding ourselves of what is true about God regardless of how we feel and regardless of what our circumstances look like. Such incredible things are made manifest in our lives as we increase in our understanding of Who God really is. *Grace* and *peace* be yours in abundance through *the knowledge of God and of Jesus our Lord*. His divine power has given us everything we need for a godly life *through the knowledge of Him* Who called us by His own glory and goodness. Through these He has given us His very great and precious promises, so that through them you may participate in the divine nature, having escaped the corruption in the world caused by evil desires. (2 Peter 1:2-4 TNIV, emphasis is mine)

How easy it is to take advantage of the fact that here in America we have been given a great foundation of what God is like. A few years back I spent some time in Nepal. A friend and I got to explain the gospel to a Nepalese man named Ram. He recognized that he was guilty before God for not being perfect and surrendered his life to Jesus, receiving forgiveness. He asked us to come to his village to tell his family about Christ. So we agreed and began the exciting and sometimes terrifying journey to his village. Our 24-hour journey started on a bus bursting with people, luggage and chickens. During the bus ride a strange Nepalese lady who was a complete stranger got tired and rested her head on my lap as if that were totally normal. We continued through an extremely windy mountain pass with a huge drop off on one side of the road, going what seemed to me 70 mph until we came to a halt for quite some time. The road had washed away and they had to rebuild it quickly. We then became the "guinea pig" bus to test the newly built road. We got off at the end of the road and our 22-mile uphill trek began.

At the time I thought I was in shape, but boy was I wrong! It was like walking up stairs wearing a giant backpack. I could only take a few steps without having to stop for a breath. Ram, who was much smaller than I, started carrying my backpack, and we began a bit quicker pace. On our walk up this 12,000-14,000-foot mountain and over a long wooden bridge that you would expect to see in an Indiana Jones movie, we would see men carrying couches and fridges on their backs. Most of my time on the hike was spend in shock. At one point we talked about praying. Ram had no idea what prayer was, so we told him it was just talking to God. So he did. He began to describe to God where we were, what we were doing, what the day was like and so on. Later I realized that Ram had no idea that God knew everything. What a huge understanding of God that I totally took for granted. But the truth is, many people in other countries have no understanding of God at all. The more interesting thing is that in the United States though we are greatly blessed with a lot of knowledge of Who God is, we can sometimes act just like Ram, thinking God knows nothing of our situation and is powerless to do anything about it.

Heart to Understand

In Bill Bright's book, *GOD: Discover His Character,* he says, "I am more convinced than ever that there is nothing more important to teach another believer than who God is, what He is like and why or how He does what He does. In fact, everything about our lives-our attitudes, motives, desires, actions, and even our words-is influenced by our view of God. Whether our problems are financial, moral, or emotional, whether we are tempted by lust, worry, anger, or insecurity, our behavior reflects our beliefs about God. What we believe to be true about God's character affects our friendships, our work and leisure activities, the types of literature we read, and even the music to which we listen." A.W. Tozer wrote, "The low view of God entertained almost universally among Christians is the cause of a hundred lesser evils everywhere among us. With our loss of the sense of majesty has come the further loss of religious awe and the consciousness of the divine presence...It is impossible to keep our moral practices sound and our inward attitudes right while our idea of God is erroneous or inadequate. If we would bring back spiritual power to our lives, we must begin to think of God more nearly as He is."[2]

> *Think of a couple of recent circumstances you have faced. What was your mental and emotional response? What does it show you that you were/are believing about God?

> *God's Word is an incredible gift He has given us to reveal Himself. He longs to help us see, know and understand Him more through it. What does your quantity and quality time in the Word show you that you believe about God?

---

2   Tozer, A.W. (1978). *The Knowledge of the Holy: The Attributes of God: Their Meaning in the Christian Life.* New York, NY: Harper Collins Publishers

*If someone were to ask you, "How do I live my life believing what is true about God instead of living by my feelings and circumstances?" what would you say to them?

*How can you become quicker to believe what's true about God in every situation you face?

Find a place alone where you can get comfortable. Through prayer, ask God to reveal Himself to you. List some circumstances in your life at this moment and think through what is true about God in regards to these circumstances.

Here is a helpful resource to remind us what is true about God. Of these attributes, are there any qualities of God that strike you or relate to your current circumstance? Consider challenging yourself to pick a verse describing that attribute of God and commit it to memory.

Some of God's Attributes

Holy (1 Peter 1:16)
Just (Zechariah 9:9)
Righteous (Psalm 7:9; Psalm 119:172; Romans 3:21-22)
Faithful (Deuteronomy 7:9; 1 Corinthians 1:9)
The One Who will never fail you (Deuteronomy 31:6; Joshua 1:5)
The One Who will never leave you (Hebrews 13:5)
Sovereign (1 Timothy1:17, Jeremiah 10:10)
The One Who has the authority to control all things (Matthew 28:18)
The One Who has the power to control all things (Job 42:2; Colossians 1:16-18,)
The One Who is able to make you adequate (John 15:5; 2 Timothy 3:17)
The One Who made you (Genesis 1:26-31)
The One Who provides (Genesis 22:9-14; Matthew 6:33)
The One Who protects (Psalm 60:12; Psalm 62:2)
The giver of wisdom (James 1:5)
The source of knowledge and truth (1 Samuel 2:3; 2 Chronicles 1:11-12; John 14:26; John 17:17)
The One Who can turn the king's heart where He wants (Proverbs 21:1)
Consistent (Romans 3:22, Romans 10:11-13)
Never changing (Hebrews 13:8 James 1:17)
The One Who can and will make you complete (Colossians 2:10; 1 Thessalonians 5:23-24, Jude 24)
All knowing (Psalm 139:1-4; Hebrews 4:13; 1 John 3:20)
Everywhere, always (Psalm 139:7-12; Jeremiah 23:23-24)
The One Who created everything (Genesis 1; Acts 17:24; Colossians 1:16)
The One Who holds all things together (Colossians 1:17)
The One Who forgives (Psalm 103:12; Colossians 2:13; 1 John 1:9)

The One Who gives second chances (Jeremiah 29:12-14; Hosea 14:1-7; Acts 9:1-6,15; 1 John 1:9))
The One Who makes success possible (2 Corinthians 3:5; 2 Corinthians 9:8; Philippians 4:11)
The One Who changes hearts not just actions (2 Corinthians 5:16-17; Galatians 5:22-23)
True Love (1 John 4:16)
The One Who accepts/approves you (Romans 12:1)
The Authority over even evil (Job 1; John 16:33; Colossians 2:10; 1 John 4:4)
The One Who cares (1 Peter 5:7; Psalm 8:4)
The One Who wants what is best for you (Jeremiah 29:11; Rom 8:28)
The One Who has authority over death (John 11:21-45)

Take a few minutes to observe your surroundings and jot down what you see. Then take some time to think through each individual observation and what it shows you about Who God is For His invisible attributes, namely, His eternal power and divine nature, have been clearly perceived, ever since the creation of the world, in the things that have been made. (Romans 1:20) Jot down what you see and what it can show you about what God is like and how He chooses to reveal Himself to us.

Pursuing

Week 1

Day 4

Jehovah-M'Kaddesh, the One Who sanctifies. We are in need, and desire for You to make us more like You. As we fix our eyes on You, the Author and Perfector of our faith, please transform us to reflect You more and more. We surrender our wandering and distracted minds and choose to connect with You. Meet us here, Lord.

On day 3 we talked about how believing what's true about God affects everything about us, especially our attitude and feelings. In *It's Not About Me*, Max Lucado describes Moses' prayer to see God's glory as "Flex your biceps. Let me see the S on your chest. Your preeminence. Your heart-stopping, ground-shaking extra-spectacularness. Would you stun me with your strength? Numb me with your wisdom? Steal my breath with a brush of yours?" And our great God answers with a Yes! He then, in Exodus 34:6-8, gives Moses a glimpse of Who He is, revealing Himself to him. "The Lord passed before him and proclaimed, The Lord, the Lord, a God merciful and gracious, slow to anger, and abounding in steadfast love and faithfulness, keeping steadfast love for thousands, forgiving iniquity and transgressions in, but Who will by no means clear the guilty, visiting the iniquity of the fathers on the children and the children's children, to the third and fourth generation and Moses quickly bowed his head toward the earth and worshiped." Seeing Who God truly is brings us to an attitude of worship, an attitude of praise.

Eyes to See

Read 1 Samuel 2:1-11

*After Hannah dedicated her son to the Lord by giving Him up, describe her attitude, thoughts and feelings.

*What truth/truths of God is she praising Him for?

*Which of these truths have you seen in your life?

Take some time to adore Your Father using His Word. Jot down verses that talk of how awesome God is and then read them out loud. If not many come to mind, use the ones written below.

Adoring our God motivates us toward thankfulness. Write out the following verses in your own words:

Psalm 79:13

Psalm 118:1

What insights about giving thanks do these verses give?

Philippians 4:6

Ephesians 5:20

Colossians 3:17

1 Thessalonians 5:18

Ears to Hear

God's will is for us to live thankful lives.

The tendency for me when I read that I am to be thankful in all things is to think that I can only be thankful for what is good or that I have to conjure up some excitement about being happy for some hard situation. But what God has helped me understand is that nothing besides Him and His Word is all good and nothing except the Deceiver is all bad. So in my circumstances, though at times it feels like they are all bad, there is something good I can thank Him for. There are also good things coming from any circumstance that I can thank Him for.

Joni Eareckson Tada broke her neck in a diving accident and became paralyzed. She is now a speaker, writer, and painter. She is an amazing example of a woman who is living out God's will to live a thankful life. Listen to her perspective on her life. "Years ago, when I began to see the power of God's Word applied to my own experience in a wheelchair, I wrote a mission statement for my life: 'I want to be God's best audiovisual aid of how His power shows up best in weakness.' I believe that what I have learned in my own paralysis is being passed on to thousands of other disabled people and their family members through Joni and Friends. That's wonderful mission for life! Heaven is the bottom line for any Christian. Everything I do here on earth, every godly response to every trial has a direct bearing on my capacity for joy, worship, and service in heaven. I don't want to get to heaven, look in my rear view mirror and think, 'Why did I waste my hardships?!' In heaven, we will finally see how our suffering on earth will serve us in eternity, gaining for us an eternal reward that far outweighs the inconvenience of pain. Five minutes in heaven will be worth it all."

Heart to Understand

From the time you and I get up in the morning till we go to bed there are plenty of opportunities to express a critical, discontented heart. Some days I can look back over the whole day and see that my heart's criticalness grew as I fed it by dwelling on it or verbalizing it. It's like the analogy of the dogs: Two dogs get in a fight-one whose owner fed it every day for the past month and the other that is a street dog that hasn't eaten in a week. Of course the dog that was fed is going to win the fight. The same is true with our critical and negative attitude. When we feed it by complaining in thought or word it grows. Not only does that affect us individually but also affects those around us. Through the enablement of the Holy Spirit, cultivating a thankful heart will result in thankful words. So let's practice thankfulness.

*What are some material blessings God has provided for you?

*What are some material things God has not given to you right now?

*What good is there in not having these right now?

Spend some time thanking God for the things you have written above.

*List some spiritual blessings God has given you. (If you need help getting started, look at Ephesians Chapter 1)

Thank God for these spiritual blessings and the implications they have in your life.

> *Make a list of your family members and by their name write the qualities you appreciate about them.

> *Write down other individuals who have encouraged, inspired or challenged you.

Spend some time expressing your thanks to the Lord for these people and the influence they have had in your life.

> *As you look around at your surroundings, what are some things you have never thanked God for? Of those things, write down why you could be thankful for them.

Perhaps something came up in your mind or heart that is very difficult to be thankful for. John 15:5 tells us that apart from Christ, we can do nothing. This is true even in regards to giving Him the thanks and praise He is worthy of. But as we ask for the Holy Spirit to enable and empower us, we are able to live out the heart of Christ.

Lord, please enable us to be praisers of You and to give You thanks in all things as You desire. Continually show us how to be thankful in all things.

Pursuing

Week 1

Day 5

Jehovah-Tsidkenu, God our righteousness. You have given us such an incredible gift of Your Son, Who laid down His life on the cross so we could be forgiven for not being perfect, giving us the privilege of standing right before You. Thank You for choosing to love us sacrificially when we did not deserve it. We are grateful to be called Your children and want to live as ones bought with a price.

Reflecting on the week:

1. Hannah took her whole heart to the Lord and was honest about what she really thought and felt.

2. When she believed what was true about God and acted on that truth, her emotions followed.

3. God's will is for us to live thankful lives.

Each of these things involves prayer, so today your time is going to be spent connecting with the Lord through a prayer experience.

Individual Prayer Experience:

You will need to take a few minutes to gather a few things: some personal photos (preferably from the last 6 months to a year), a dark marker, and some rocks (big enough to write on, but small enough to carry).

Read Joshua 3:14-4:24
We have the incredible gift of talking about what God has done for us, sharing with others how He has come through for us. Spend some time looking through your photos and asking God to show you

how He has shown Himself in your life. When things come to your mind write on one side of your rock what He did and on the other side what that shows you to be true about Him. Take a prolonged period of time to do this. When you can't possibly think of anything else spend some time telling the Lord how you feel about each act He has done.

Empowering

Week 2

Day 1

King, Creator and Sustainer, what an incredible gift we have to meet with You today, to have time to hear from You and to be changed by You. What an awesome God You are to step into our lives and to be so intimately acquainted with all our ways. This week please make us people who would live dependent and surrendered to You, and who get to see and understand You more as a result.

Page Jumpers

Read 1 Samuel 2:1-36
List things that jump off the page (verses that stand out to you):

-
-
-
-

Cloud of Witnesses

Log onto www.BeholdingHimBecomingMissional.com and follow the link to a video under week 2.

This week we are going to see how:

1. We are desperate for the Lord's empowerment.

2. God is able to empower us.

3. God directs and empowers us as we submit to and depend on Him.

Here Am I

To prepare our heart to hear from the Lord this week, consider the questions below.

*If someone asked you what the Spirit-filled life is, how would you respond?

*How often do you think you manifest the Spirit-filled life? How do you know?

Lord, we want to humbly come to You with teachable hearts seeing and understanding You in a fuller way. Where there is resistance to You in regards to letting You live Your life through us please soften us. Make us people consumed with really knowing You to the depths of who we are. Give us a glimpse of how and why You want us to know You. Lord, give us pure and sensitive hearts that are quick to relinquish our rights. Make us to be people quick to depend on Your enablement instead of our own. Write on our hearts how desperately we need Your ability and give us a passion to live our time here on earth by the strength of the Holy Spirit. Lord, make us to be people who clearly hear and are confident in knowing Your voice.

Empowering

Week 2

Day 2

Giver of Life and all that is good, what an honor it is to get to meet with You today. What a privilege to get to read Your Word. Thank You for putting us in a country where Your Word is so accessible. Thank You for Your Spirit Who enlightens our minds and teaches what we do not know. Thank You for Your promise that when we call out to You, You will answer us. We do call out to You now and ask that You would let us understand more than we currently do what it means to be empowered by Your Spirit. Help us lay down our pride and arrogance that makes us think we have nothing else to learn. Wow us, Lord, with how much we need You.

Eyes to See

Read 1 Samuel 2:1-36

> "The normal practice at Shiloh was for the priest to receive whichever part came up from the boiling pot on the end of the fork. Eli's sons insisted on taking what they wanted, when they wanted it. Their ritual offenses came in three areas: (1) their selection of the best parts for themselves; (2) their preference for the meat being roasted rather than boiled; and (3) their refusal to yield the fat for burning on the altar." *The IVP Bible Background Commentary Old Testament*

*Explain what Eli's sons were doing.

*Can you think of anything Hophni and Phinehas' actions can be compared to in our day and culture?

*How would you feel if you were the person coming to give a sacrifice? How would you respond to the priests?

*How long was it before Eli got involved in dealing with his sons' sins? What did God think about this?

*How would you describe Eli at this point in his life?

Ears to Hear

For ten years of my Christian life I truly believed I could live the Christian life if I just tried hard enough. I approached the Bible as a book of do's and don'ts. I remember one time when I was pretty irritated at God because of how He organized the Bible. I could not understand why He didn't just make a huge long list for me, making it easier to live the Christian life. I thought that if I had this list of everything I should do and everything I shouldn't do, then I would be the best Christian to ever walk the planet. Why? Because I would know what was expected of me, and I believed that if I just knew, then of course I could do it.

I approached the do's and don'ts of God as the Pharisees did, acknowledging what needed to be done and trying to get it done in my own strength, not relying on the Holy Spirit. As this misunderstanding of how to live the Christian life grew, I made a chart for myself in hopes that it would help me be a perfect Christian. At the end of the day I would turn my little arrow poked into a paper plate to the degree I was a good Christian. My thought was that as I got into this habit, my external motivator would make me a better and better Christian. As I tell you this story now, I am a bit embarrassed by my pride and arrogance.

I do believe my motives and desires were to be pleasing to the Lord but that is not the problem. I also knew that I was truly accepted by my Father regardless of my actions, but I didn't trust Him to bring about the transformation in my heart. Rather, I took on the responsibility of sanctifying (being made more like Christ) myself. I believed that it was by grace that God has rescued me from hell, but it was by my effort and trying really hard that I lived the good Christian life.

Write out the verses below in your own words.

Galatians 3:3
How foolish can you be? After starting your Christian lives in the Spirit, why are you now trying to become perfect by your own human effort?

Romans 3:20
For no one can ever be made right with God by doing what the law commands. The law simply shows us how sinful we are.

God in His faithfulness and generosity stepped in and rescued me from my unbelief and self-sufficiency. Through a series of events and steps of faith, I found myself on a mission trip in Katmandu, Nepal. As I would meet with Him in the morning, He would open up His Word to me like I had never understood it before, teaching me about living the Spirit-filled life. I would share what I was learning with the team leaders and my friends, and they would just sit staring at me with open mouths. I still wonder to this day what they were thinking.

As I returned home, the transition was pretty tough. Each time I heard a sermon it would end with the dos and don'ts to be a good Christian. The action points were good, but the power source was not talked about. Each time I was left thinking, *I just need to try harder, I just need to do these three things*. After hearing this week after week, I began to doubt what the Lord had taught me in Nepal through His Word. It was pretty radical, I thought, that we couldn't do anything in our own strength and that life wasn't about trying real hard.

But before I totally threw out my understanding, God brought people and authors into my life who said the exact things that the Lord had spoken to me in Nepal. One of those people was Russ Akins, the director of Master Plan Ministries in Durango, Colorado. When I returned from Nepal, I started working with a college ministry that was associated with Campus Crusade for Christ. Russ was a godly man who talked about the Spirit-filled life more than anyone I had ever met. He had worked with Campus Crusade for twenty years and then started Master Plan and had been leading it for fifteen years. God had given me an incredible gift of getting to learn from Russ. Not a week would go by that he wouldn't bring everything back to being directed and empowered by the Holy Spirit.

No matter how long we have been Christians, and no matter where we have come from or what positions the Lord has given us, **we truly are desperate for the Lord's empowerment.** Why? Because we are far worse than we ever dared imagine.

There is nothing you and I are not capable of doing. Murder and adultery seem like the "biggies" in our culture. So let's use those as an example. In Matthew 5:21, 27-28, Jesus addresses these "biggies" as well.
"You have heard that our ancestors were told, 'You must not murder. If you commit murder, you are subject to judgment.' But I say, if you are even angry with someone, you are subject to judgment... You have heard the commandment that says, 'You must not commit adultery.' But I say, anyone who even looks at a woman with lust has already committed adultery with her in his heart."

*What do you hear Jesus saying?

The root of anger and lust is already in our hearts and given enough time and exposure to temptation, we would walk it out to the degree of committing murder and murder. This is what we truly are capable of. If we live our lives as though we aren't that bad and would never do anything "that bad," then why would we live dependent on God's strength instead of our own? Why would we need Him, if we had it covered ourselves?

> *Have you ever realized that you are capable of murder and adultery? What thoughts and feelings are aroused as you think about this?

Not only are we in desperate need of Him because we are capable of doing what we never thought possible, but also because we can't do anything of eternal value apart from Him. We can't conjure up great motives, unconditional love, joy, peace, patience, kindness, goodness, faithfulness, gentleness, and self-control apart from the Holy Spirit.

> *Using a dictionary or thesaurus, use other words to describe the fruit of the Spirit.

> *Looking at the words above and realizing that those are only results that come from the empowerment of the Holy Spirit, do you have any new insights?

What does God say to us in the verses below about our ability apart from Him?

John 15:5

2 Corinthians 3:5

Colossians 1:29

Philippians 4:13

Heart to Understand

It is pretty easy to look at Hophni, Phinehas and Eli and think, "*Come on guys, get it together. What the heck were you thinking? That is pretty lame that you would live so selfishly. You're supposed to be the leaders*". It is so easy to point the finger at others instead of realizing that you and I are just as desperate for a Savior and Sanctifier as they are.

The fruit of the Spirit is like a temperature gauge of our hearts. Since each of these characteristics can only be produced in a true sense by the Holy Spirit, when we are not being loving, patient, self-controlled or gentle it is evidence to us that we are in desperate need of the Holy Spirit to empower us. When He is not empowering us, it is because our hearts are not yielded to Him resulting in what Galatians 5:19 calls fruits of the flesh. These are things like jealousy, anger, and selfishness.

*Think of a few situations you were faced with in the last couple of days. What were some characteristics of your heart attitude in these situations?

*Generally, in what types of situations do you tend to depend on the Holy Spirit's help? Why? Why not other situations?

*What specifically keeps you from turning to the Lord in dependence on His ability instead of your own strength? Why?

As we live our lives dependent on the Holy Spirit, we get to see Him come through for us by rescuing us, sustaining us, restoring and reviving us, bearing fruit through us that lasts for eternity, giving us His strength, ability, wisdom, understanding, knowledge, and pure motives. Basically, He wants to give us every good thing, and He says that no eye has seen and no ear has heard what He wants to give us. (See 1 Corinthians 2:9) He wants to transform us into the image of Christ more and more, and he wants us to experience these things more and more.

*Describe a current situation where you are desperate for the Holy Spirits' enablement.

*What would be the internal result of letting Christ give you His ability in this situation?

Oh, God, we truly are desperate for Your enablement to live life in a way that makes You known. Burn this truth into the deepest part of who we are, that we would be motivated to turn to You more and receive the good You have for us.

Empowering

Week 2

Day 3

Our God Who enables us, we truly are desperate for You to enable us to hear from You today. Through Your Spirit, help us to see how You are extremely able to give us everything we need for life and godliness through Your Spirit. Give us a glimpse of Your strength and ability today.

Eyes to See

Read 1 Samuel 2:1-36

    *In verses 1-11:

        *What things does God do for those who depend on or need Him?

        *What happens to the people who trust in and depend on their own strength?

        • How can you see Hophni and Phinehas reflected in these verses?

    *From verse 12 on, what is said about Samuel?

    *What was the faithful priest that God was going to raise up going to be like?

Ears to Hear

I want to share a great conversation published in *Postcards to Corinth* called "Learning, The Lost Art of Making People Feel Stupid" that took place between Will Walker and a couple of college guys.

"Yeah, we all know too much," I said. "I had a group of pledges one year that grew up in a really good church, but what they knew and what they experienced were two different worlds. I told them at our first meeting that I thought they were all full of crap. Let me ask you what I asked them."

I continued. "If Jesus were here physically and were your discipler this semester instead of me, do you think you would have a better shot at growing spiritually than you do now with me as your discipler and His Spirit living inside you?" Casey smirked and asked, "What do you mean 'here physically'"? "I mean here, physically. He could be right by your side as much as you wanted him to be." "Well, then I'd take that," said Casey. "Why?" "Because he would be straight with me, you know. He could see into my heart and just tell it like it is. There wouldn't be any question about what I'm supposed to do." "So this seems like a no-brainer to you?" I asked. "I guess," responded Casey, confident but suspicious. I turned to Michael, "What about you?" "Well, I know the right answer is the Holy Spirit but since that is what I have had all along, and that hasn't worked out so well, I would honestly say Jesus just to try something new."

They chose the same answer but for different reasons. Michael knew the "right answer." Casey was left wondering why his answer was "wrong" and wishing he hadn't been so sure of himself. Someone was going to look stupid, and nothing creates tension like the potential of looking stupid.

What people know does not impress me anymore. I want to know what they want. In this case, they wanted Jesus as their discipler instead of me, but at the expense of having His Spirit inside them. This scenario has its apparent advantages, but it reveals something about them at the level of their desires. I already knew at this point what it says about them, but again, what I know will very rarely change anyone. They have to discover it. So we continued:

I asked both of them, "If you would be better off having Jesus with you instead of in you, why didn't God establish life that way?" I got blank stares. So I continued. "I mean, the disciples wanted Jesus to stay and he told them at least twice that it was better for them if He left." Casey, probably sensing that he might be the one to look stupid, questioned, "When did He say that?" I showed him the verses. "So why is it better?" (I.e. why were you wrong?) More blank stares.

Let's review. I could have explained all this to them on the front end and avoided hurting anyone's self-esteem. They would know having the Holy Spirit is better, but it would only be head knowledge. Instead, I asked two simple questions and it surfaced that deep down they really just wanted Christianity to be easier.

"Okay, Casey, you said you would like it because Jesus would shoot straight with you. He could look in your heart and tell you that you are full of crap. Then what would you do about it?" "What do you mean?" Casey asked. "Think about it this way. If Lebron James was your personal coach in basketball, could you play in the NBA?" "No." "Why not? You would have one of the best players in the world teaching you." "But that doesn't mean I could play like him." "What if somehow Lebron could live inside you and play through you? Then could you play in the NBA?" Casey gets an epiphany, "I get it. If I didn't have His Spirit in me, I couldn't do what he tells me I need to do. It wouldn't matter that Jesus was here telling me to do it."[3]

We serve a very powerful God. To get a glimpse and reminder of God's ability, write down in your own words what God is able to do as seen in the verses below.
Job 38-40

God is able to empower you

If God is powerful enough to do all of this, of course He is powerful enough to give you strength to live the Christian life. He reassures us through the apostle Paul of His ability to do so. The Spirit of God, Who raised Jesus from the dead, lives in you. Just as God raised Christ Jesus from the dead, He will give life to your mortal bodies by this same Spirit living within you. (Romans 8:11) The Holy Spirit that raised Christ from the dead is also able to make us more like Him and empower us to bear fruit for eternity.

He is also able to empower us to live godly lives because He knows us perfectly and intimately. He knows our thoughts, motives, strengths, capabilities, weaknesses, why we do what we do, and why we think what we think. He knows exactly how He has designed each one of us and exactly what we need at each moment. He knows how we feel right this moment and how the emotion was brought about and how long it will last. He knows how intense it is and every other emotion associated with it. He knows our hurts, rejections, and our pressures. He also knows the purpose of our trials. Because He knows us so well, so perfectly, He knows what we need in order to live the life He desires for us and exactly how to change us so that we can better experience and know His love for us.

Heart to Understand

It seems there are numerous situations where we need to be given God's ability, otherwise things will turn out very badly - things like managing our time, our talents, our money, having a good attitude, evidencing the fruit of the Spirit like we talked about, accomplishing everything that God has called us to, not being lazy but not being a workaholic either.

Austin and I just adopted our second son, Uriah John. When Uriah was born Asher was only a year old. So the first few weeks of my life with Uriah all I was finding time to do was feed babies, change diapers, pick up the house and if I got lucky I made a meal. Sometimes that is how life feels. I don't have time to do anything other than running around like a chicken with my head cut off. But sure enough a few weeks went by and the Lord taught me how to rearrange my schedule so I could get the things done that He has set before me to do. His grace truly is sufficient. But the wonderful thing is that He gives us what we need when we need it. He doesn't give me more or less. So when I think about my friend Christina who has four kids and think "I would never be able to do that," I need to remember that God's grace would be sufficient then, too, just as it is now.

---

3   James, Rick. *Postcards to Corinth*. Orlando, FL: CruPress.

*In what areas are you most in need of God's ability to empower you?

*How do you feel when you think about God being able to empower you to live a godly life? (If you need some help, think about what it would be like to have God give you the ability you need in a few specific situations.)

*Of the things that you wrote down for the very first question on this day, which of those have you seen God do in your life and when?

*What are some examples of when you trusted in your own strength and abilities instead of depending on the Lord's empowerment? What were the results?

*Describe a situation in which you are still waiting to see victory. How often are you depending on the Lord's empowerment for the victory?

Spend some time talking to the Lord about this situation. Tell Him your hopes and fears regarding it.

Empowering

Week 2

Day 4

Jehovah Jireh, our Provider, what a gift You give us of being able to approach You so boldly and receive the grace that we need. We desire to present to You every part of who we are. Where we are hesitant, give us willingness and strength, and where we are blind to our need for You, and give us Eyes to See. Meet us here today, Lord, that we might connect with You and offer ourselves as living sacrifices, holy and pleasing to You.

Eyes to See

*Write out Colossians 2:6-7 and tell how it compares to Galatians 3:3 which we looked at on Day 2.

*The Pharisees tried by their own power to be what God wanted them to be, and therefore could not receive God's ability to change them. Describe a time when you tried to give someone something that they really needed but they would not receive it from you because they thought they could do it on their own.

*Read the following verses and rewrite them in your own words.

1 Corinthians 3:1-3

Galatians 5:16

Galatians 5:22-25

Ears to Hear

So we know that we are in desperate need of the Holy Spirit to produce the life of Christ in us, and we know that God is completely able to empower us to live godly lives, so why is it that God transforms us sometimes and not others, or in some areas and not others?

God directs and empowers us only as we submit to and depend on Him.

As we go through life in community as a follower of Christ, Jehovah Jireh, our Provider, will open our eyes little by little to our sin. He will allow us to see parts of our hearts that we have never seen before which exposes our ickyness. He shows us our stubbornness, our dishonesty, our pride, our selfishness, our rebelliousness and not honoring and submitting to authority, our unkind thoughts toward people, our lack of prayer, fearing what others think of us, wasting time, our lust, our anger, and our unforgiveness. When He shows us, we can agree with Him, accept responsibility and choose not to blame others or make excuses, or we can ignore Him. We cannot and never will be able to live the Christian life by our own strength continually trying harder. We will never be able to change ourselves and be more like Christ in our own effort. Only God can change us; the way we let Him change us (if He chooses), is by humbling ourselves.

Humility is being honest about who we really are, which then enables us to confess and surrender, and brings the Holy Spirit's enablement.

The founder of Campus Crusade for Christ came up with a helpful illustration to explain the Spirit-filled life. It is the best tool I have come across to simply lay out what the Spirit-filled life is and how someone can live a Spirit-filled life. This is the illustration.

The Bible tells us that there are three kinds of people

1. Natural Person (someone who has not received Christ.)

Natural Person (Self-Directed Life)

Self is on the throne, directing decisions and actions
(represented by the dots), often resulting in frustration.
Jesus is outside the life.

"But the people who aren't spiritual can't receive these truths from God's Spirit. It all sounds foolish to them and they can't understand it, for only those who are spiritual can understand what the Spirit means." (1 Corinthians 2:14).

2. Spiritual Person (one who is directed and empowered by the Holy Spirit.)

Spiritual Person (Christ-Directed Life)

Jesus is in the life and on the throne. Self is yielding to Jesus.
The person sees Jesus' influence and direction in their life.

Spiritual Person

Christ-centered
Empowered by the Holy Spirit
Introduces others to Christ
Effective prayer life

Understands God's Word
Tusts & obeys God
Experiences love, joy, peace,
patience, kindness, faithfulness,
gentleness, goodness & self-control

Some spiritual traits which result from trusting God:

3. Carnal Person (one who has received Christ, but who lives in defeat because he is trying to live the Christian life in his own strength.)

Carnal Person (Self-Directed Life)

Jesus is in the life but not on the throne. Self is on the throne, directing decisions and actions (represented by the dots), often resulting in frustration.

"Dear brothers and sisters, when I was with you I could not talk to you as I would to spiritual people. I had to talk as though you belonged to this world or as though you were infants in the Christian life. I had to feed you with milk, not with solid food, because you weren't ready for anything stronger. And you still aren't ready, for you are still controlled by your sinful nature. You are jealous of one another and quarrel with each other. Doesn't that prove you are controlled by your sinful nature? Aren't you living like people of the world? (1 Corinthians 3:1-3)

A carnal Christian cannot experience the abundant and fruitful Christian life, and trusts in his own efforts to live the Christian life.

Some or all of the following traits may characterize the Christian who does not fully trust God:

Carnal Person

Unbelief
Disobedience
Poor prayer life
No desire for Bible study

Legalistic attitude or critical spirit
Impure thoughts, jealousy, guilt
Frustration, aimlessness
Worry, discouragement
Loss of love for God and others

Jesus promised the abundant and fruitful life as the result of being filled (directed and empowered) by the Holy Spirit. If you become aware of an area of your life (an attitude or an action) that is independent from Christ, then it is a matter of confessing and surrendering. A good analogy for this is called spiritual breathing. Just like there are two parts of breathing, inhaling and exhaling, there are two parts to living the Spirit-filled life.

1. **Exhale**-confess your sin-agree with God concerning your sin and thank Him for His forgiveness of it, according to 1 John 1:9 and Hebrews 10:1-25. Confession involves repentance-a change in attitude and action. You are not confessing to receive more

forgiveness (since you were completely forgiven the first time you asked and gave the control of your life to Christ). Rather, we confess to restore our fellowship with Him.

2. **Inhale**-surrender the control of your life to Christ. That He now directs and empowers you according to the command of Ephesians 5:18 and the promise of 1 John 5:14, 15.

Heart to Understand

Log onto www.BeholdingHimBecomingMissional.com and under week 2 watch the video, "How do I live a Spirit-filled life?"

Doing throne checks throughout the day is a great reminder to live a life dependent on the Holy Spirit. A throne check is taking a few moments and asking God to show you if there has been anything that you have been trying to do in your own strength or independent from Him. If things pop into your mind, confess them and surrender them. Then you are able to go about your day confident that the Holy Spirit is living His life through you.

"This High Priest of ours understands our weaknesses, for he faced all of the same testing we do, yet he did not sin. So let us come boldly to the throne of our gracious God. There we will receive his mercy, and we will find grace to help us when we need it most" (Hebrews 4:15-16).

God opposes the proud (James 4:6): those who are self-sufficient, those who try to manage their lives without Him, those who struggle and strive to live the Christian life on their own, and those who are too proud to acknowledge their need. "But He gladly, freely lavishes His grace, all His divine favor and resources on those who are humble. We demonstrate humility by acknowledging our helplessness and our need to Him and others, and by crying out to Him for grace." Nancy Leigh DeMoss

> *Are you in a habit of doing "throne checks"? If not, is that something you want to be in a habit of doing? (If so, begin to pray that God would bring it about then make some goals to develop the habit.)

Empowering

Week 2

Day 5

God Who we are so desperate for and Who is able to direct and empower us, live Your life through us today. Give us Your perspective and Your heart. Let us meet with You today and change us to make us look more like You. Each distraction that comes up, please enable us to submit it to You and cry out for You to help us not be overcome by it. Give us a bigger glimpse of what You are like today.

Reflecting on the Week:

Summarize the three points of this week and write down what stuck out to you.

1. We are doomed to fail and are desperate for the Lord's empowerment.

2. God is able to empower us.

3. God directs and empowers us as we submit to and depend on Him.

The bad news is that you are worse than you dared dream, but the good news is that God wants to direct and empower you so that you can better love and be loved by Him. He is able to direct and empower you because of His great ability and knowledge of you. He will direct and empower you as you humble yourself. As you do, you will find that all of the resources of heaven and all of the Spirit's power are at your disposal, and unless heaven's riches can be exhausted or the Spirit's power can be found incapable, over time you will find you will not come up short.

Take some time to do a throne check and let Him show you what specific ways you have been trying to change yourself on your own, apart from humbling yourself by recognizing your need for Him and acting as He leads.

Intimate

Week 3

Day 1

Oh, Ever Present One that is continually presenting Yourself to us, what a gracious God You are to show Yourself to us, to give us a glimpse of Your greatness and majesty. Lord, this week please enlighten our minds and mold our hearts to truly understanding and being convinced to the depth of who we are that You want us to know You, that we can be confident in hearing You speak to us and that Your word is critical to our lives.

Page Jumpers

Read 1 Samuel 3:1-21
List things that jump off the page (verses that stand out to you):

-
-
-
-

Cloud of Witnesses

My husband's best friend, Nate, grew up as a missionary kid in Columbia and Romania. His family would frequently take ministry trips to other countries. On one of their trips to Machu Picchu they were in a large market carrying their suitcase containing everything important, including all of their money and passports. Nate's dad set the suitcase down to call his parents and let them know they had arrived safely and the bag disappeared. Imagine the fear that would sweep over you not having any money, passports or visas and a family you had to take care of. He started praying that God would show him where the bag was. At that moment it began to rain heavily and every person in the market began putting tarps over their tables to keep the items they were selling from being damaged. Nate's dad was walking through the hundreds of tables in the rain and finally stopped at one of the tables. He felt God tell him to look under this particular table. When he lifted the tarp, his bag was sitting right there.

This week we are going to see how:

1. God wants us to know Him.

2. We can grow in confidence in hearing God's voice.

3. God's Word is necessary for our lives.

Here Am I

To prepare our heart to hear from the Lord this week, spend time considering the questions below.

*How confident are you in hearing God's voice and why?

*How would you know if what you thought to be God's voice really was?

Intimate

Week 3
Day 2

Lord, thank You for letting us approach Your very presence with confidence. We desire to meet with You today and are anxious to hear what is on Your heart and mind. Enable us to see and hear today.

Eyes to See

Read 1 Samuel 3:1-21

> *What are some things you would expect to be true of Samuel or his life being raised by a spiritual leader?

> *How many times did God call to Samuel? What is different about the last time?

> *Describe some things that are true of God that you see in these verses.

What an amazing God we have that He persists in making Himself known to us as He did with Samuel. Growing up with the priest as your caretaker and sleeping in the temple, Samuel knew about the Lord. He celebrated all the feasts which were reminders of all the ways that God had acted on behalf of His people, but yet, he didn't recognize God's voice. He lacked intimacy with the Lord.

How true that can be of our lives as well. We can go to church or Bible Studies and learn more facts about God without ever interacting with Him.

*Would you describe your relationship with God as intimate? Why or why not?

*Aside from what you know about God, do you have examples of times you have experienced Him in a personal way?

Ears to Hear

God wants us to know Him. Psalm 23 gives us a beautiful picture of this. The end of verse 5 says my cup overflows. In the culture of that day when you were at someone's house for a meal the host would let you know how long you could stay by how full they kept your cup. If they poured you a full cup, they were saying "I'm enjoying your company, stay longer." If they poured your cup less than full, it meant it was time for you to go. God pours our cup to overflowing. The point was unmistakable.

God does not weary in getting Samuel's attention. He is persistent, desiring to make Himself known. God calls to Samuel and after He uses the means necessary to get his attention, He then comes and stands there with Samuel calling to Him. How comforting that God knows and does what it takes for us to hear and recognize His voice. Then when He gets our attention, He shows up to reveal Himself.

What are some similarities between the verses below and 1 Samuel chapter 3?

> Now Moses was tending the flock of Jethro his father-in-law, the priest of Midian, and he led the flock to the far side of the wilderness and came to Horeb, the mountain of God. There the angel of the Lord appeared to him in flames of fire from within a bush. Moses saw that though the bush was on fire it did not burn up. So Moses thought, "I will go over and see this strange sight-why the bush does not burn up." When the Lord saw that he had gone over to look, God called to him from within the bush, "Moses! Moses!" And Moses said, "Here I am" (Exodus 3:1-4 NASB).

> "Now that same day two of them were going to a village called Emmaus, about seven miles from Jerusalem. They were talking with each other about everything that had happened. As they talked and discussed these things with each other, Jesus himself came up and walked along with them; but they were kept from recognizing him. He asked them, "What are you discussing together as you walk along?" They stood still, their faces downcast. One of them, named Cleopas, asked him, "Are you only a visitor to Jerusalem and do not know the things that have happened there in these

days?" "What things?" he asked. "About Jesus of Nazareth," they replied. "He was a prophet, powerful in word and deed before God and all the people. The chief priests and our rulers handed him over to be sentenced to death, and they crucified him; but we had hoped that he was the one who was going to redeem Israel. And what is more, it is the third day since all this took place. In addition, some of our women amazed us. They went to the tomb early this morning but didn't find his body. They came and told us that they had seen a vision of angels, who said he was alive. Then some of our companions went to the tomb and found it just as the women had said, but him they did not see." He said to them, "How foolish you are, and how slow to believe all that the prophets have spoken! Did not the Messiah have to suffer these things and then enter his glory?" And beginning with Moses and all the Prophets, he explained to them what was said in all the Scriptures concerning himself" (Luke 24:13-27 TNIV).

Heart to Understand

*God persisted in revealing Himself to these people. How do you feel knowing God persists in making Himself known to you as well?

*Why do you think God wants you to deeply know Him more?

*How does knowing Him more relate to our purpose of displaying His glory?

*How do you think you personally can get to know God better? (How do you get to know a friend better?)

Lord, is there anything else You would like me to understand about Your desire for me to know You?

Make note of anything that comes to mind.

I am truly amazed when I think that if I did nothing in my whole life but discover more about God, I would still not even scratch the surface. To think that for all of eternity the same could be true. Oh, the depth of our God! To think He so desires us to see Him and know Him that He has surrounded us with things that give us a glimpse of what He is like. What a gift!

>*Visit www.BeholdingHimBecomingMissional.com and look at the pictures under week 3. Write down what truths about God the images remind you of.

Oh God, give us Eyes to See You more and more, to understand Your heart and Your passions. Let us understand Your desire for intimacy with us. Whatever keeps us from recognizing You, remove it so we can behold Your glory.

Spend some time telling Him what You think and feel about the things you have just thought about Him.

Intimate

Week 3
Day 3

Immanuel, our God Who is with us, what a comfort to know that You never leave us or forsake us, that You are right here with us, no matter what we face, no matter how far we feel from You. It is amazing that You desire to be intimate with us, that You want to let Yourself be known to us, though we won't always treat You the way You deserve. Thank You for being willing to share Your heart with us and for being willing to communicate with us, Your creation. Your ways are so unfathomable to us, yet You want to communicate to us in a way that we can understand. What a truly great God you are! Oh Lord, make us quick and able to recognize Your voice as You say Your people can. Let our lives be lived in an intimate relationship with You. Open our Eyes to See and our Ears to Hear. Let us hear You speak to us even today.

Eyes to See

Read the following stories and summarize how God communicated in each of them.
Acts 10:1-7

Acts 16:6-10

Numb. 22:21-35

Joshua 1:1-9

2 Samuel 12:1-12

Luke 3:21-23

Acts 20:16-24

*Why do you think God communicates in different ways to different people and different circumstances?

Ears to Hear

An important part of any relationship is communication. Since God desires a personal and intimate relationship with each of us as His children, He will communicate with us in a way that we can understand.

Write out John 10:27 and jot down what it says about God communicating with us.

If you are a believer, it proves that you have "heard God's voice." You have understood the truth that only He offers that you were in desperate need of forgiveness because you stood guilty before God. You understood that through Jesus' life, death and resurrection you could receive that forgiveness and the Father greatly desired you to ask for it. You heard Him call you and you responded.

*What feelings arise knowing you have heard God's voice?

God communicates in a lot of different ways. The biggest and most obvious is through His **Word**. Ya know, "His Words." 2 Tim. 3:16-17 says that Scripture is God-breathed; whether we feel like they are or not and whether we feel like He is talking/communicating to us or not, He is.

Another way that God communicates with us is through people. Isaiah, Elijah, Elisha, Micah, Nahum, Jeremiah, Obadiah, Ezekiel, Nathan, and Jonah are just a few of the people God used to communicate to people. Even today God still uses people to share His thoughts. There have been many times that God has used speakers at conferences to speak to me in a very real and personal way. One time in particular has been burned into my mind. It was as if the speaker was talking right to me and saying exactly what I needed to hear. I was so encouraged that I was a blubbering mess and sometimes still wonder what the people around me must have been thinking.

As we live yielded to the Holy Spirit, our thoughts are another way that He communicates with us. 1 Corinthians 2:16 says that He has given us the mind of Christ. He leads our thinking in seemingly small things to rather big things. Fill in the blanks for Jeremiah 33:3_____to me and I will

_____you and_____you great unsearchable things you do not know. I do this a lot, asking Him where I have misplaced things like my keys and every time right after I ask Him where my keys are a thought of where they could be pops into my head. I look there and sure enough there they are. Or when I am reading His Word, I love to ask Him, "Lord, why did you do it that way?" or "What do you think about that?" or "How does that relate to me?" and sure enough some neat thought pops into my head.

My husband, Austin, and a friend were walking around the college campus seeing if they would be able to get into any spiritual conversations with some students. They ended up talking with a guy named John. They started talking about spiritual things and Austin got to share the gospel with him. Throughout the discussion, John kept saying, "I just can't believe it, I was just thinking about this."

As we saw in the verses above, God can also communicate to us through visions. Twice in my life God has communicated to me through a vision and both times moved me to love Him more and live more devoted to Him.

The first was before I was a Christian. A friend invited me to her church to watch her in a play. After the play they had a time of worship. I had never been part of something like that. As the band was playing I saw a hand over the worship team and thought "God must be happy and involved with these people and maybe He wants me here." I went home and talked to my mom and asked if we could start going to church there since we had no involvement in church until that point. The next week we went to that church the Pastor approached me, a little eleven year old girl, and shared the gospel with me. For the first time, it made sense why I needed to make a personal decision to give the control of my life to Jesus.

Sometimes circumstances are a way that God uses to communicate to people as He did in Egypt with the plagues. He was communicating that He was God. Another example which I read today in my time with the Lord is in 1 Kings. Elijah desires King Ahab and the people to see that God truly was God and called fire down from heaven. God sent fire to devour the drenched offering that was made in the presence of King Ahab and all the people. The people were able to see that God is the One and only true God and their god Baal was not. Though not all circumstances are God communicating to people, there are times that He uses them.

I was in need of a new Bible since 'Genesis' was falling out. I obviously wanted a Bible with Genesis in it, so I went to the Christian bookstore. There were so many to choose from. I was narrowing it down to the version I wanted and then went from there. During the process I was asking God which one He would like me to have. Finally I found the one I wanted. I had pulled it off the shelf and looked through it and decided this was the one. But something nagged at me. *The cover wasn't just right* I thought. So I looked at all the covers staring at me from the display case and I decided on the one on the top shelf corner. I pulled it down and took it out of the see through box. At the bottom of the box was a handwritten small piece of paper with nothing but LAURA written on it. God sure knows how to make us smile.

In hearing God's voice, there are some things we need to be cautious of. In the Old Testament, people were stoned for saying something God had said when He hadn't said it, or for being just slightly wrong. God considers it a big deal when we put words in His mouth that He didn't say, making Him out to be a liar.

Another caution Paul warns us of is to not exceed what is written that we wouldn't become arrogant having an I'm better than you attitude. It is better to just stick with what we know for sure God said in His Word.

In the end the most important thing is to let scripture be our authority. If we see a vision, or someone says something or we think God is leading our thoughts but it is contrary to scripture, we can be 100% sure that it is not God communicating with us. God can not lie or disagree with Himself. Oh, that we would be like the Bereans in Acts 17 who received the message with great eagerness and examined the Scriptures every day to see if what Paul said was true.

We can grow in confidence in hearing God's voice.

The way I grew the most in recognizing God's voice was through practice, through training my ear to what His voice was like. Here are some helpful tips:

> *Make your mind available to Him by knowing His Word. Hebrews 5:14 says that maturity in Christ is having our senses trained to discern good and evil. The only way to get trained in what God thinks about things is by reading and memorizing His Word.

> *Ask God questions (which shows a humble heart) and journal the thoughts that come to mind after you ask Him.

Heart to Understand

God's voice is closely linked with action. What comes from His mouth will always be successful in accomplishing what He desires. Therefore it makes sense that His voice is closely tied to decision making.

> *Of the verses you looked at above of God communicating, what were the desired actions as a result of hearing from God?

Romans 12:1-3 speaks of giving ourselves entirely to the Lord, having our minds (thoughts, hopes and dreams) yielded to Christ. Then, we will know and be an example of what God's will is. Some things that are helpful to ask ourselves when discerning God's desire in a decision we are making are: Is there any un-confessed sin that has broken your fellowship with Him? Are you being fully controlled by the Holy Spirit through faith?

Here is an easy to remember acronym to help you make a godly decision.

G.A.S. Gives the "fuel" (or confidence) to walk out what God has for us.

God's Word. God's written word is our ultimate source of authority in all areas of life. Relating to your specific situation, what things has God already given clear direction in the Bible? Ask God to lead you to specific passages of how you fit into His plan. Psalm 32:8, 119:105, Matthew 7:24.

Ask mature believers. Ask for advice from mature Christians, from someone who knows you well, someone who will be objective with you and someone who knows and walks with God and knows His ways. Proverbs 11:14, 12:15, 15:22.

Spirit-filled reasoning. With your heart and mind yielded to Christ, think strategically. He has given us a sound and sanctified mind and desires us to love Him with it and be a good steward using it. Using wisdom and reason we will follow the examples of the apostles:

1 Thessalonians 3:1-2 "we thought it best…"
Philippians 2:25, 26 "I thought it was necessary…"
1 Corinthians 16:3-4 "if it is fitting…"
Acts 6:2-4 "it is not desirable…"
Acts 15:22, 28 "it seemed good…

Summarize the following verses and jot down how this relates to letting God lead our thinking.

Proverbs 14:15-16

Matthew 25:14-30

1 Peter 4:10

Proverbs 3:3-5

Ask yourself questions:

*How does it fit in the overall plan of God? What would be the most strategic choice as an investment of my life? How much _____ will it take? Is there a need? What would prepare and develop me? What are my motives? Is it to gain approval or acceptance from someone, money, power or to stay comfortable? Does it fit with what I am passionate about?

Misconceptions about discerning God's will:

Putting authoritative reliance on subjective means. An example of this is "the open door policy," saying that God's will is whatever opportunity works out for you. Moses was leading the Israelites out of Egypt and ran into the Red Sea. That very well could have looked like a "closed door. Sometimes a "closed door" may just be an opportunity to give God more glory. Just because an opportunity comes up doesn't mean it is the best option for your time and resources. In Acts 16:22-40, what would have happened if Paul and Silas believed that whatever happened was God's will, living by the open door policy?

Another example is judging God's will by your "feelings of peace." If our feelings were the authority of God's will, Jesus would not have died on the cross. See Luke 22:42-44, Hebrews 12:1-4 God can use our feelings and often times our desires can be in line with His desire, but when making decisions, it is unwise to use them alone. Read Acts 20:22-23, 21:10-14. Paul knew the Lord wanted Him to go to Jerusalem but the Christians let their feelings of sadness for him try to govern Paul's decision. Paul would not let the fear of hard times change his decision.

   *How do you generally interact with the Lord when it comes to making decisions and why?

   *Is there a present decision you need to make? Use the space below and the GAS acronym to help you think it through with the Lord.

Faith is not waiting until you know 100%. Genuine faith is moving in the direction it seems God is leading, putting confidence more in God's ability to guide or re-direct than in your ability to decide. Making a decision in faith means putting your trust ultimately in God and not in self, circumstances, or others. The more we grow as Christians the more decisions we will make by faith in God, from seemingly big ones like who you'll marry, to seemingly small ones like what should you watch on TV. It is important to be ready to trust God in your decision whether it turns out the way you expected or not.

Intimate

Week 3

Day 4

God, you are our Creator and Sustainer, and yet are willing to put Your heart on paper for all to see. Wow. You are a great and wonderful God. Your Word is an incredible gift to us, but we so often take it for granted. Oh Lord, please renew our vision, open our Eyes to See the truth and soften our hearts to the precious gift of Your Word. Give us an unquenchable passion to seek You out and to know You in an intimate way. Make our hearts receptive to what You say to us and how You say it through Your Word. Cause us to love interacting with You through Your Word more than we dreamed possible.

Eyes to See

Read 1 Samuel 3:11-4:22

    *Summarize what is happening

    *What is significant about Eli and his sons' deaths?

    *Write out 3:21 in a couple different versions and jot down your thoughts about it.

    *4:3 says, "Why did the Lord bring defeat on us today before the Philistines?" Describe a time you thought something was going to happen and it turned out you were just deceived?

Ears to Hear

While I was in college a friend of mine took me ice climbing. I wonder if you have ever been ice climbing? Basically you stick some claws on your feet that enable you to climb sheer ice. Then you are given an axe that you strike into the waterfall that has turned to ice and with the aid of your harness you start climbing. I enjoyed ice climbing much more than regular climbing because it felt a bit more secure having more to hold on with than just your finger tips.

But this first time ice climbing was also my last. I was at the bottom of the 50 foot sheer face of ice and I was belaying my friend as he climbed to the top. I had never belayed anyone before and he was about 20 pounds heavier than I was. He made it to the top and let me know that he was coming down. As he put his full weight on the rope it threw me into the air and I loosened my grip on the rope. I hit the ground and realized that my friend was falling. I could not remember which hand I was supposed to grip tight with in order to catch him. I picked a hand and squeezed, but it ended up being the wrong hand. The rope burned the skin off my hand as my friend continued to fall. Eventually he hit the ground, and I rushed over to see if he was ok. He was unconscious. I called 911 and it seemed like it took forever for the ambulance to come and to hoist him out of the ravine. He died in the ambulance on the way to the hospital.

The best part about this experience is that it is not true. I did have a friend take me ice climbing and I did belay him and end up dropping him, but he did not hit the ground that hard and was fine, head to toe.

*What were your initial feelings when you discovered that I had lied to you?

If I were you, I would probably feel some intense anger. I hate when people lie to me. I feel taken advantage of and it takes me awhile to get over it. I imagine that you don't like being lied to either. None of us want to buy into a lie. But chances are good that you and I both are buying into some lie of the deceiver. It seems one of his most prominent lies is that we don't need God's Word. Have you bought into the lie? You can tell by examining how often you read it. Do you live as though it is your daily bread, your daily sustenance for living?

God's Word is necessary for our life.

There are a multitude of reasons why God's Word is necessary for us, but we are only going to have time to look at three of them.

God's Word **comforts** us.

This is my comfort in my affliction, that Your Word has revived me. Psalm 1119:50 Comfort is to be reassured and freed from pain and anxiety. Jesus told us that this life is going to be hard. In the world you will have trouble, but take courage; I have overcome the world. John 16:33 The goal in this life is not to avoid pain so we are going to need comfort.

*So how does His word comfort us?

Did you mention that God's Word shows us what is true? It shows us God's heart and God's ability which gives us strength, confidence, eternal perspective, peace and hope. This is the kind of comfort that leads to perseverance and courage.

> *How are these verses examples of God's Word providing comfort that leads to perseverance and courage?
> "Nevertheless I am continually with You; You have taken hold of my right hand. With Your counsel You will guide me, and afterward receive me to glory. Whom have I in heaven but You? And besides You, I desire nothing on earth. My flesh and my heart may fail, but God is the strength of my heart and my portion forever." (Psalm 73:23-26 NASB)
>
> "The Lord who delivered me from the paw of the lion and from the paw of the bear, He will deliver me from the hand of this Philistine." (1 Samuel 17:37 NASB)

God's Word also **transforms** us.

"Sanctify them in the truth; Your word is truth." (John 17:17 NASB) Scripture by the work of the Holy Spirit is a means God uses to make us more like Him. "For the Word of God is living and active and sharper than any two-edged sword, and piercing as far as the division of soul and spirit, of both joints and marrow, and able to judge the thoughts and intentions of the heart." (Hebrews 4:12 NASB) We cannot change or be changed until we see that there is a need to be changed. Scripture helps us to see ourselves as we really are by giving us a standard by which to measure ourselves.

I have known my friend, Janna, since high school. I had the privilege to live with her in college which always seemed to provide some excitement to life. With four girls in a house, once in a while there was some drama. One day I pulled a very immature act and got jealous that Janna was spending more time with our other friend and roommate than she was with me. Janna looked me in the eyes and said, "Laura, do you love me?" I answered "Yes." She said "Love is not jealous." It was true, and it was exactly what it took for me to see my sin. Scripture showed me where I needed to change and brought about humility. The humility enabled me to surrender to the Lord and receive His empowerment to love Janna in a non-jealous way.

> *How have you seen God use His word to bring about transformation in a situation?

The last one we have time for is that God uses His Word to **communicate** with us. God spoke directly, personally and audibly to Adam and Eve. But then sin was brought into the picture and their intimacy with God was broken. But because of God's great desire to be known and have an intimate relationship with us, He still pursued communication with people but mostly through dreams, visions, and prophets. Before God put on flesh, came to earth and communicated face-to-face with people and lived the perfect life on earth, hearing from Him was not an everyday thing. Now since Jesus is in heaven at the right hand of the Father, the most clear and accessible way He communicates to us is through His Word. We are the most blessed of all time. EVER! Before Jesus lived on earth as

100% man and 100% God, people would get to hear God once and that was it. But not us, we get to have Him communicate with us however often we want! Wow.

So exactly how does God communicate to us through His word? "He will bring glory to me by taking from what is mine and making it known to you. (John 16:14 NIV) It is actually the Holy Spirit making our minds understand what God is communicating when we read Scripture. As you spend time in God's Word and store it in your heart, then in timely ways the Holy Spirit brings God's word to your mind and speaks to you in your heart.

*Describe a time that the God spoke to you through His Word.

God communicating with people is a huge deal. We have bought into a lie if we have even an ounce of doubt that His Word is no big deal. Oh, that we would see His Word for what it is, that we would value His Word more than other people's opinions, our own opinions, books, the culture, or any other thing.

"Now these (Bereans) were more noble-minded than those in Thessalonica, for they received the word with great eagerness, examining the Scriptures daily to see whether these things were so." (Acts 17:11 NASB) They didn't come with their opinions to the Scriptures to prove their point but they went to God's word teachable. My prayer is that we would be more noble minded than all others in our culture… that we would receive the Word with great eagerness, and examine the scriptures daily. My desire is that we wouldn't only be the one talking to Him, but that we would let Him talk straight to us by going to His Word ourselves.

Heart to Understand

Summarize what these verses have to do with God's Word and what this would practically look like in your everyday life.

Psalm 19:7-8

Psalm 37:31

Proverbs 6:20-23

Matthew 4:4

John 17:17

John 20:31

Romans 15:4

*What do you think are the most common reasons for not spending time in God's Word on a regular basis?

*What is a graceful and true response to these reasons?

*Which one(s) do you most relate with?

Here's what I think would top the list. I wonder if these were your responses, too.
1. Not enough time.

2. I don't get anything out of it. I don't want to.

3. Intimidation. I don't know what to read.

Let's play the 'what's true' game.
What is true and what is the deception of the 1st one, that you don't have enough time?

What is true and what is the lie of the 2nd one; not getting anything out of it?

What is true and what is the lie of the 3rd one; not knowing what to read?

If you don't already spend chunks of time in Scripture on a regular basis, what would intrinsically motivate and keep you motivated to feast on God's Word in a regular way? Are there steps you should take toward this?

Some encouragement from John Piper in regards to spending time in God's Word is from his book *When I Don't Desire God.* "One of the ways we can fight against the inclinations that lure us from the Word of God to computers or television or any other substitute pleasure is to remind ourselves often of the immeasurable and superior benefits of the Word of God in our lives. We must put the evidence before us that reading, pondering, memorizing, and studying the Bible will yield more joy in this life and the next than all the things that lure us from it."

Spend some time talking with God about spending time hearing from Him. This would be a great time to ask Him to give you motivation to devote yourself to His Word even more.

Intimate

Week 3

Day 5

Lord, here we are, perhaps not feeling totally together, but desiring to meet with You. Remind us that we stand before You as pure, holy, dearly loved and in desperate need of You. Write on our hearts that You want us to know You intimately, give us confidence in hearing Your voice and convince us that Your Word is necessary for our life. You are God and we are not. We yield to You today.

Reflecting on the week:

This week we saw through 1 Samuel chapters 3 and 4 that God wants us to know Him so our confidence can grow in hearing His voice, and that His Word is necessary for our lives.

Look back through the week and jot down the things that struck you the most.

How did God reveal Himself to you this week?

Lectio Divina is Latin for holy reading. It is a classic approach to drawing near to God through His Word. Let's spend some time today doing that. Here's how:

It is a slow, contemplative praying of the Scriptures that enables the Word of God to become a means of union with God and consists of four distinct stages.

1. Lectio: Reading and Listening

When we read God's Word, we should allow ourselves to become men and women who listen as God speaks to us with His gentle but specific nudging. The practice of Lectio Divina requires that we first quiet our anxious thoughts in order to hear God's Word to us. This is different than speed-reading, or scanning, as we might do with a daily newspaper.

2. Meditation: Meditating

Once we have found a word or passage in scripture that speaks to us in a personal way, stop right there. Forget the rest of the chapter. Re-read the key thought, ruminate on it. In this kind of meditation, we don't "empty our mind" as in Eastern meditation but rather, reflect on it. As you re-read the thought, it may help to emphasize different words.

3. Oratio: Prayer

Next, talk to God about what you have been reflecting on. Ask Him questions about it. Tell Him what you think and feel about it.

4. Contemplatio: Contemplation, Acceptance

Journal your questions, thoughts and the thoughts that come to your mind after you ask God your questions and compare your thoughts to Scripture. Think about what this would look like practically in your heart and life. Ask God how He would like you to respond to Him.

So now, pick a chapter and let's meet with God. Make sure to write down below what God opened your Eyes to See.

Holy

Week 4

Day 1

Elyon, You are supreme and You rule over all things. You are the Maker of all and therefore Master of all. There is none that is greater than You. How often we act like we are God and You are our servant. Oh, give us a glimpse of Your holiness that we would then have a proper view of ourselves.

Page Jumpers

Read 1 Samuel 5-8 and as you read, use the space below to draw a picture describing these chapters to help you get a feel for what is going on. As you go, jot down thoughts, ideas or verses that stick out.

Cloud of Witnesses

Read 2 Kings 18-19 and Psalm 99:1-5. As you read, think through how you see God's holiness.

This week we are going to look at God's holiness, our depravity, and God's commitment to His glory.

Here Am I

"In the year that King Uzziah died, I saw the Lord seated on a throne, high and exalted, and the train of his robe filled the temple. Above him were seraphs, each with six wings: With two wings they covered their faces, with two they covered their feet, and with two they were flying. And they were calling to one another; "Holy, holy, holy is the Lord Almighty; the whole earth is full of his glory." At the sound of their voices the doorposts and thresholds shook and the temple was filled with smoke. "Woe to me!" I cried. "I am ruined! For I am a man of unclean lips, and I live among a people of unclean lips, and my eyes have seen the King, the LORD Almighty." Then one of the seraphs flew to me with a live coal in his hand, which he had taken with tongs from the altar. With it he touched my mouth and said, "See, this has touched your lips; your guilt is taken away and your sin atoned for." Then I heard the voice of the Lord saying, "Whom shall I send? And who will go for us?" And I said, "Here am I. Send me!" (Isaiah 6:1-8)

Spend some time asking God to give you a glimpse of His holiness this week. Ask Him to let you see Him as high and exalted. Ask Him to give you eyes to see and a heart that understands Him more through the Holy Spirit.

Holy

Week 4

Day 2

Exalted above all gods, Your ways are above our ways and it is such a privilege to humble ourselves before You, and to get to meet with You and hear how You have shown Your glory long before we ever existed. Let us see You and know You more today through Your Word. Enlighten our minds to see the wonderful things about You. Help us lay down our misconceptions of Who You are and take up a right view. Move us to live in truth that You are the Most High and we are not.

Eyes to See

Read 1 Samuel 5-6:21

> *What is the first thing God does when the ark is brought to Ashdod?
> What are your thoughts concerning the significance in this?

> *What were the ways the people responded when God showed Himself as the Most High?

> In the ancient Near East, the heads and/or right hands of slain enemy soldiers were often brought back to the victors' camp as trophies of war. TNIV footnotes.

> *In what ways do you see this to be similar to today?

> *What was finally understood about God as a result of all the death?

Read Psalm 96-97

*Write down the things it says to do.

*What aspects of God cause us to do these things?

*What do you most commonly find yourself praising God for? Have you ever thought of praising God for destroying His enemies?

What do the verses below show us God wants us to understand about Him?
Jeremiah 9:23-24

Jeremiah 10:5-16

Daniel 4:28-37

Ears to Hear

A.W. Tozer says, "The essence of idolatry is the entertainment of thoughts about God that are unworthy of Him. And the history of mankind will probably show that no people has ever risen above its religion and man's spiritual history will positively demonstrate that no religion has ever been greater than its idea of God."

God exposes where we believe things that are not true about Him. The people living in Ashdod were no exception. They were putting their hope and trust in a false god called Dagon. This was keeping them from understanding the truth about Who God really was. So God went straight for the falsehood, exposing it for what it really was. My hope is that this week He will also expose to us where we are believing things that are not true about Him, especially in regards to His justice and holiness.

God is holy. This means that He is separated from sin and devoted to seeking His own honor.[4] Often people claim that in the Old Testament God was holy and showed His wrath but He is different and not like that in the New Testament. Let's examine what is true.

---

4   Grudem, Wayne (1995). *Systematic Theology: An Introduction to Biblical Doctrine* Grand Rapids, MI: Zondervan

Write out the general idea of the New Testament verses below.
Romans 1:18

Romans 2:5

Romans 5:9

Colossians 3:5-6

1 Thessalonians 1:8-10

Revelation 6:16-17

Revelation 16:3-6

Revelation 19:15

Why do you think it is a common misunderstanding that God is more holy and just in the Old Testament and not so much in the New Testament?

Throughout time God has been, is, and will continue to be completely holy and just in showing His wrath. The book of Ezekiel mentions 48 times the purpose of His wrath: to show Himself as God and to bring people to repentance.

Heart to Understand

Joshua is another book that clearly shows God's holiness resulting in His wrath. I was reading through Joshua recently and got a glimpse of God's holiness. When I read scripture I really enjoy trying to picture myself there and therefore end up asking a lot of questions. What would it be like to be there? What would the atmosphere be like, what would be the attitude of the people? What would I be feeling? As I read Joshua in this way God used it to show Himself to me in a way I had not understood before. Look at chapter 8 with me and I will show you what I mean.

Joshua 8:1-29
Write out the gist of what happened as if you were in Joshua's army.

Now describe the situation as if you were a resident of Ai and the possible feelings and reactions that would have taken place.

I can't imagine anyone reading this from the Ai resident point of view and not having your heart at least somewhat moved to sadness. Chapter 7 tells us that Ai is a small town that defeated the 3,000 men Joshua sent to attack the city. Imagine the jubilation of the Ai people. Imagine the feeling of beating the great army of Joshua not only once but actually sent them running twice! This happened right after the walls of the huge city of Jericho came tumbling down. Surely the little town of Ai was scared spit less of Joshua's great army until they defeated it two times. If I were an Ai resident I would feel pretty confident. All the men of the small town were most likely enthusiastically chasing out Joshua's army, sensing victory was theirs. Then the scene changes. The other part of Joshua's army that was waiting in ambush sets the city on fire. The men of Ai look back and see the fire destroying their city. Oh, imagine the confusion and the worry about their families. The army they were chasing starts pursuing them, and the ambushers of the city start coming after them until they are surrounded. Other than the King of Ai, not one person is left living.

If you are anything like me, this is likely very hard for you to read and not feel angry and sad about these seemingly innocent people dying. But what this attitude shows is that I, and perhaps you, don't really have a grip on or deep understanding of God's holiness. If we were like Isaiah, who got a glimpse of God's holiness, rather than having an "I deserve or they don't deserve" attitude, we would join him in falling to the ground saying, "I am ruined. For I am a man of unclean lips, and I live among a people of unclean lips." I think we would have a very different perspective and response to what happened in Ai.

When we see perfection, we are faced with the reality of how imperfect we really are. God is completely perfect and completely just, so He gives people what they deserve. Habakkuk 1:13 says "Your eyes are too pure to look on evil; You cannot tolerate wrong." God's holiness demands that there be consequences for sin. Because He is a perfect and just judge, He cannot excuse or ignore sin. Imagine if someone did something very terrible to you (get something in your mind), and they stood before the court and the judge decides to let what they did slide. Imagine if the judge said, "Well, that is ok, I will let it go today; just be nicer next time." That would be a bad judge since his job is to uphold justice. Since God is perfect, He will never fail at being a perfect judge, and the consequence of sin is His wrath.

It seems that when God's wrath is directed at the sin of our offenders, it is a wonderful thing that we are grateful for. But when that same wrath is pointed at us, it is so easy to throw up our defenses and plead that we don't deserve it.

*How do you feel about God's holiness and wrath?

*When we are feeling like we/they don't deserve wrath, what does that show us we are believing about God? About mankind?

Let's look at one more place where God will express His wrath. Read Ezekiel 38:18-23. This is telling of the time when Russia will attack Israel in the last days.

*If you saw this happen in your lifetime, what would be your thoughts and feelings?

Oh Lord, please rescue us from our self-centered lives. It is so hard for us to see that we actually deserve all the evil that is in the world because we have offended you. It is so hard to understand that because You are good, You punish evil. It is so hard for us to see that this life is about You and Your glory. God, we don't want to be morbid in delighting in your wrath, but we don't want to condemn You to justify ourselves either. We want to honor You rightly, because You are worthy. By Your Spirit would you enable us to understand the depths of who we are and what we deserve apart from You. You deserve every part of our life to be about making You known and reflecting You. Oh God, please humble us that we wouldn't be demanders and justifiers of ourselves but that we would fully rest on the work of the cross. Make us people that would see what we deserve and be driven to our knees in worship. Give us a glimpse of Your holiness and justice. Help us to humble ourselves under your mighty hand.

Holy

Week 4

Day 3

God, You are Holy. We can say that with our lips but it is so hard to really understand that deeply. Please give us a glimpse of Your holiness like You gave Isaiah that we would see ourselves rightly in relation to You. It seems we come to You so often with an "I deserve" attitude. Oh, Lord, only You can change us from the inside out and move us to approach You rightly. Today, we ask that Your Spirit would explain to us in a way that we can understand what we truly deserve apart from what Jesus did on the cross for us.

Eyes to See

Read 1 Samuel 4-6:21

> *What are some misconceptions the people in Ashdod and Ekron believed about God?

> *How did what they believed about God affect the way they acted toward Him?

> *How do you see God's holiness in these verses?

Ears to Hear

Everyone who is called by my name, whom I created for my glory, whom I formed and made (Isaiah 43:7 TNIV).

Isaiah shows us that we are created for God's glory. This means that we were created to display God's heart, His character, His greatness in the way we act and live.

But the reality is:
For all have sinned and fall short of the glory of God (Romans 3:23 TNIV).

We screwed up in doing and being what we were created to do and be. **We fell short of displaying who God was and therefore we are under His judgment**. It is kind of like being hired for a job. When you are hired to accomplish a certain thing and you don't accomplish that for which you were hired, you fail and in all reality should be fired. Why pay someone for what they were supposed to, but didn't do? This is sin, not being perfect in reflecting Who God is, not fulfilling that to which we were made.

Sinning and falling short of His glory can seem a bit abstract and unclear. But God in His grace didn't leave this open for uncertainty. He provided the Ten Commandments to help us recognize that we truly have fallen short. Any of us can look at that list and say, Yup, I don't measure up.

There is no one righteous, not even one (Romans 3:10-11 TNIV).
This means that throughout the span of time, not one person could stand before God being totally blameless. Not one person could stand before Him and say they lived completely perfectly in reflecting Who God is to those around them. Therefore, we deserve judgment. The wages of sin is death (Romans 6:23). Our wage or payment is death. We earned it. Our rightful consequence is separation from God and His goodness, here on earth and for all eternity. We rightfully deserve His wrath. We absolutely deserve what the small town of Ai received.

This is a big deal. Because unless we really see our sin, how can we see our need for someone to rescue us from our sin? Ray Comfort has a great analogy of this. There are two planes each full of passengers and flight attendants. On the first plane, the flight attendant hands out parachutes telling people that they should put them on because it will make their flight better, it will give them joy, fulfillment and peace, not even telling them why they should put the parachute on. So, people take the parachutes and put them on. After some time these people start getting cramped up from having the parachute on their back and not being able to sit up straight. Then some others on the flight start making fun of them and mocking them. You can imagine the frustration these people feel after being told that this parachute is going to make them happy and peaceful. So one by one they start removing the parachutes and when the plane crashes none live. On the second plane, though it is also full of people and they know they are going to crash, the flight attendant tells people, "We are going to crash" as she hands out the parachutes. People put them on, and after a few hours they too start cramping and people start making fun of them, but they are not fazed by it because they know their life is going to be saved by the parachute. Unless we see our need to be saved, how can we be? This is why it is so important that we truly understand that none of us can stand before God as innocent.

*How do you think a person becomes convinced they are in need of being saved?

*How does Romans 3:20 answer this question?

Jesus reminded the proud of the law, and reminded the humble of His grace to forgive. This really is the crux of the matter. We so desperately need to go from being guilty to being forgiven by the One we failed to measure up to. But what if this part is left out? What if we just tell people they need to have a relationship with God or ask Jesus into their heart without understanding their guilt and need of a Savior? What if a random person came up to you saying they just paid $5,000 worth of your traffic violations? I would think, "*What the heck are you talking about!*" I would think this person was crazy, I would think they were utterly foolish and would be a bit offended that they would assume that I was guilty of $5,000 worth of traffic violations. However, if first this person told me how I was just caught going 55 mph in a school zone where in fact there was a conference for blind kids going on and they told me of 8 outstanding parking tickets I had, then they told me they had paid that fee for me, I would be incredibly grateful. I would not think they were foolish and I would not be offended that they thought I did something illegal because I would know the fact that I had and deserved to pay $5,000. Romans 1:18 says, "The cross is foolishness to those who are perishing."

> *Do you believe someone can go from guilty to innocent without understanding they are guilty in the first place? Why?

Heart to Understand

Think back to the people living in the little town of Ai. Not one person living in that town was innocent before God. Since each and every one of them was guilty, they deserved to be punished under the wrath of God. Let's take it to a personal level. You and I and even the nicest person you know all deserve the same exact judgment that those people received. Ouch! We are all guilty and deserve God's wrath. I wonder if it is hard for you like it is hard for me to not jump to the "but Jesus" part of the story.

I was on student staff with Young Life for a while, and from experience I think the way they present the gospel at camps is pretty incredible, allowing high school students to really get a glimpse of what we are talking about here. At camp there are generally four talks about God's holiness, our sin, God's response and our response. The talk about our sin is generally at night time, and they do not share about the hope of being forgiven for not being guilty until the next day. It gives the students a chance to contemplate if they really are guilty and feel the effects of their sin.

> *Read John 3:36. What are your thoughts and feelings about God's wrath being toward a non-believer?

My hope is that you have seen more of how holy God is and understood a bit more of why we deserve His wrath. What we have been talking about is the beginning of life as a follower of Christ. Recognizing our guilt before God and repentantly turning to Him for forgiveness. But this is not the end of seeing God's holiness and seeing our sin. The entire Christian life will be filled with seeing more and more what God deserves and more and more of how we don't measure up and how we need Him more than we ever imagined. It will be filled with seeing more of how holy God is, and how inadequate we are without Him. At our first step of turning to Him, He did forgive us of all of our inadequacies, but throughout our life He is committed to reflect Himself through us which will mean showing us the inadequacies we were not aware were there, for the purpose of drawing us to depend on Him more.

       *What would happen in your life if you didn't believe God really was holy and will always act completely just?

       *What would happen if you didn't believe your sin was really that bad and nothing really needed to be done about it?

       *Since the time you made the decision to admit your guilt before God and receive His forgiveness, how has your view of God's holiness changed? How has your view of your own inadequacies changed?

       *Do you see that you have grown in seeing more of how holy and deserving God is and how undeserving you are? What has influenced your growth or lack of growth in this?

Oh Lord, we do not deserve to stand before You. We have failed to reflect and display You. We have not lived up to or measured up to what we were created for. God, You are so incredibly deserving. You deserve every part of who we are to glorify You. Thank You that our eyes are opened to how desperate we really are for you to rescue us from ourselves Lord, please prepare our hearts for what You want to communicate to us tomorrow.

Holy

Week 4

Day 4

Righteous Judge, we are grateful that You judge rightly, and that You can't be won over or bought over, but rather You give what is deserved. We are grateful that You can see so clearly and don't get confused about what is right and what is wrong. But God sometimes we don't like that You are completely just when we are the ones You need to discipline. But we do thank You anyway, that You will always do what is right and best, even if it is painful. Lord, please help us to better understand the justification that You bring. Give us eyes and hearts to recognize You and thereby be in awe of You today.

Eyes to See

"The created universe is all about glory. The deepest longing of the human heart and the deepest meaning of heaven and earth are summed up in this: the glory of God. The universe was made to show it, and we were made to see it and savor it. Nothing less will do. Which is why the world is as disordered and as dysfunctional as it is. We have exchanged the glory of God for other things" (Rom. 1:23).[5]

Skim through chapters 4-6 again

> *In what ways do you see God's commitment to His glory?

In the following verses, describe the situation for the people and explain why God acted or did not act.
Ezekiel 20:6-9

---

5   Piper *Seeing and Savoring* pg. 13

Ezekiel 36:16-23

Daniel 9:17-19

Psalm 79:9

Psalm 25:11

Psalm 106:8

1 John 2:12

1 Samuel 6:19

Philippians 2:9-11

Ears to Hear
God is committed to His glory

"You can learn a lot about someone when you find out what things get them fired up. When you see their heart's desire, it is like seeing right into them. When you talk to someone it doesn't take very long to see what they are passionate about. When we take a genuine interest in another person, we want to know what their life purpose is, their goal in life, the one thing they are striving for. Should our relationship with God be any different? Have you ever asked, *What is the one thing that God is most passionate about? What is the one thing that will always motivate Him to act?* Or in other words, *Why did God create the world? How does He act in it today?*

When we understand why God created, then we can understand what sin is. Romans 3:23 says, For all have sinned and have fallen short of the glory of God. Sin is failing to reflect the glory of God. It is the pursuit of satisfaction outside of Him, for we glorify the things we take satisfaction in. We have not glorified God the way we should. Instead of seeking our satisfaction and joy in Christ we have sought it elsewhere, in money, friends, sex, etc.

God's glory is of infinite worth. If He values anything of lesser worth above Himself, He is an idolater. For an idolater is one who places anything above that which is supremely valuable (God). If God belittles His glory by valuing something else above it, He would be unrighteous, thus He would no longer be God."[6]

"God either loves Himself supremely, or He over-loves something lesser than Himself, which is the very definition of idolatry. So God appropriately loves Himself, and He loves the public display of His excellence with a white-hot, relentless passion that never ends, never diminishes, and never dims. He created us for His glory (Isaiah 43:7). He liberated His disobedient people from Egypt for the sake of His name (Ezekiel 20:8-9). He promised restoration in the coming of Jesus out of concern for His holy name (Ezekiel 36:20-38)."[7]

Heart to Understand

Read Judges Chapters 14 and 15 and summarize it below.

Samson judged Israel for 20 years. It seems that he began a bit before Eli died and the ark was taken, and ended not many years before the battle at Mizpah we will read about in 1 Samuel 7.

This is just crazy to me that Samson and Samuel lived at the same time! They both were miracle babies given to women who were barren and both were set apart for serving God. It is an interesting thing to note that one did serve the Lord whole-heartedly and the other lived a very pleasure-driven life. One used the unique circumstances God had given him for encouraging the people to depend on the Lord, and the other used his unique abilities to please himself.

"Though Samson is impressive as an individual, he turns out to be anything but a military hero. He never leads Israel out in battle; he never engages the Philistines in martial combat; he never experiences a military victory. All his accomplishments are personal; all his victories, private."[8]

In Judges Chapter 14 and 15, Samson was looking to marry a Philistine woman. How sad that instead of believing that God wanted to deliver him and his people from the oppression of the Philistines, Samson didn't seem to care. He wanted what he wanted, not what God wanted.

"Samson's self-will ironically yielded no satisfaction for him. By disregarding his God-given privileges, he lost his bet with the Philistines, his wardrobe, his wife, and his honor. Samson's basic problem was that he did not submit to God's authority over his life. This authority problem manifested itself first in his refusal to submit to his parents' authority (14:3; cf. 17:6; 21:25). Samson did not exercise self-discipline. He let his passions control him (cf. 1 Cor. 9:27). Self-discipline is essentially a matter of submission to God's authority, not a matter of self-denial. Separation is essentially unto God, not just from things."[9]

"God's Spirit motivated Samson to slaughter the 30 Philistines in Ashkelon (14:19). Samson was not just taking personal revenge for what his Timnite guests had done to him. He was perhaps

6   Shramek, Dustin. Retrieved from http://www.geocities.com/Athens/Delphi/8449/passion2.html

7   McDonald, Dan. Retrieved from http://www.wrf.ca/comment/article.cfm?ID=459

8   Block, Daniel I. (1999). *Judges, Ruth. The New American Commentary series.* Nashville, TN: Broadman & Holman Publishers.

9   Constable, Dr. Thomas L. *Judges* Retrieved from http://www.soniclight.com/constable/notes.htm

unwittingly fulfilling his role as a judge in Israel by slaying the enemies of God's people. This was an act of holy war though Samson appears to have carried it out with carnal vengeance. He did God's will but for the wrong reason. God had chosen Samson as His instrument to begin defeating the Philistines, and He would use him for that purpose even though Samson was a reluctant servant. Thus we see God's providence overcoming the problem that Samson posed."[10]

Samson was not all bad. At some points in his life he did demonstrate some faith in God even though "the exploits of Samson read like the actions of an uncontrollable juvenile delinquent."[11] "However his unwillingness to remain dedicated to God resulted eventually in his loss of strength, his enslavement, and his death."[12]

*What do you recognize about the spiritual condition of the Israelites through Judges 14-16?

*Who do you most relate with: Samson, Samuel, the Israelites or the Philistines and why?

"The men of Judah did not respond to Samson as a judge whom God had raised up to deliver them from the Philistines. Instead of supporting him they meekly bowed before their oppressors and took the Philistines' side against Samson (v. 11-13). They rebuked Samson for jeopardizing their safety by attacking the Philistines. They were content to live under the Philistines' heel."[13]

"Gaza lay on the sunny Mediterranean coast in the heart of Philistine territory. It was probably a popular vacation site for compromising Israelites as well as the Philistines.

Perhaps Samson went there to enjoy the amusements that flourish in such places and to show off his physique on the "muscle beach" of his day. As the judge assigned to destroy the Philistines, his presence there for recreational purposes was inappropriate to say the least. It also reveals his great self-confidence since after 20 years of judging Israel he was undoubtedly a wanted man in Philistia. In contrast, Samuel, who was only a few years younger than Samson, was at this time ministering as a faithful circuit-riding judge in Israel's heartland."
Dr. Thomas L. Constable.

*All of us have some sort of authority in our life. Have your actions toward them resembled that of the men of Judah in any way? If so, how?

*How does what God did through Samson's life show us that He is committed to His own glory?

10   Constable, Dr. Thomas L. *Judges* Retrieved from http://www.soniclight.com/constable/notes.htm
11   Cundall, Arthur E. (1968). *Judges and Ruth. Downers Grove, IL:*.InterVarsity Press.
12   Constable, Dr. Thomas L. *Judges* Retrieved from http://www.soniclight.com/constable/notes.htm
13   Constable, Dr. Thomas L. *Judges* Retrieved from http://www.soniclight.com/constable/notes.htm

God tells us that He ultimately will be glorified. He tells us every person who has ever existed will see Who God truly is and will bow in confession of that fact.

>   *What is the point of living for God's glory now versus waiting until that day? (Feel free to use Samson and Samuel in your explanation.)

Great and Glorious, we see that throughout time You have been committed to Your glory, to showing the world Who You really are. Thank You for letting us see and know You. What an incredible gift. God, it is hard for us to understand Your ability to show wrath, but please continue to expand our minds to understand more of You. In our everyday lives, please make us aware of times that You are showing Your glory. Give us eyes that see and hearts that understand. How desperate we are for you.

Holy

Week 4

Day 5

Lord, here we are, presenting ourselves before You, the only One perfect in holiness, desperately dependent on You. Continue to let us see and understand Your holiness and how much we need You, and let us see Christ's sufficiency filling the gap for us.

Reflecting on the week:

This week we looked at God's holiness, the fact that no one is righteous apart from Christ and that God is committed to His own glory.
Look back at some of your answers for this week. What things stick out the most?

How has reflecting on these things influenced your relationship with God?

As we spend time with God and reflect on our lives, God uses it to let us see Him as more holy than we imagined and to see our depravity as worse than we thought it was. This then can lead us to the cross where we find grace (which we will look at next week.), Let's allow God to expand our understanding of His Holiness and our depravity today through personal reflection.

Read Jeremiah 5
In this chapter God is dealing with four sins of the people. Let's use it to examine our own lives.

Verses 1-6 show us the people were **ungodly**.

In these verses God tells Jeremiah to search for godliness/righteousness among the people. The test: does the person practice justice and truth?

Verses7-9 show us the people were **ungrateful**.
"They used His gifts in order to commit sin and serve their idols. The goodness of God should have brought them to repentance (Rom. 2:4), but they were ungrateful for His blessings (Hosea 2:4-13). Instead of acting, like men and women made in the image of God, they became like animals in heat."[14]

Verses 10-19 show us the people were **unfaithful**.
"This is the heart of the matter: Since the people did not believe God's Word, they turned their backs on God and went their own way."[15]

Verses 20-31 show us the people were **unconcerned**.
"The prophets' description of the people must have angered them, but it didn't shake them out of their complacency." Because they did not fear God "the courts were corrupt, the prophets were liars, the priests went right along with them-*and the people approved what was done and enjoyed it*!"[16]

Personal Reflection over the last week:

If you are anything like me and can't seem to remember the last week, you might want to get out your planner to help you reflect.

Godliness-

*How have you stood up for what was true? How have you not?

*How have you done what was right even to your own hurt? How have you not?

*In what situations have you dealt honestly and sought the truth? In which ones have you not?

Gratefulness-

*What are some resources that God has blessed you with? Have you treated them as more important than God?

14 Wiersbe, Warren (2007). *The Wiersbe Bible Commentary: Old Testament*. Colorado Springs, CO: David C. Cook
15 Wiersbe, Warren (2007). *The Wiersbe Bible Commentary: Old Testament*. Colorado Springs, CO: David C. Cook
16 Wiersbe, Warren (2007). *The Wiersbe Bible Commentary: Old Testament*. Colorado Springs, CO: David C. Cook

*Have you used them to sin? If so, how?

Faithfulness-

*What actions have shown that you believed God's Word?

*What actions have shown that you didn't believe God's Word?

Concerned-

*In your sphere of influence, have you done things to please people rather than God?

*Have you used your sphere of influence to please yourself rather than God?

*When you have seen other people doing what is not right, what was your response?

Gracious

Week 5

Day 1

God of Abraham, Isaac and Jacob, the beginning and the end, thank You for what You did in our hearts last week by giving us a glimpse of Your holiness. We are absolutely desperate for Your continued enablement to be pleasing to You. We want to be people that are godly, grateful, faithful and concerned. This week as we spend time with You and get into Your Word, please open up our Eyes to See and our Ears to Hear that we might gaze on Your grace and be a reflection of it to those around us.

Page Jumpers

Read 1 Samuel 7:2b-10:8
List things that jump off the page (verses that stand out to you):

-
-
-
-

Without seeing God's holiness, the worthiness of Jesus cannot be fully perceived. Last week we spent time thinking and reading about God's holiness which leads to His wrath. Hopefully the result we have come to see is how holy God is, what He truly deserves, and what we truly deserve. In light of that, as we look at His incredible grace this week, we will be in awe of His worthiness of our adoration.

This week we are going to look at how God shows His grace in different ways. We will look at examples of His grace given to the people, to Samuel, and to Saul.

Cloud of Witnesses

I was headed to Nepal for a 2-month-long mission trip. I tried my hardest to raise support but I was still $2,000 short. My plane ticket was already purchased, and I was told that if I didn't come up with the money, I would have to pay it back and not go. It was the day of departure and there were discussions happening about when I should go back home. The final plan was that I would go to the airport and then take a bus home. I was loading my bag on the bus to get to the airport, and within a matter of five minutes $2,100 came in. I experienced shock, tears and excitement all rolled into one. God had not only provided above what I needed but also had given me something I had always wished for, a story of how He does awesome things.

Gifts of money and material possessions provide great examples of grace when they are given as gifts, not earned. Sometimes I get overwhelmed with the grace we are shown. I wish I could write about every time God showed His grace through people's gifts to us - like my parents paying for my college, or last week when someone left $200 on our door step, or when we were given furniture/ musical instruments/ cars, or when Austin's parents helped us with the down payment on our home, or when I have been pulled over by a cop and he has not given me a ticket, (or when I deserved a parking ticket and didn't get one). None of this we earned, none of this we deserved. All of this demonstrates how so often we are given things we truly don't deserve.

Like we talked about last week, I have offended God. I have not measured up to His standard of perfection and have not lived up to perfectly reflecting Him, which is what I was created for. I have utterly failed and deserve His wrath. But He stepped in, He opened my eyes to see my failure and moved me to repentantly cry out to Him for His forgiveness. He forgave me, removing my sins as far as the east is from the west, and continues to fill my life with things that I do not deserve.

How can I not tell of our most precious gifts, our two boys? In our first week together reading 1st Samuel Chapter 1, I told you the story of Asher and how God brought him to us. Nine months later Asher's birth mom called us to tell us that she was pregnant again and wanted us to consider another adoption. That next summer our second son, Uriah John, was born. We did not earn these beautiful babies; heck, we weren't even involved in the conceiving them. We really did nothing to deserve them. God's grace is overwhelming.

Here Am I

Review Day 2 of last week and read Psalm 96 and 97 again.

To prepare our hearts for the week, put the following verses in your own words.
Romans 3:20-26

1 Corinthians 15:1-4

Ephesians 2:12-13

Colossians 1:15-23

Revelation 5:6-14

Gracious

Week 5

Day 2

Worthy King Who deserves everything we are, thank You for Your Holy Spirit that enables us to understand You. Lord, this week as we meditate on Your grace, let us see Your choice to bruise Your Son for our sin as more valuable than we have ever imagined. Let us come to say worthy, worthy, worthy is the Lamb from a mind and heart that understand. Break through our apathy and hardness of heart that makes us not see You as You truly are.

Eyes to See

Read 1 Samuel 7:2b-4

Baal was the Canaanite god of fertility and was associated with lightning and thunder. The Canaanites thought that he was in charge of providing what they needed for their crops. The rain is what would give them fertile ground which would give them wealth. Baal is who they thought would do this for them if they did enough to please him.

The people thought Baal would go back to the underworld which would make the land lose its fertility. In the spring time (they hoped) Baal would come back to life. They thought the offering of blood was what brought him back to life. So they would offer their own babies as sacrifices on the hot burning coals of the altar. If Baal came back to life and had sexual relationship with Asherah (the female half of Baal), then fertility of the land would be assured. As a result the Canaanites did horrible sexual acts on the high places in front of other worshippers to seduce or arouse Baal to have sex with Asherah. After this happened on the altar, all the members of the adult community would engage in intercourse with prostitutes. The whole community perverted two of the most beautiful gifts of God: the gift of a baby and the normal sexual relationship of a man and a woman within the confines of marriage. Their relationship to Baal was not one of love or grace but one of appeasement and fear.[17]

> *Do you think it was easy for the Israelites to destroy their idols? Why or why not? Describe what their various feelings and thoughts could have been.

---

17 VanderLann, Ray. *Faith Lessons on the Prophets and Kings of Israel*. Ray VanderLaan. Retrieved through Focus on the Family.

It seems this happens over a span of time. It must have taken quite some time to destroy the Ashtoreth's and the Baal's, to travel to Mizpah (7.5 miles from Jerusalem) ,and then to wait for everyone else to get there. Then they spend time corporately with the Lord, fast and confess. (Interesting to think that after a long hike with probably some gear, they must be hungry. But they choose to fast.)

*What do their actions over this span of time show you about their repentance?

Read 1 Samuel 7:7-17

*What could possibly be some fears the Israelites had when they heard the Philistines were coming to attack them?

*Try your best to put yourself fully in this scenario. Imagine that God had called you to smash your idols (think of what that is for you; what gets your attention more than God?) Then you walk eight miles with your family, carrying all of the necessary provisions for camping. When you arrive, you fast and confess your sin. Then you hear of terrorists coming to the exact place where you are with the intent of destroying you. How would you react? What would you feel? What would you be thinking and saying?

I think it is pretty neat how, as they were worshipping the true God, He used thunder (what their idol Baal was thought to control) to drive out their enemies. How reassuring to them that God was the one true God, the One that could provide what they needed.

Ears to Hear

The Israelites wanted Baal's blessing of fertility on their crops so badly that they were willing to offer the life of an innocent baby for their personal, financial, and material success. How similar this is to our culture, which does the same thing over 1,000 times every day for personal gain and convenience through abortion. Have you wondered how the Israelites could stand by and do nothing while they are doing these horrible acts? Yet, aren't we doing the same thing in our culture today?

Or think about the world's 148 million orphans (which has grown from 70 million just since 2002.) That is one child in every thirteen, think of the 10 million single moms with kids under the age of 18 in the United States, or the 700,000 women who become widows each year. How have you responded to their needs? How have you displayed God's heart to protect and provide for them? "God does not judge a nation simply because of the wickedness of the ungodly. He also judges a nation because of the disobedience of His own people."[18] I don't know about you, but thinking about this sure brings conviction to my heart. *Oh God, let us be people who love, people of active love.*

---

18   Fehsenfeld, Del (1993) *Ablaze With His Glory!* Nashville, TN: Thomas Nelson.

He gave justice and help to the poor and needy, and everything went well for him. Isn't that what it means to know me?' says the Lord (Jeremiah 22:16). So what is an example of how they were murdering the innocent? Look a few verses back at 19:4-5. "For Israel has forsaken me and turned this valley into a place of wickedness. The people burn incense to foreign gods-idols never before acknowledged by this generation, by their ancestors, or by the kings of Judah. And they have filled this place with the blood of innocent children. They have built pagan shrines to Baal." To defend the poor and needy is to rescue innocent children.

To know God, to walk intimately with Him, is reflected by our active concern for the orphans and widows. Tom Davis addresses this in his book *Fields of the Fatherless*, "If you searched the Bible from front to back, you'd find many issues close to God's heart. But you'd notice three groups of people that seem to come up again and again. Allow me to introduce you to those people God wants us to put at the top of our priority list: the orphans, widows, and aliens (strangers). These are the weak, the underprivileged, and the needy among us, and they all have a desperate need of provision and protection. Scripture mentions the importance of caring for these individuals more than sixty times! Clearly, the protection and well-being of these people is one of God's great and constant concerns. He actually defines Who He is by His promises to them. Consider His promise to provide: *A father of the fatherless, a defender of widows* (Psalm 68:5)."[19]

Our passivity and complacency of taking care of the orphans, widows and foreigners is sin. It is not reflecting Who God is. We talked last week about how our sin, personal and corporate, will not go unpunished. On the topic of our sin, Henry Blackaby says, "God knows full well-as we could never know-the appalling destructiveness of sin. He knows what sin has done to us; He knows how it hurts and impairs us. For every sin we've committed, He understands the full harm done to ourselves and to others, as well as the awful affront which it is to Him."[20] God was not content to let sin go unpunished. "God through the death of His Son, purposed to deal radically with sin… In the graciousness of God, every moment of experiencing His continuing judgment provides us an opportunity to remember how tragic sin is, how it turns us into His enemies, and how costly it is for God to deal with it."[21]

How do these verses describe Jesus, Who God was pleased to crush in order to punish sin?

Colossians 2:9

Colossians 1:15-18

Hebrews 4:15

> The seven holidays as listed in Leviticus 23 are called the "feasts of the Lord". Christ can be clearly seen each of the feasts and collectively tell the story of God's redemption of man. Many scholars agree that the first four feasts Christ has already fulfilled while the last three are yet to come.

1 Peter 2:22

19 Davis, Tom (2008). *Fields of the Fatherless*, Tom Davis Colorado Springs, CO: David C. Cook
20 Blackaby, Henry (2005) *Experiencing the Cross: Your Greatest Opportunity for Victory Over Sin.* Colorado Springs, CO: Multnomah Books.
21 Blackaby, Henry (2005) *Experiencing the Cross: Your Greatest Opportunity for Victory Over Sin.* Colorado Springs, CO: Multnomah Books.

Hebrews 12:2

Philippians 2:10

Titus 2:13

"When we recall the horror and frightful injustice of God's pure and blameless Son being crucified, the question often comes; *Why?* We want to know: could there not have been some other way? Was there no other way to save us from sin? If you haven't yet done so, I urge you to stand in the presence of God and ask Him, "Why did Jesus have to die?"[22]

Heart to Understand

An interesting observation can be made in verse 6.
"So they gathered at Mizpah and, in a great ceremony, drew water from a well and poured it out before the Lord."

The final feast of the Jewish year was the feast of Tabernacles. This was a time where the family would retreat for eight days. They would build huts as a reminder of the temporary housing that God provided for the Israelites when He led them out of Egypt, and would hang fall crops in the booth as a reminder of God's faithfulness. The first and the eighth days were set apart to worship and present an offering to the Lord. Each day of the Feast of Tabernacles was filled with festivity. Each day, the high priest along with all of the priests would descend from the Temple Mount to the pool of Siloam to fill a pitcher of water and head back up to the Temple Mount by a different route. In the midst of a "great ceremony", the high priest would pour the water out of the pitcher onto the altar. They did this to ask for God's blessing on their nation so that He would provide His life-giving water. How amazing that Jesus called out to the people in John Chapter 7 to come to Him or to present themselves to Him during this feast of tabernacles so that He could cause life-giving water to flow out of them. This must have shaken their understanding, that if they presented themselves to Him (which that in itself is them admitting He is God) that He would bless them and change them from the inside out. Perhaps this could be the heart attitude of the people in verse 6. Perhaps they were turning to God in repentance and were asking for His blessing of life.

In Acts 2 Peter gives a message to the people about how Jesus really is God. After he convinced many that Jesus was God, he tells them they are the ones who crucified Him. The response was "Peter's words pierced their hearts, and they said to him and to the other apostles, 'Brothers, what should we do?' (Verse 37) They became deeply aware of their own sinfulness which led to repentance. "This became the central call of early Christian preaching. Repentance (*metanoia*) involves primarily a radical change in a person's central affections, convictions, and life direction. It signifies a recognition

---

22   Blackaby, Henry (2005) *Experiencing the Cross: Your Greatest Opportunity for Victory Over Sin.* Colorado Springs, CO: Multnomah Books.

that one's life has been oriented around self and sinful pursuits and an embracing of God's will and priorities."[23]

Repentance is a key ingredient in revivals. We see it in Acts 2:14 through the end of the chapter. Another example of revival occurred in Wales, starting in 1904. The great call to the people was to confess any known sin to God and to make any wrong done to others right, put away any doubtful habit, to obey the Spirit promptly, and to confess faith in Christ publicly. This is how that movement was explained. "The movement went like a tidal wave over Wales, in five months there being a hundred thousand people converted throughout the country. Five years later, Dr. J. V. Morgan wrote a book to debunk the revival, his main criticism being that, of a hundred thousand joining the churches in five months of excitement, after five years only seventy-five thousand still stood in the membership of those churches!

The social impact was astounding. For example, judges were presented with white gloves, not a case to try; no robberies, no burglaries, no rapes, no murders, and no embezzlements., District councils held emergency meetings to discuss what to do with the police now that they were unemployed.

As the revival swept Wales, drunkenness was cut in half... There was even a slowdown in the mines, for so many Welsh coal miners were converted and stopped using bad language that the horses that dragged the coal trucks in the mines could not understand what was being said to them. That revival also affected sexual moral standards. I had discovered through the figures given by British government experts that in Radnorshire and Merionethshire the illegitimate birth rate had dropped 44% within a year of the beginning of the revival. The revival swept Britain, Scandinavia, Germany, North America, Australia, Africa, Brazil, Mexico, and Chile. As always, it began through a movement of prayer."[24]

Nineveh is another example of revival. The prophet, Jonah, was called to encourage them to turn from their sin and to tell them of the wrath that God was going to bring on them lest they repent. After initially rebelling, Jonah rebels God's call no longer and goes to the wicked city of Nineveh telling them what God wants him to say. They respond the same way the Israelites did, by fasting and turning from their evil ways. They are an example of 2 Chronicles 7:14 that says If my people who are called by my name will humble themselves and pray and seek my face and turn from their wicked ways, I will hear from heaven and will forgive their sins and restore their land. However, not a hundred years later after this great repentance, they reverted back to extreme wickedness, cruelty and pride. God again in His grace sent Nahum the prophet. This time they did not turn as they did in Jonah's time, and they were completely destroyed. Nineveh no longer remains today.

*What would it *look like* for our nation to repent and honor God above all else?

*What do you think it would *take* for our nation to repent and honor God above all else?

---

23   Arnold, Clinton E. (2009) *Illustrated Bible Backgrounds Commentary*. Grand Rapids, MI: Zondervan
24   Orr, J. Edwin. *Prayer and Revival*. Retrieved at http://www.jedwinorr.com/prayer_revival.htm

*What is your responsibility as a believing citizen in your nation?

*What is the hope 2 Chronicles 7:14 offers and how can you personally live it out?

Oh Lord, You are incredibly gracious to allow us to recognize our need for You. You don't stop there, You even enable us to repent and then give us forgiveness. We do not deserve Your forgiveness. We do not deserve the abundant life You offer, yet You lavish these things on us. What can we do but praise You, telling You that You are worthy, worthy, worthy!

Gracious

Week 5

Day 3

God of grace, You offer us what we don't deserve, not only us, but all people of all time. You offer us what there is no way for us to earn. Thank You for Your grace in showing us what is true about You and what is true about us. Thank You for your gift of forgiveness and innocence that You offer us. Thank You for the opportunity to get to know You so intimately and to be acquainted with Your ways. Thank You for what You are doing in our lives right now and what You will continue to do in the future. Help us to not heap up information but let You do the work of transformation in our hearts.

Eyes to See

Read 1 Samuel 8

*What are your thoughts about the elders wanting Samuel to appoint a king to lead them?

*Why do you think Samuel was displeased with them asking him to do this?

*What was their underlying reason for wanting a king as recorded in vs. 19-20?

Ears to Hear

>*Have you ever been discouraged by people you are serving getting mad at you for helping them turn away from the bad and toward what is actually best for them? What was the situation and how did you feel about it?

This is what was happening to Samuel. It was his job to serve these people and lead them to love and obey God. Instead the people he ministered to wanted to be like other nations and rely on a man instead of God. They didn't want to trust God but looked to other things for security. They rejected God's authority in their lives. (God was going to give them a King, in His timing, not theirs.) No person is able to fulfill all of our hopes, only God is. Samuel knew this and it broke his heart for the people because God was not being honored.

Like God, Samuel spent his entire life serving these people and then he received the ultimate rejection from them. Let's look at how God meets Samuel in his rejection and disappointment.

>*What does God say to Samuel? Do you think it was helpful for Samuel to hear? Why?

God encouraged him in what is true and told him how to respond. I have experienced similar encouragement. I remember one day when I was extremely discouraged. I had just had someone I ministered to say very hurtful things to and about me. I was so discouraged that I couldn't think or talk about anything. Austin turned to me and said "Let's play the 'what's true' game". That had always been helpful in the past, so I unenthusiastically agreed. He began quoting verses, and none of them were specifically resonating with this particular situation until he said, "Consider it pure joy my brothers whenever you face trials of many kinds because you know the testing of your faith develops perseverance" (James 1:2-3 NIV). For some reason that gripped me and gave me hope. It reminded me of the big picture and gave me perspective. Basically God was playing the 'what's true' game with Samuel, giving Him perspective and direction.

How encouraging that God did not get mad at Samuel because of the bad attitudes of the people he was entrusted to shepherd. I have talked with many young women who have led small group Bible studies that have been very successful and others that have struggled to have just one or two people there. These women have taken the initiative to steward what God has entrusted to them. Praise God! But sometimes it can be embarrassing if the results don't turn out like we hoped. When I have been in this position, I have been fearful of what others thought about me. I feared that they would see me as a failure. Perhaps this is how Samuel felt.

Founder of Campus Crusade for Christ, Bill Bright used to always say that effective evangelism is taking initiative in the power of the Holy Spirit and leaving the results up to God. How true that is in whatever God calls us to. The things God puts before us to do is not about the results but rather is about your obedience in stewarding that responsibility.

Heart to Understand

God gives us what we don't deserve. How gracious of God to tell Samuel the truth, giving him proper perspective of the situation and telling him how to handle it.

Let's look at another example of God's graciousness in remarkably reminding people of what is true. Read Acts 12:1-18

*What is your favorite part of this story? Why?

This took place during the Jewish Festival of Unleavened Bread which was seven days after Passover. The Festival of Unleavened Bread was celebrated to remember how God had brought the Israelites out of slavery in Egypt, and called them to live as holy, not being influenced by the world and getting involved in sin by those who surrounded them. This foreshadows Jesus as our Unleavened Bread. He is called the Bread of Life and was without sin. Ok, but get this. What a great teacher God is! He orchestrates this great visual reminder of what is true. During the very festival they are to be focusing on these things God actually leads Peter out of slavery. How gracious and able God is to remind us what is true and change our perspective. Oh, let us offer our minds and hearts to Him more often for Him to do this work.

This was the very thing Samuel was discouraged about. Instead of the people being led out of slavery, they were willfully choosing to be led back into slavery by asking for a king on their terms. When we insist on things our way, on our terms, it only leads to bondage. Romans tells us that God allows us to go our own way and be led into this bondage in order to bring us to repentance.

Write out the first half of 2 Chronicles 16:9

"These people have the rare quality of wholeheartedness, single-mindedness, and genuine sincerity. The prophets of old were ablaze with God's glory. They did not come representing themselves. They came representing God alone. They feared only Him and, therefore, were fearless in their preaching. God is not looking for better programs. He is looking for better men and women whose hearts are wholly His. The Bible urges us to be single-minded in our devotion to God. It also warns that a double-minded man will be "unstable in all his ways" (James 1:8). Unstable men are driven by impulse, circumstance, or the fear of others. But those with perfect hearts have set their minds, wills, and affections on the one supreme objective-to know, love, honor, and obey God with all their hearts. Such wholehearted devotion will not flirt with love of money, self, pleasure, or the praise of men. Their lives are under the control of the Spirit, who makes their days purposeful, their minds disciplined and clear, and their spirits alert, sensitive, and energized by God Himself. Such people are more concerned about building God's reputation than their own. They are committed to building His kingdom rather than seeking a personal following of their own. Their focus is not on security in this life, but on one day hearing their Master say, "Well done, thou good and faithful servant."[25]

Take some time to tell God what is on your heart in regards to these things. Feel free to write it down if that would help to keep you from getting distracted.

25 Fehsenfeld, Del (1993) *Ablaze With His Glory!* Nashville, TN: Thomas Nelson.

Gracious

Week 5

Day 4

Holy, Gracious and Worthy God, thank You for the conviction You bring in our hearts. We know that it is a sign that You do care about us enough that You are not willing to leave us the way we are. Help us to be receptive to Your work in our life. Help us to recognize when we are being prideful and not receiving Your grace. Help us to delight in You more and more all of our days. Help us to see the gifts You continually offer to us. Teach us today through Your Spirit as we submit to You.

Eyes to See

Read 1 Samuel 9:1-10:8

 *Describe what we are told about Saul.

The tribe of Benjamin had almost been destroyed because of their rebellion against the law (Judges 19-20). Despite what Saul says, his family was very powerful and wealthy, owning much real estate, cattle, and servants. Saul's perseverance in finding the animals shows that he is not a quitter, but there in no indication of any sort of spiritual life. Saul lived within 5 miles of where Samuel lived but had no idea of who this spiritual leader was. It doesn't seem he was against religion; he simply did not make knowing the Lord a vital part of his life.

 *There are many ways God's grace is shown to Saul in this chapter. What are some of them?

*In verse 21 when Saul says that his tribe is the least of all the clans, what does that reveal about Saul?

*What things happened to Saul that he would have found to be strange?

During my time in Nepal there were a number of strange things that happened to which I did not know how to respond. One of these situations happened as three of us were walking around the city. We had gone a bit too far and were lost. We were in a huge city where we didn't speak the language and didn't have access to a car. We began praying and walking, hoping God was leading us back home. We came to a colorful building and wondered what it was. As we continued we came to a giant building with a fence around it. Our curiosity was sparked, so we peeked in at the gate, trying to see what it was. As we peeked in, intimidating guards approached us. Not seeing this as a time to run, we stood there, like deer in headlights. When they got to us they stopped, then came a young boy dressed in a red toga-like outfit. When he reached us, he motioned for us to follow him. Because we were young and curious, we did. After a walk across the parking lot, we could see into the building where there were scores of young boys bowing down and chanting. We knew then that we were at some sort of monastery but had no idea where this boy was leading us. We went inside and began the walk up flights and flights of stairs and started asking each other in little spurts, "Where are we going?" Finally we reached the top of the stairs and were motioned to sit down and wait at a door. After a while a boy dressed just like the first boy opened the door and ushered us into a room full of gold statues and introduced us to the lama. We were shocked, wondering, *What do we do?* There we were with a Buddhist lama (much like the Dali lama) who spoke English. I thought, *What a great opportunity to share the gospel with him.* That didn't work out so well. He was one of the most unreceptive people I have ever spoken with. He probably saw me as an ignorant, impertinent young lady. His driver knew where our hotel was and drove us home. I recount this story to you because perhaps the feelings I experienced that day in Nepal were similar to Saul's feelings during his time with Samuel.

Ears to Hear

God's grace to Saul is an example of how God gives us what we don't deserve, often in contrast to our feelings. Who knows what someone rich and handsome like Saul was had to be insecure about, but he seemed to show us he was. His insecurity would grow and give him problems for the rest of his life because he never turned to the Lord with it. In spite of his feelings of insecurity, God provided him with directions to get to Samuel, helped him in his current mission of finding donkeys, gave them food to eat (which was much needed since they had run out of food), told him about his future, and anointed him king. Although God did all of this for a man who was full of insecurity, Saul lived for the praise of men rather than for the praise of God. The grace of God truly is overwhelming.

*How would you describe what it looks like to live for the praise of man, rather than for the praise of God?

*What are a few examples from your own life?

*How is living for the praise of man rather than the praise of God related to pride?

It is easy to think of pride as only arrogance, describes as someone thinking they are better than others. Though this may be arrogance, it is not the whole picture of pride. Another side of pride is pretending that you are less than what you really are. Arrogance and false humility are really fruit of the same heart condition of pride.

"Pride causes us to make ourselves the exception to the rule. It feeds on self-gratification, self-satisfaction, and self-promotion. Pride causes us to think that what we know in our heads, we actually have in our lives. This is one of the greatest weaknesses of today's church. We have more information than any generation in church history, but we lack the depth and character of previous generations. The more we know, the more we think we have accomplished."[26]

Humility, on the other hand, is what captures and displays God's heart. Listen to this "When Jesus heard this, He was amazed. Turning to the crowd that was following Him, He said, 'I tell you, I haven't seen faith like this in all Israel!' (Luke 7:9)

What caused God in the flesh to be amazed? It was the humility of the centurion. Read Luke 7:1-10

Stop at…
"this man deserves" In reality, he does not deserve anything, but this comment is evidence of this man's character that people would say this about him.

"his master valued highly" For a master to value a servant, it either speaks well of the master or the servant. We would tend to think the servant was pretty awesome, but the master's attitude toward Jesus reveals that he was exceptional.

"I do not deserve to have you come under my roof." How he viewed himself was very different than how others viewed him. He didn't put himself on a pedestal like others did. He didn't have an "I deserve" attitude thinking he should get whatever he wanted.

"do this and he does it" He sees himself rightly when he lives as though Jesus is his authority.

---

26 Fehsenfeld, Del (1993) *Ablaze With His Glory!* Nashville, TN: Thomas Nelson.

The centurion is a great example to us of humility (not to mention a great reflection of God-but that is a topic for another day). He was honest about who he really was no better, no less.

Read 2 Kings 6:1-7
For a long time this story was so confusing to me, but not long ago God really encouraged me through it. Imagine you join a crowd to cut down some trees. You are not very experienced with an axe and have to borrow one from someone else (they were too expensive for you to buy). You're chopping away at a tree when the axe flies off the handle and into the water. You panic, not sure how to retrieve the axe head, and thinking you can't afford to replace it. Imagine the embarrassment of having to ask for help from the person you admire the most, the person you want to think you're really great. Not only do you have to ask for help, they ask you pointed questions about your mistake. But it is beautiful that because this guy humbles himself by admitting his need, and God helps him in his mistake. Jesus died for mistakes, too.

Another way God showed grace to Saul was by authenticating Samuel's words, giving him many signs that were fulfilled to show that what Samuel said was true. For Saul to tell others he would be king could possibly be grounds for people to kill him. God gave him everything he needed to stand with confidence.

Heart to Understand

"We need to see first and foremost that God is God. He is perfect and complete in Himself, He is overflowing with happiness in the eternal fellowship of the trinity, and that He does not need us to complete His fullness and is not deficient without us. Rather we are deficient without Him; the all-sufficient sacrificed Son, is the stream of living water that we have thirsted for all our lives. Unless we begin with God in this way, when the gospel comes to us, we will inevitably put ourselves at the center of it. We will feel that our value rather than God's value is the driving force in the gospel. We will trace the gospel back to God's need for us instead of tracing it back to the sovereign grace that rescues sinners who need God."[27]

Every day there is the tendency to have our hearts drawn away. CJ Mahaney describes three ways this can happen.[28]

1. Legalism which is basing our relationship with God on our own performance.

2. Condemnation, which is being more focused on our sin than on God's grace

3. Subjectivism, which is basing our view of God on our changing feelings and emotions.

    *We obviously cannot see Saul's heart, but from his attitude and actions, which of these three possibilities do you assume he has a tendency toward?

---

27   Piper, John (2000). *The Pleasures of God.* Colorado Springs, CO: Multnomah Publishers.

28   Mahaney, C.J. (2002) *The Cross Centered Life: Keeping the Gospel the Main Thing.* Colorado Springs, CO: Multnomah Publishers.

*Which one do you have a tendency toward?

*What keeps you from receiving God's grace?

*Is there a situation right now that is preventing you from receiving God's grace?

Lord, we acknowledge that we cannot do anything worthwhile apart from You enabling us. We need to be receivers of Your grace everyday but our hearts are so proud that it makes it hard. Please help us to yield, to humble ourselves like the axe-thrower, and to see You help us in our mistakes. Oh Lord, please help us to have the habit of receiving freely what You offer.

Gracious

Week 5

Day 5

Oh gracious God, Your grace truly is sufficient. Thank you for the different ways you show Your grace and how You've offered Your grace so freely as we can see in Scripture. What a great and mighty God You are!

Reflecting on the week:

Look back at what you discovered this week. What things stick out the most?

This week we looked at how God showed His grace to the Israelites, to Samuel, and to Saul.

> *Who do you find yourself relating to the most as you receive what you don't deserve from God?

God's grace abounds to us. Here is a sample of the blessings God has given you if you have turned to God and let Him forgive you. These are things you do not deserve. These are truths that you have not earned but are gifts to you from God. Highlight the ones that strike you. As you go through the list, spend some time praising and thanking God for what He has given you, remembering that each one is an undeserved gift of His grace to you.

93 things true of the follower of Christ.[29]

1. I am a child of God (John 1:12)

2. I am a saint (1Corinthians 1:2)

3. I am the salt of the earth (Matthew 5:13)

4. I am the light of the world (Matthew 5:14)

5. I am protected by the power of His name (John 17:11)

6. I am set free by the truth (John 8:31-33)

7. I am eternally secure in Christ (John 10:27-31)

8. I am kept from the evil one (John 17:15)

9. I am one with God the Father and Jesus the Son (John 17:23)

10. I am God's gift to Christ (John 17:24)

11. I have peace with God (Romans 5:1)

12. I have been justified by faith (Romans 5:1)

13. I have access into the sphere of God's grace (Romans 5:2)

14. I can rejoice in trouble. (Romans 5:3)

15. The love of God has been poured out in my heart. (Romans 5:5)

16. I am reigning in life with Jesus Christ (Romans 5:17)

17. I have been reconciled to God through the death of Jesus (Romans 5:10)

18. I have been raised to walk in the newness of life (Romans 6:4)

19. I have been united with Christ through His death and resurrection (Romans 6:5)

20. My old self was crucified with Christ (Romans 6:6)

21. I am alive to God in Christ Jesus (Romans 6:11)

22. I am not under the law, but under grace (Romans 6:14)

23. I have eternal life in Christ Jesus (Romans 6:23)

24. I am freed from the power of sin (Romans 6:18)

25. I am free from condemnation (Romans 8:1)

26. I am a servant of God (Romans 6:22)

27. I am free from the power of sin and am a servant of righteousness (Romans 6:18)

---

29 Adapted from Freedom in Christ Ministries

28. I am free from the vicious cycle of sin and death (Romans 8:2)

29. I am indwelt by the Holy Spirit (Romans 8:9)

30. I am led by the Spirit of God (Romans 8:14)

31. I am a joint heir with Christ (Romans 8:17)

32. I can be confident that all things work together for good (Romans 8:28)

33. I am being conformed to the image of Christ (Romans 8:29)

34. The Holy Spirit helps my infirmities (Romans 8:26)

35. The Holy Spirit makes intercession for me (Romans 8:26)

36. God foreknew me (Romans 8:29)

37. I have been given all things (Romans 8:32)

38. I am inseparable from the love of God (Romans 8:35)

39. I am more than a conqueror through Christ (Romans 8:37)

40. I am God's temple (1 Corinthians 3:16-17)

41. I am washed, sanctified, and justified by the blood of Jesus (1 Corinthians 6:11)

42. I have been bought with a price (1 Corinthians 6:20)

43. I am the image and glory of God (1 Corinthians 11:7)

44. I am triumphant in Christ (2 Corinthians 2:14)

45. I am a sweet aroma manifesting the presence of God wherever I go (2 Corinthians 2:14-15)

46. I am adequate for anything because my adequacy comes from God (2 Corinthians 3:5)

47. I am a new creation in Christ (2 Corinthians 5:17

48. I am an ambassador for Christ (2 Corinthians 5:20)

49. I am strongest when I am weakest (2 Corinthians 12:10)

50. I am crucified with Christ and the life I now live is His (Galatians 2:20)

51. I am redeemed from the curse of the Law (Galatians 3:13)

52. I have access to the fruit of the Spirit, love, joy, peace, patience, kindness, goodness, faithfulness, gentleness, self-control (Galatians 5:22-23)

53. I am in Christ Jesus (Ephesians 1:1)

54. I am blessed with every spiritual blessing (Ephesians 1:3)

55. I am chosen by God to be holy and blameless (Ephesians 1:4)

56. I am predestined to adoption through Jesus (Ephesians 1:5)

57. I am accepted in the beloved (Ephesians 1:6)

58. I have redemption through His blood (Ephesians 1:7)

59. I am forgiven of all my sins (Ephesians 1:7)

60. He has made known to me the mystery of His will (Ephesians 1:9)

61. I have wisdom as I try to know His will (Ephesians 1:8)

62. I am predestined according to His purpose (Ephesians 1:11)

63. I have obtained an inheritance (Ephesians 1:11)

64. I am filled with the Holy Spirit of promise (Ephesians 1:13)

65. I have the spirit of wisdom and revelation in His knowledge (Ephesians 1:17)

66. My eyes have been enlightened (Ephesians 1:18)

67. I know the hope of my calling (Ephesians 1:18)

68. I know the exceeding greatness of His power to me (Ephesians 1:19)

69. I know the riches of His inheritance in the saints (Ephesians 1:18)

70. I am made alive with Christ (Ephesians 2:1)

71. I am raised with Christ and seated in the heavenlies (Ephesians 2:6)

72. I have been saved by grace through faith (Ephesians 2:8)

73. I am God's handiwork created in Christ Jesus for good works (Ephesians 2:10)

74. Once afar off, I am now made near by the blood of Christ (Ephesians 2:13)

75. I have access through Jesus to the Father (Ephesians 2:18)

76. I am a fellow citizen with the saints in God's household (Ephesians 2:19)

77. I am able to walk boldly into Christ's presence (Ephesians 3:12)

78. I am strengthened with power through His Spirit in the inner man (Ephesians 3:16)

79. I am receiving exceeding abundantly above all that I ask or think (Ephesians 3:20)

80. I can speak the truth in love (Ephesians 4:15)

81. I can grow up in all things under Him (Ephesians 4:15)

82. I have been renewed in the spirit of my mind (Ephesians 4:23)

83. I have put off the old man (Ephesians 4:22)

84. I once was darkness, but now I am light in the Lord (Ephesians 5:8)

85. I am able to walk as a child of light (Ephesians 5:8)

86. I am able to be strong in the Lord and the power of His might (Ephesians 6:10)

87. I can choose to put on the whole armor of God and stand (Ephesians 6:13)

88. I am able to quench all of Satan's darts (Ephesians 6:16)

89. He who started a good work in me will finish it (Philippians 1:6)

90. The mind of Christ is in me (Philippians 2:5)

91. God is working in me both to desire and to do His good pleasure (Philippians 2:13)

92. My citizenship is in heaven from which I eagerly await His coming (Philippians 3:20)

93. I can rejoice in the Lord always (Philippians 4:4)

El Shaddai

Week 6

Day 1

El Shaddai, God of might even over the frailty of man, knowing You is the greatest treasure that we could ever know. Your power and might far exceed anything we understand. Though we don't even understand the tiniest bit of Your power, we know that because of Your power and might You are able to help us see You and help us understand. We long to know You more; please open up our eyes to treasure You as our El Shaddai.

Page Jumpers

Read 1 Samuel 10:9-12:25
List things that jump off the page (verses that stand out to you):

-
-
-
-
-

Cloud of Witnesses

Log on to www.BeholdingHimBecomingMissional.com and watch the "Journey to the edge of the Universe" video under week 6. It is a great eye opener to the power of God. He is powerful enough to create things beyond what you or I could ever even imagine and things we didn't even know existed.

This week we are going to look at God's power and strength in revealing truth to us, in delivering us, and in making us adequate for His service.

Here Am I

Read Luke 14:25-35, Mark 1:16-20 and Matthew 16:24-27.
Write out some specifics below of what it costs to be a follower of Christ.

What is the purpose of the cost?

Spend some time sharing your thoughts and feelings with the Lord regarding these things, and ask Him to show His power and might in speaking truth to you, delivering you from a self-focused life and preparing you for the direction He desires for you.

El Shaddai

Week 6

Day 2

El Shaddai, Powerful and Mighty God, how small our understanding of Your power is. How incapable and weak we think You are sometimes. In reality You are stronger and more powerful than we will ever come to know. This week as we read Your word and spend time gazing at You, let us truly see You. Our minds and hearts are not big enough to understand, but we can understand in part. Please reveal Yourself to us. Give us a glimpse of Your glory.

Eyes to See

Read 1 Samuel 10:9-27

> *What would your reaction be if someone you knew previously did not have any sort of relationship to the Lord and suddenly he begins reciting verses and telling people what God said about things?

> *What insights do you gain from reading that Saul does not present himself to Samuel as he was told to do, but rather hides with the baggage?

> *Why do you think Samuel starts talking about how God brought them out of Egypt?

> *What does this process of selection show about God's knowledge?

*Read verse 19 again. What do you suppose they were thinking and feeling when Samuel said this?

Read Mark 5:21-24, 35-43

*What do these verses show you about God's ability to fully know, engage and meet our needs?

Read Mark 5:24-34

*What do these verses show you about God's ability to fully know, engage and meet the need?

*Now that we have looked at these verses from Jarius' and the bleeding woman's point of view, think about them from the disciples' point of view.

"O Lord, you have examined my heart and know everything about me. You know when I sit down or stand up. You know my thoughts even when I'm far away. You see me when I travel and when I rest at home. You know everything I do. You know what I am going to say even before I say it, Lord. You go before me and follow me. You place your hand of blessing on my head. Such knowledge is too wonderful for me, too great for me to understand!" (Psalm 139:1-6)

He knows us perfectly and intimately. He knows our thoughts, motives, strengths, capabilities, weaknesses, why we do what we do, and why we think what we think. He knows exactly how He has designed each one of us, and exactly what we need at each moment. He knows how we feel right this moment, how it happened, and how long it will last. He knows how intense it is and every emotion associated with it. He knows our hurt, rejection, and our pressures. He also knows the purpose of our trials. Because He knows us so well, so perfectly, He knows what will change us so that we can better experience and know His love for us. He knows how to cause us to better reflect Him.

Ears to Hear

Like we see in Mark God is powerful enough not only to fully know, engage and meet whatever need their might be, He is also powerful enough to show us and convince us of what is true.

God's power and strength to reveal truth.

"As the rain and the snow come down from heaven, and do not return to it without watering the earth and making it bud and flourish, so that it yields seed for the sower and bread for the eater, so is my word that goes out from my mouth: It will not return to me empty, but will accomplish what I desire and achieve the purpose for which I sent it" (Isaiah 55:10-11).

How amazing is it to think that God cannot speak without purpose. When He speaks, action follows.

*Think of scenarios in the Bible where God spoke; what was the action that followed?

*What emotions were aroused in you as you thought about this?

Now look at the verses that precede what we just read.
"Why spend money on what is not bread, and your labor on what does not satisfy? Listen, listen to me, and eat what is good, and you will delight in the riches of fare. Give ear and come to me; listen, that you may live" (Isaiah 55:2-3a).

I feel a bit like a kid being invited to a candy store when I read these verses. I had the "I cannot believe I actually get to…" feeling. Because we just read how God's Word is always with purpose, it will always have a point and be worth it. We are invited to listen, and not only to listen, but to be filled. We are not just invited to be filled with a temporary filling like with bread, but filled in a way that will sustain us, not just here on this earth but in heaven forever. Life is what will result from listening to Him. How refreshing that is. It seems that on TV and in movies and even in nature, all around us, we are surrounded by death. How refreshing that a relationship with Him will be life-giving to us and to others around us. Oh, life!

I am not very good at saying hard things when they need to be said. I know a lot of people that are and I admire them greatly, but I am not, and never have been. Therefore, it is so encouraging to me that God is absolutely strong in this. Nothing can or will hinder Him from speaking up. When He speaks up it will bring life! He is not afraid that He will offend someone. He sees beyond temporary hurt to the ultimate value of the truth spoken. How wonderful to know that God cannot be controlled by people's feelings. God will give life. You know the embarrassment of walking around with your zipper down all day and nobody told you. Well, it can never be that way with God. He will speak truth. I hope that is as refreshing to you as it is to me. He has our backs. He will not lie to us.

Heart to Understand

Because we have such a generous God, He gives us the opportunity to be life givers as well to reflect Him by sharing His life-giving words. He does not give this privilege just to a select few. At the moment you surrendered your life to Him, He blessed you by commissioning you.

If you are a believer, God has called you to reach the world for Christ. That will look different for each of us (which we will talk about in depth next week), but His heart for multiplication in evangelism and discipleship will be the same. He has sent us to bear fruit that will last (John 15:16).

From the mouth of Paul he says, "I urge you to live a life worthy of the calling you have received" (Ephesians 4:1). We have been given the very mission Jesus had. "As the Father has sent me, I am sending you" (John 20:21).

What was Jesus' heart and mission? Underline the parts of the verse that answer this question.

"Father, I want those You have given me to be with Me where I am, and to see My glory" (John 17:24).

"I have come into the world as a light, so that no one who believes in Me should stay in darkness" (John 12:44-46).

"I have not come to call the righteous, but sinners to repentance" (Luke 5:32).

"I have come that they may have life, and have it to the full" (John 10:10). Life- Greek *Zoe* meaning eternal life

"For even the son of Man did not come to be served, but to serve, and to give His life as a ransom for many" (Mark 10:45).

Why are the miracles and good deeds Jesus did written down for us to see? "Jesus performed many other signs in the presence of His disciples, which are not recoded in this book. But these are written that you may believe that Jesus is the Messiah, the son of God, and that by believing you may have life in His name" (John 20:30-31).

The miracles and good deeds Jesus did were to give evidence of Who He really was. They were not the end goal but a means to the goal. Jesus' passion was bringing the lost to the light, and He has commissioned us to do the same. "Then the eleven disciples went to Galilee, to the mountain where Jesus had told them to go. When they saw Him, they worshiped Him; but some doubted. Then Jesus came to them and said, "All authority in heaven and on earth has been given to Me. Therefore go and make disciples of all nations, baptizing them in the name of the Father and of the Son and of the Holy Spirit, and teaching them to obey everything I have commanded you. And surely I am with you always, to the very end of the age" (Matthew 28:16-20).

So since God has sent us, what does He promise? Does He promise that it will be easy and great all the time? No, in fact He promises the opposite.

"In this world you will have trouble. But take heart! I have overcome the world" (John 16:33).

But He also has promised that He is everything we need. He is our sufficiency, and will provide all we need.

"My grace is sufficient for you, for My power is made perfect in weakness" (2 Corinthians 12:9).

"His divine power has given us everything we need for a godly life through our knowledge of Him Who called us by His own glory and goodness" (2 Peter 1:3).

And He promised to be with us.

When God called Moses to go to Pharaoh and lead the Israelites out of Egypt, God said "I will be with you" (Exodus 3:12).

When God called Joshua to lead the people into the Promised Land, He said, "As I was with Moses, so I will be with you; I will never leave you nor forsake you. Be strong and courageous" (Joshua 1:5).

When God calls Israel to actively trust Him for the future, He said to them, "So do not fear, for I am with you; do not be dismayed, for I am your God. I will strengthen you and help you; I will uphold you with my righteous right hand" (Isaiah 41:10).

When God calls Jeremiah to speak truth and tell of His coming judgment, He says to him, "Do not be afraid of them, for I am with out and will rescue you" (Jeremiah 1:8).

When God tells Paul to keep speaking, He says, "Do not be afraid, keep on speaking, do not be silent. For I am with you" (Acts 18:9-10).

Every time someone was commissioned, God promised He would be with them. Now when God says He will be with us, it is not like when we say it. When we say it, we often mean, "Let me know if you need anything." But God means He will show up; He will reveal Himself; He will do what only He can do. When we make ourselves available to Him, He does the heart and life changing work.

Remember, God says the same thing to us. "All authority in heaven and on earth has been given to me. Therefore go and make disciples of all nations, baptizing them in the name of the Father and of the Son and of the Holy Spirit, and teaching them to obey everything I have commanded you. And surely **I am with you** always, to the very end of the age" (Matthew 28:16-20).

*What are some fears and hesitations you may have about being called and commissioned?

*How can you actively trust God with these fears and hesitations?

El Shaddai

Week 6

Day 3

Oh Lord, yesterday was a tough day to swallow. Fear and doubt are so easily present in our lives. Please help us to recognize and turn to You for Your enablement and to believe what You say is true. As our El Shaddai, You are able to deliver us from our fears and our doubt. Let us see that to be true today.

Eyes to See

Read 1 Samuel 11:1-11

> The Philistine threat to Israel in the west presented the Ammonites with an opportunity to move against Israel from the east with supposed impunity. TNIV study Bible.

   *Summarize these verses.

   *What are your thoughts about how quickly the men of Jabesh seem to ask for a treaty and offer to be their captivity?

   *How would you feel if you were in these people's shoes? Would you have responded differently? Describe what this could look like in our day.

   *What do you think about how Saul motivates the men to come fight in the army against the Ammonites?

*When the people of Jabesh heard they would be rescued, I love how it says, "They were elated." Yeah! Why do you suppose they told the Ammonites they would surrender instead of telling them they would fight them?

*What were the deep fears and doubts the people of Jabesh had?

*When thinking about living out the mission God has called you to, what are your deep fears and doubts?

Ears to Hear
God's power and strength to deliver us from our fear and doubt.

Read Luke 14:25-35

*What sticks out to you?

*When Luke starts talking about salt, does vs. 34 feel out of place to you? Why?

*Why does he talk about salt in this context?

If we were to keep reading, we would see that after Jesus makes it very clear that anyone that follows Him will need to sit down and calculate the cost, He begins to share His passion for the lost. He begins telling parables: the parable of the lost sheep, the lost coin, and the lost son. This is not a coincidence that counting the cost for really being a Christ follower has to do with caring about the lost and thereby sharing your faith. The end of these parables ends with We had to celebrate this happy day. For your brother was dead and has come back to life! He was lost, but now he is found! (Luke 15:32) After sharing His passion for the lost being found, He goes on. He begins to talk about being good stewards of what we have been entrusted, to invest in our eternal future instead of things that will not be around in our future. How it makes sense to use what we have been entrusted toward Jesus' passion of seeing the lost come to know Him!

Read 1 Corinthians 2:1-5

*How do you feel knowing that even the great apostle Paul was fearful?

The vast majority of people who are alive today have not heard or understand the gospel. It doesn't matter what country you are in; many only have a vague idea of Who Jesus is and why He came, died and rose again. Most are searching for authentic understanding of who they are and how they fit into this world. Many wonder about God and if He likes them or is happy with them (not something you want to find out at the end of your life). Most suffer from a lack of personal acceptance, low self-esteem, and security. When people are exposed to the Gospel, God is able to reach them, and to change their motivations, attitudes, and actions from the inside. As a result they are transformed by the ultimate truth of the Bible through the power of the Holy Spirit.

"We would all agree that there is a lost world to reach with the redeeming news of the gospel. China has a billion unreached. Europe is still addicted to post-modern philosophy. The cracks are barely visible in the Muslim world. Missionaries are slugging it out, one person at a time in Japan. The battle for the hearts of the Russian people still rages. And if it were not enough that the world beyond our borders is dying for the message of Christ, we look down our own streets and see moral decay. In America, 30 percent of all births are illegitimate. Heinous acts of crime accost our senses through the media each week. National condom week is "celebrated" each February on hundreds of college campuses. Racial divisions still run deep. Generation X has become "Generation Why?" as absolute truth gives way to moral relativism."[30]

When He saw the crowds, He had compassion on them, because they were harassed and helpless, like sheep without a shepherd. Then He said to his disciples, "The harvest is plentiful but the workers are few. Ask the Lord of the harvest, therefore, to send out workers into His harvest field. (Matthew 9:36-38)

"The gospel of Jesus Christ is as powerful, as needed, as relevant to our times as it has ever been. What will it take to make disciples of all nations? The heart of Jesus beat with compassion when He saw the multitudes. He saw disease and sickness. He saw people who were harassed and helpless. But His solution was astonishing: not more technology, more strategies, or more programs, but "Ask the Lord to send out workers." God's plan has been, is, and always will be people reaching people. We don't need today's workers to work harder. We need reinforcements who will come join the harvest."[31]

I had a friend tell me that on his mission trip to Nepal, his team went to small villages where they later heard the entire village came to put their trust in Jesus. I have another friend who told me about her trip to Africa where she said a girl's arm was healed as she prayed for her. I have another friend who had the opportunity to share the gospel with the Pope and was invited back by him to train others how to share their faith. Multiple friends have told me of people who have said, "I can't believe you are here. I was just praying that someone would come teach me how to start a ministry."

---

30   *Sending Developing Life-Long Laborers*. Retrieved from www.godsquad.com
31   *Sending Developing Life-Long Laborers*. Retrieved from www.godsquad.com.

But not only does God do so much in other people's lives when we make ourselves available to Him and go, but He also does so much in our own hearts. The most common thing I hear from people when they return home from a mission trip is that they think God did more to help them than He did to help others.

Here are some examples of the vision and maturity that is built by going.

Gratitude- Austin and I took a team of twenty students to Russia to share our faith, disciple students, and start a college ministry. The trip was great and we got to see God do amazing things in Russian student's lives as well as the lives of the students that came with us. But this trip like no other gave me such gratitude for our country and how there is a desire for justice. There were multiple instances in Russia that made it obvious that justice was not something their country values. As an example, a Russian student told us that 14 of the 17 students in her class paid the teacher off to have their grade raised. This is absolutely normal everyday stuff.

Willingness to give- On a trip to Africa, we spent time with a group of women from the poorest tribe in the country. As we were sitting with them in their hut made of trash, they joyfully insisted on giving us their small bananas (which actually tasted like potatoes). They had next to nothing, yet the little they did have, they were willing to give. An experience like this will cause you to see into your own heart.

Mission trips build confidence, deepen a relationship with God, and expand our small view of God.

Heart to Understand

Read Romans 10:13-16. List the things you are currently doing to participate in this process.

*What are some things that would keep you from going on a short term mission trip?

*Are any of these things rooted in fear and doubt?

Please don't let these things keep you from going. Each objection rooted in fear and doubt can be overcome by our El Shaddai, God Who is full of power and might, even over the frailty of man. As you take it to Him, He will be with you. He will come through for you. He will show Himself as God.

In a college class when asked, "What makes you unique?" I would answer that I had absolutely no desire to travel. God changed my heart by once again using my curiosity. I heard of all the amazing things God was doing in Africa and I wanted to be there, I wanted to see first hand. So a friend of mine and I went. We stayed with some missionaries to see what they did. The gentlest way I can put it is that I really did not enjoy it. I never wanted to go to another country again. But I wanted to be involved in ministry so I did a discipleship training school and part of the training was to go on a mission trip. That trip revolutionized my heart for going. Since that trip I have been on many, even this last one to Russia for two months with a 1 year old. When you seek to further His kingdom He will provide what is needed (even diapers, formula and baby items.)

"God's desire is to bless His people so they can also be a blessing. Part of being a blessing is taking the news of a relationship with God to people who don't know Him. Ministries which include being a blessing as a non-negotiable value will reflect more life and vitality than ministries which solely focus on being blessed. Furthermore, a worldwide focus further intensifies the life and vision of a group of believers. A world vision can only add to what God is already doing in people's lives."[32]

Log on to www.BeholdingHimBecomingMissional.com and watch the video "Send Me"
Spend some time with the Lord. Share with Him your thoughts and be open to His leading. Write down the things He brings to mind.

---

32 Campus Crusade for Christ staff web resource

El Shaddai

Week 6

Day 4

God of all strength and power, give us hearts to say, Send me I'll go." Give us faith to trust that You will come through, You will show Yourself as God. Please give us Your eyes and Your ears and Your heart for the nations. Oh Lord, rock us out of our apathy and complacency and living for the pleasure of this life. Oh Lord, help us invest our split second in eternity on earth for the greatness of telling people about You. Expand our vision, enlarge our hearts to feel what You feel toward the lost. Empower us to say "no" to unbelief and walk by faith in You, the Author and Perfecter of our faith. God we are desperate for You.

Eyes to See

Read 1 Samuel 11:12-12:25

*What is the point Samuel is trying to get the people to see in his sermon?

> Samuel perceives that it is now the appropriate time for the people to renew their allegiance to the Lord. The kingship he speaks of is the Lord's, not Saul's. Samuel calls for an assembly to restore the covenant relationship between the Lord and his people. TNIV study Bible.

*What is the result of this speech?

*What was Samuel's great desire for the people?

*After the people recognize their sin and turn to God, Samuel talks about not serving idols. How does this relate?

Ears to Hear

"Missions is not the ultimate goal of the Church. The glory of God is the ultimate goal of the Church because it is the ultimate goal of God. The final goal of all things is that God might be worshipped with white hot affection by a redeemed company of countless persons from every tribe and tongue and nation. Missions exists because worship doesn't. When the Kingdom finally comes in glory, missions will cease. Missions is penultimate (the next most important thing); worship is ultimate. If we forget this and reverse their roles, the passion and the power for both diminish."[33]

When we have our eyes and hearts turned toward bringing glory and honor to our awesome God and His worldwide objective of recruiting the nations to be His totally on-fire worshippers, we will not be lured by the things of this world.

There are more people alive today than ever before throughout all of history. When Dawson Trotman, founder of the Navigators was asked, "What is the need of the hour?" he did not respond by saying we need more money, bigger buildings, better communication, more effective tools, or better transportation. He said, "What is the need of the hour, you ask? God is the God of the universe and He will supply every need we have to pull it off. The need of the hour is an army of soldiers dedicated to Jesus Christ, who believe that He is God and that He can fulfill every promise He ever made, and that nothing is too hard for Him. The need of the hour is men who want what Jesus Christ wants, and who believe He wants to give them power to do what He has asked. Nothing in the world can stop these men."

The main thing we need in order to do what God has called us to do are not skills or training. God will provide those for us. The main thing we need is a heart that is willing. Steve Shadrach in his moving book, *The Fuel and the Flame* lays out how each believer has a role in the Great Commission. He says, "Every believer is to pray, give, witness, and disciple, but are we called to do more, to find a specific role (or calling, if you will) in Christ's global cause?". The answer, of course, is yes. He goes on to lay out four "habits" to develop in our lives while asking the Lord to make it clear which our primary role is right now.

World Christian Roles:

1. The Goers. The frontline warriors.

2. The Senders. The financial rope holders.

3. The Welcomers. Ministers of hospitality-ministering to the world from your own country (international students)

---

33 Piper, John (2010) *Let the Nations be Glad: The Supremacy of God in Missions.* Grand Rapids, MI: Baker Academic.

4. The Mobilizers. The strategic motivators.

    *Which of these gets you excited?

In Day 3 we talked about the importance of going on a short term mission trip.

    *Why do you think going on a short term mission trip is important no matter which of these roles is your primary role?

Heart to Understand
God's power and strength are able to make us adequate.

"By now you've realized the Great Commission is not a spectator sport. You need to get out of the stands and onto the track and find the race that God has for you."[34]

Hebrews 12:1-2 exhorts us to get up, strip down, dig in, and, move out: "Therefore, since we have so great a cloud of witnesses surrounding us, let us lay aside every encumbrance and the sin which so easily entangles us, and let us run with endurance the race that is set before us, fixing our eyes on Jesus, the author and perfected of faith, who for the joy set before Him endured the cross, despising the shame, and has sat down at the right hand of the throne of God."

    *How has God been leading you?

    *What steps can you take to walk by faith in how God has been leading you?

Take the rest of your time today to reflect on what God is doing in your heart and spend some time talking to Him about it. It might be helpful to use the space below to write some things down.

Now to Him Who is able to do immeasurable more than all we ask or imagine, according to His power that is at work within us, to Him be glory in the church and in Christ Jesus throughout all generations, for ever and ever! Amen Ephesians 3:20-21

34 Shadrach, Steve (2003). *The Fuel and the Flame*. Tyrone, GA: Authentic

Not that we are competent in ourselves to claim anything for ourselves, but our competence comes from God.
2 Corinthians 3:5

But thanks be to God, Who always leads us as captives in Christ's triumphal procession and uses us to spread the aroma of the knowledge of Him everywhere. 2 Corinthians 2:14

El Shaddai

Week 6

Day 5

What an incredible God You are! That You loved us so deeply and intensely that You gave it all to bring us into relationship with You. Thank you for calling us to join You in doing what Your heart beats for. You are so generous to let us partner with us, though we are weak and You know we are but dust. Thank You for the incredible gift of sharing the most important news with people who don't know. Thank You!

Reflecting on the week:

*Sum up what we studied this week.

*What stood out the most to you this week? Why did it stand out?

Not only can God use you around the world but also right in your own backyard.
Identify your personal sphere of influence:

*Sharing your faith. What people do you regularly come in contact with who may not know Christ yet?

*What would it look like to share your faith within your sphere of influence?

*What new or young believers do you know who you could potentially begin discipling?

*What would it practically look like to spend time with these people to help them become multipliers for God's kingdom?

*What more mature believers do you know who you could train to share their faith, disciple other women and encourage to reach the world for Christ?

Begin to pray for these people that you have listed and make it a priority to be involved in their lives. If you would like practical resources to help you share your faith and disciple women visit

www.MissionalWomen.com
www.looktoJesus.com
www.growingleaders.com
www.perspectives.org
www.CruPressGreen.com
www.cm07.crusade.org
www.shorttermmissions.com
www.evangelismtoolbox.com
www.thetravelingteam.org
www.thetask.org
www.eternityimpact.com

I highly recommend reading the book, *The Fuel and The Flame,* by Steve Shadrach to help you practically prepare your heart as well as come up with a plan and implement your ministry.

Revealing

Week 7

Day 1

The Great I AM, what a privilege to get to see your glory, to get to behold You and reflect You as we run with endurance the race marked out for us. As we bring our minds and hearts before You, let us see You as You truly are. Show us Your glory today that we would be transformed to reflect You better and more clearly to this world that desperately desires to see You. This week give us eyes to see and ears to hear and tender hearts to be molded as we look at how You reveal Yourself through us as we live on purpose.

Page Jumpers

Read 1 Samuel 13:1-14:23
List things that jump off the page (verses or thoughts that stand out to you):

-
-
-
-
-

Cloud of Witnesses

Durango, Colorado, is a small college mountain town of about 25,000 people. There are very interesting dynamics of this town that Austin and I had the privilege of experiencing for ten years. One of those dynamics was the passion for the Lord that His people evidenced. I believe that because Durango can be a very hard place to live for the Lord, it brings out a refinement and strength. On a very small scale it is similar to what is happening in China, where extreme numbers of people are coming into relationship with the Lord which many credit to the Lord allowing persecution. During our season in Durango, Austin and I had the privilege of befriending a godly young man and woman (who we will call Matt and Julie) who are now married. About a year ago, they picked up their young lives and moved to East Asia where they are serving as "teachers". They are both gifted in teaching and desire to see young people come to know Christ and become multipliers for His kingdom. I just got a letter from them explaining what I will call a Jonathan step (taking a risk for God). They have a passion to see God's Word read and spread to the people who do not have access to it. Their passion is fueled by seeing 90% of the young people they work with love to read and have deep existential questions they cannot answer. But they do not have access to the book that will help them discover answers. Even if God's Word was available to them, they could not afford it since one third of the female students prostitute themselves to pay for school. For most of them splurging involves buying a milk tea for about 30 cents. Our friends have dreamed about what could be, dug in to get all the information they could about how to accomplish their dream, and are diving in to open up a place that will offer God's Word to these young people. As they have taken Jonathan steps, God has shown up and done what only He can do in bringing the details together for His name and character to be known.

This week we are going to look at how God reveals Himself to us and through us as we live purposefully. This week we will take Jonathan steps of our own to Dream, Dig and Dive into displaying God's heart and character to the world.

Here Am I

To prepare your mind for recognizing how God reveals Himself through our lives, log onto www. BeholdingHimBecomingMissional.com and reflect on the how the pictures reveal God's heart and character.

What are some of your thoughts, excitements, fears or anxieties having to do with this upcoming week's study?

Is there anything keeping you from presenting a willing heart to the Lord?

Spend some time telling God where you are at and asking for strength and for Him to align your perspective with His.

Revealing

Week 7

Day 2

Our God Who is able to motivate us, what a pleasure to get to connect with You today, to get to meet with You and to hear what is on Your heart. We submit ourselves to You, willing to hear, willing to understand. By Your Spirit, enlighten our minds and motivate our hearts.

Eyes to See

Read 1 Samuel 13:1-14:23

*Describe the scene of chapter 13.

> Could you imagine a grown man hiding in the dark etching on a wall, "Spare me, O merciful God, spare me, O Yahweh," and "Save, O Yahweh." That is what was found in a cave near the Judean fortress city of Lachish.
>
> The IVP Bible Background Commentary.

*How many soldiers had run off in fear? Where did they go or hide?

*Using your imagination, what would you picture a troop looking and acting like if they were "quaking with fear" (13:7)?

*Who had weapons and who didn't and why? How do you think this affected the soldiers and why?

*Describe how you would feel if you were the only one with the responsibility to protect and defend an entire army?

*What was Jonathan moved to do? Why?

Ears to Hear

What an example Jonathan is of a guy that knows God and ventures in faith to reflect Him. I think this has to be one of my favorite stories of taking a risk for God and seeing Him come through. Let's put ourselves in the story and try to see and feel what Jonathan may have been going through. Jonathan wins a battle against the Philistines with 1,000 men. The Philistines want revenge so they assemble a bigger army to retaliate. Imagine watching this huge mass of thundering chariots and soldiers march toward you as far as you can see, with the intent of mercilessly destroying you. A little scary. But there is hope. Samuel the prophet is coming. He is going to give a sacrifice and pray for God to be on your side. Day after day goes by and the Philistines are getting more and more numerous. Perhaps you begin to wonder, "Where is the inspiration and encouragement from our great leader, Saul?" After a few days the mounting discouragement and fear provoke our imaginations to wonder what the Philistines are going to do to us when we are captured. What kind of torture will they use? The rumors begin of what they did to so and so's friend when they were caught. Then worry starts to set in. Why is Samuel not coming? Is it because the Lord will not support us? Is it because the Lord is not on our side? After an entire week Samuel hasn't shown up. In direct disobedience Saul makes the offering in Samuel's place. Sure enough, after the offering was made, here comes Samuel. Saul is too proud to admit his foolishness and rather than taking responsibility for it, he tries to cast blame everywhere except where it is due. Samuel begins to say, "You have done a foolish thing… You have not kept the command the Lord your God gave you; if you had, He would have established your kingdom over Israel for all time. But now your kingdom will not endure." Hearing this would bring me to shake in my boots. My leader has not brought God's favor but rather brought His judgment by acting foolishly. I would wonder, 'What in the world does 'your kingdom will not endure' mean?' I would surely think,"This is it, we are going to die. "Though I wish I would be the brave courageous Jonathan, I fear I would take off for the cliffs just the like the rest of the army, scratching in the rock, 'Oh God, please save me'.

But our friend Jonathan acts. This, is an appropriate time to remember Jonathan is human just like us. He has fears and insecurities and weaknesses just like us. I am sure he was scared witless being one of the only ones with a sword. But in his fear, he acts. He takes his armor-bearer (carrier of the military equipment and likely Jonathan's apprentice) to scope out the situation. He gathers information and makes a decision to step out and see what God does. Why? He believes what is true about God and decides to trust Him. He recognized that "Nothing can hinder the Lord from saving, whether by many or by few." So he decides to give God an opportunity to show His greatness. He says, "Come, let's go over to the outpost of those uncircumcised fellows. Perhaps the Lord will act in our behalf."

Jonathan's actions were based on His understanding of the Lord. He understood life was about God and His name and character being made known. No one else was doing what needed to be done, so rather than sitting back complaining and pointing fingers, he is moved to action. He recognizes what he has and recognizes God's ability and goes for it.

Like Jonathan we exist for God's glory to see Him and to display Him to the world or, in other words, to know Him and make Him known. Before Jonathan could do anything, he had to **DREAM**.

I have the incredible privilege of working with the future leaders of our country, college students. I love how they are old enough to discover who they are apart from their parents and to figure out how they personally relate to God. God has built me to love college students and I could go on all day telling you what I love about them. But I would like to share with you something I have noticed as a result of working with them (if you are in college right now, maybe you can relate.) The vast majority of students that come to college have been trained to live the common, status quo life: to just *do*, just because. They have not been trained to live for the purpose of displaying God's heart or character. So instead of coming to college saying something like," I love seeing justice brought about where there is none, and I can best reflect and display the character of God through this, so I am going to pursue a law degree". Instead, what I hear over and over when I ask why someone is studying what they are studying is "Well, it is the only major that I didn't hate. " They were told that they had to go to college in order to get hired somewhere in order to make money and it will be icing on the cake if you actually get to enjoy what you do. A life lived like this will lead to looking back on life, saying "I wish I would have experienced what I was built for, seeing and displaying the character of God."

I cannot imagine anyone saying it better than John Piper in his motivating book, *Don't Waste Your Life*: "God created us to live with a single passion to joyfully display His supreme excellence in all the spheres of life."[35] We were designed and put here for seeing and displaying God's character. God's desire is for us to know Him and therefore reflect Him. And we all, who with unveiled faces contemplate the Lord's glory, are being transformed into His image with ever-increasing glory, which comes from the Lord, Who is the Spirit. (2 Corinthians 3:18)

All throughout scripture it is easy to see God's heart for us to know Him. As we begin to really see Him, we can't help but be changed from the inside out by the Holy Spirit. In his book *Visioneering*, Andy Stanley talks about developing vision for your life. "Glorifying God involves discovering what we could and should accomplish. We were created and re-created with His purposes in mind. And until we discover His purpose—and follow through—there will always be a hole in our soul. With that in mind, rethink the implications of this familiar verse: For we are His workmanship, created in Christ Jesus for good works, which God prepared beforehand so that we would walk in them. (Ephesians 2:10)."[36] He continues, saying, "Do you know what that means? It means you are the product of God's vision. God has decided what you could be and should be. You are the outcome of something God envisioned. Through Christ He has brought about, and continues to bring about, changes in you in accordance with His picture of what you could and should be. But His vision for you is not complete. You have a part. Look at the next phrase. We have been envisioned and then crafted for a particular purpose. That purpose is to do good works which God has envisioned us doing."[37] Wow. That communicates such confidence that the God of the universe actually envisions

---

35   Piper, John (2003). *Don't Waste Your Life*. Wheaton, IL: Crossway Books.

36   Stanley, Andy (1999). *Visioneering*. Colorado Springs, CO: Multnomah Publishers, Inc

37   Stanley, Andy (1999). *Visioneering*. Colorado Springs, CO: Multnomah Publishers, Inc

me doing what I greatly desire doing. Going on, he says "As Christians, we do not have a right to take our talents, abilities, experiences, opportunities, and education and run off in any direction we please. We lost that right at Calvary. But then, why would we dream of such a thing? God has a vision for your life. What could possibly be more fulfilling than that?

At the same time, we have no right to live visionless lives either. If God—think about it—if God has a vision for what you are to do with your allotment of years, you had better get in on it. What a tragedy to miss it. Missing out on God's plan for our lives must be the greatest tragedy this side of eternity.

Granted, this world offers a truckload of options when it comes to possible visions to pursue. But you were tailor-made, carefully crafted, minutely detailed for an elected divine agenda. It is what you were created and re-created for. God's visions for your life are the things that will give your life impact beyond this life. For, as we will see, God's visions always have an eternal element. His individual vision for your life is a small part of a plan He envisioned and put in motion long before you or I came on the scene."[38]

How desperate we are to have lovers of Jesus living out how they uniquely are built! Could you imagine if there were architects going to God and saying, "Lord, in Jeremiah 33:3, You tell me to call to You and You promise that You will answer me and tell me great unsearchable things I don't know. So what is the best way to design this building?" Imagine not just architects but scientists, astronomers, environmentalists, politicians, caretakers, teachers, musicians, business workers, artists and doctors all calling out to God saying, "Oh Lord, teach me how and why." He is the ultimate source of all these things and He uses these means to reveal Himself.

Heart to Understand

"But whatever you do, find the God-centered, Christ-exalting, Bible-saturated passion of your life, and find your way to say it and live for it and die for it. And you will make a difference that lasts. You will not waste your life."[39]

Let's think through a helpful acronym that lets God lead us in how we are built to display Him. The acronym is INVEST. Interests, Nature, Vision, Experiences, Spiritual Gifts and Treasure.

Interests-

   *What (types of things) and who (could be a people group, age group etc.) do you enjoy?

   *What do you see going on around you, and every time you experience it or think about it, it deeply affects you?

---

38   Stanley, Andy (1999). *Visioneering*. Colorado Springs, CO: Multnomah Publishers, Inc
39   Piper, John (2003). *Don't Waste Your Life*. Wheaton, IL: Crossway Books.

Nature/Personality-

   *What are some of your strengths and weaknesses mentally, emotionally and socially?

Vision-

   *What is happening that you desperately want to be different?

   *What are you passionate about? How would others describe you in terms of your passions?

   *What is something you would do in your lifetime for the glory of God if you knew you would not fail?

Experiences-

   *What events or activities have shaped who you are today?

   *What circumstances have shaped what you personally value?

Spiritual Gifts-

   *What comes naturally for you to do?

   *What do you enjoy doing? What thing(s) really refresh and encourage you after you do them?

*What have others noticed you are good at?

*If you have taken spiritual gift inventory tests, what did they say your spiritual gift(s) were?

*What are some things you are confident doing because of the ability God has given you?

Treasure-

*What has God entrusted to you? What resources are you a steward of?

And perhaps the most important question. How can you used what you discovered above to make Jesus known?

These are questions designed to help you dream. There can be many things that affect us, but perhaps one stands out above the rest. Perhaps of these things you wrote above, there is something that pulls at your heart and cries for your attention and action above the rest.

*What are your initial thoughts about actually diving in to do the thing you wrote down for the question, "What is something you would do in your lifetime for the glory of God if you knew you would not fail"?

*Do you truly believe God has created you uniquely to reflect Him to the people around you? Do you believe that your passions and abilities are important for displaying God's character to those around you? Why or why not?

Spend some time telling God your fears and anxieties about stepping out in courageous faith like Jonathan. Ask Him to ready your heart for change and to make it willing to dream big, dig deep, and dive courageously. Ask Him to give you a true understanding of how you are built and why it is important to the world around you.

Revealing

Week 7

Day 3

God of all wisdom and generous giver when we ask, thank You for letting us know You, for desiring to reveal Yourself to us and to let us see who You truly are. We want to see and know You more. Oh, Lord, give us Eyes to See You, ears that hear You, and hearts that understand You. We submit ourselves to You and ask for You to do Your transforming work in our hearts to cause us to fear You, that we may grow in wisdom and walk by faith.

Eyes to See

Read 1 Samuel 13:1-14:23

*What strikes you about what Jonathan did or didn't do before he acted?

*Jot down your thoughts about Jonathan not telling his Father?

*What does it make you think when scripture addresses Saul as father of Jonathan rather than addressing him as King Saul in 14:1?

*Describe Jonathan's plan. What leads you to believe that he put some thought behind this action?

In 1 Samuel 14:2, Saul is identified as being under a pomegranate tree. It was customary for leaders to hold meetings under well-known trees.[40] The other leaders including Jonathan were probably there. Verse 3 & 4 show us he leaves the meeting and already has in his heart to go take action. What could have caused this motivation in Jonathan? Could the meeting have not been going anywhere? Perhaps the leaders were talking and planning out of fear rather speaking out of faith remembering what is true about God? Perhaps his courage was beginning to melt by being around them? Perhaps this scenario was similar to the twelve spies scoping out Jericho, ten of whom saw the task as impossible, and hindered the others from thinking in faith-filled ways. Caleb and Joshua, however, saw the potential for God to act mightily and to show Himself faithful to His promises.

Ears to Hear

God tells us in His Word that He highly values wisdom, the right application of knowledge. In Proverbs He tells us many of the benefits of getting information from the counsel of others. "For lack of guidance a nation falls, but victory is won through many advisers." (Proverbs 11:14) Proverbs 11:22 describes a woman without discretion this way: "Like a gold ring in a pig's snout is a beautiful woman who shows no discretion." The Hebrew word for discretion is *ta'am* which means intelligence, advice, behavior, judgment, reason and understanding.

Read Proverbs 2:1-4 below and underline the descriptive words used to get wisdom and jot down the thoughts that come to mind as you read.

"My son, if you accept my words and store up my commands within you, turning your ear to wisdom and applying your Heart to Understanding indeed, if you call out for insight and cry aloud for understanding, and if you look for it as for silver and search for it as for hidden treasure..."

The descriptive words used for acquiring wisdom show a pretty bold progression. Accept, store up, turn your ear, apply your heart, call out, cry aloud and then the final intensity of searching as though you were searching for hidden treasure.
"Then you will understand the fear of the lord and find the knowledge of God. For the Lord gives wisdom; from His mouth come knowledge and understanding." (2:5-6)

As we truly pursue wisdom we will get to see the Lord more, and have right understanding which is a gift from Him. As we see more of Him, we will view ourselves more and more rightly, affecting the way we interact with and display Him to others.

"We waste our lives when we do not pray and think and dream and plan and work toward magnifying God in all spheres of life. God created us for this: to live our lives in a way that makes Him look more like the greatness and the beauty and the infinite worth that He really is."[41] This takes effort to learn from the knowledge and experience of others. After we dream of what could be, we need to take the practical steps to **DIG**.

---

40   TNIV footnotes. Grand Rapids, MI: Zondervan
41   Piper, John (2003). *Don't Waste Your Life*. Wheaton, IL: Crossway Books.

Heart to Understand

"For this reason I remind you to fan into flame the gift of God, which is in you through the laying on of my hands. For the Spirit God gave us does not make us timid, but gives us power, love and self-discipline." (2 Timothy 1:6-7)

Out of Paul's great affection for Timothy, he tells him to make an effort to develop how God has built him. Isn't the expression "fan into flame" a great picture of this?! What other words could be used in place of "fan into flame"?

We can develop our passions and gifts because the Holy Spirit gives us courage, ability, right motivation and the focus and self-discipline we need to do it. We don't need more or better gifts than what we have already been given. But rather we need to act on and use what we have already been gifted with.

*Considering your dreaming on day 2, who are some people that work in the field of your dream?

Make a list of good questions to ask them. (Some possible questions could be, "How would I get started if I wanted to..." "What do you wish you had known when you were where I am...?") Set up a time to get together with them this week and run through your questions.

*How can you put yourself in places to see these people work? How can you be involved or assist them in anyway?

*What are some books you could read that would increase your understanding of the 'how to's' of seeing your dream lived out?

Revealing

Week 7

Day 4

Revealer of Your glory and the motivator of our hearts, help us believe what is true about You, and give us courage to dream big, dig in to get wisdom, and dive in and trust that You will come through and show Your character. Give us eyes that see You as You truly are and hearts that are willing to give anything, to give others an opportunity to know You as well. Do as You see fit in our hearts today.

Eyes to See

Like Jonathan, Nehemiah is another great example of someone who took a risk of dreaming big, digging for wisdom, and diving in for God's glory.
Read Nehemiah 1:1-2:18

*What was Nehemiah passionate about? How did he dream?

*How did he dig?

*How did he dive?

*What was his view of God and how did it affect his actions?

Ears to Hear

Is anyone among you in trouble? Let them pray. Is anyone happy? Let them sing songs of praise. Is anyone among you sick? Let them call the elders of the church to pray over them and anoint them with oil in the name of the Lord. And the prayer offered in faith will make them well; the Lord will raise them up. If they have sinned, they will be forgiven. Therefore confess your sins to each other and pray for each other so that you may be healed. (James 5:13-16)

This is a great example of what it means to **DIVE** in. Whatever you do, in any circumstance, do it with action-oriented faith. If you are in trouble, whether it be stress, discouragement, or conflict in relationships, pray. If you are sick, ask for others to pray for you as well. If you are happy, then sing and praise God. In whatever situation you find yourself, respond with action, leaving the results up to God. This is what it means to dive in - to walk out your dream in action-oriented faith to display God's glory, His very heart and character.

It is so easy to back down and not actually take steps in the direction of doing what God has built us with a passion to do, to mask our fear or laziness in comments like, "It is just not God's time yet" or "God has told me to wait." These may very well be true but are perhaps the exception and not the rule. From scripture we see that God desires for us to be in motion, taking steps and trusting Him to come through, not sitting passively waiting for a mystical experience to confirm to us we are on the right track. Whatever comes our way, we are to act with action-oriented faith.

I think there are a few ways to cultivate active faith. One is by to think through each circumstance we are in and to respond in faith. Just this evening Austin and I were distressed over the natural disasters that have been destroying many people on our planet. What are we to do about 100,000 dying? "If anyone is in trouble, he should pray" or if anyone is sick, he should have others pray for him. The only way at that moment for us to respond actively to our sad hearts was to pray. In an effort to cultivate active faith, I recently spent a day trying to take inventory of each circumstance that came up, and note my response to it. What I found was very eye- opening. My first responses are often not action-oriented faith. I believe as I train myself to respond with active faith by the enablement of the Holy Spirit, I will begin to dive in more aptly. Will you consider experimenting with me and taking inventory of your circumstances and responses, and choose to respond in action-oriented faith?

A second way I think we can grow in our willingness to dive in whole-heartedly to what God has for us is by getting to know Him more and more. "But those who know their God will display strength and take action." (Daniel 11:32) Our courage will falter as time goes on if we don't constantly put before ourselves what is true about God. Not much in our media and everyday life is blatantly telling us what is true about God, though it is in front of our eyes all day. "For His invisible attributes, eternal power and divine nature are being clearly seen, through what has been made." (Romans 1:20) It takes His Spirit revealing Himself to us, which we don't see or understand when we are not listening. When Moses cried out "Now show me your glory" in Exodus 33:18, he was basically saying, Oh God, I want to know You, I want to see you. What God did was amazing. He let him see parts of His character in a more deep and full way. "And he passed in front of Moses, proclaiming, 'The Lord, the Lord, the compassionate and gracious God, slow to anger, abounding in love and faithfulness, maintaining love to thousands, and forgiving wickedness, rebellion and sin. Yet he does not leave the guilty unpunished… Moses bowed to the ground at once and worshiped." (Exodus 34:6-8) How can we get to know God more if we don't intentionally spend chunks of time with Him? I doubt Moses would have understood His Lord in this new way just in passing. It was because he carved time out just for him and the Lord.

*Practically what would you need to do to prioritize carving out time for getting to know God more?

*What are some verses related to your dream that remind /show you what is true about God? Take some time to write them in the space below and on a 3x5 card and memorize them, making them usable weapons in the face of discouragement and leaking vision.

Heart to Understand

"Do not be like the horse or the mule, which have no understanding but must be controlled by bit and bridle or they will not come to you" (Psalm 32:9).

Ten years of my life were spent performing on horseback so I grew up with an understanding of how horses act. The horse I rode for many years loved to run. The group I performed with would charge in to a stadium at a run with our bright costumes and music blaring as the sixty riders rode patterns. Before the start of each show we would wait at the gate. As we would wait, my horse "Moon" would get so excited that he would jump up and down, which was not the most comfortable thing in the world. I had to keep a very tight rein on him because he was so excited to run in. If I had let up on the reins at all he would have probably charged right through the gate. On the other hand, I have not had much exposure to mules but what I have seen of them is that they are very stubborn. It seems that they prefer to stand, and are not big proponents of moving. To get a mule to take a step forward when they don't want to move is probably a lot like the feat of getting an elephant to pull a cart.

*Do you tend to act more like a horse where you have to hold back the reins, or more like a mule where you have to shove it to get it to take even the tiniest step?

*On the flip side, what does it take to stop you? Once you are on track of being a good steward of what God has given you, what would stop you from this great pursuit?

This makes me think of Daniel in the Bible who dreamed of how God could use him even in politics for the government who had just conquered his city. He dug in to learn as much as he could, being extremely teachable. Then he dove in, responding in active faith pursuing opportunities to speak up and declare God's triumph.

In order to reflect the glory of God, revealing his character to those around us, we need to have the perseverance of Daniel. We need to not throw in the towel but rather reject the lies like "Well, I guess it just wasn't meant to be." We need to keep actively pursuing what God has called us to steward. When we fail or are rejected by the enablement of the Holy Spirit, we need to keep rising like Proverbs 24:16 which says, "A righteous man falls seven times but rises again."

*What are the things that are going to keep you from continually taking steps in active faith to pursue your passion for displaying God's character?

*Who can you communicate your desires to that would motivate you to keep walking by faith?

*What are some specific, realistic, measurable, with an end-in-sight goal you can make related to what God has been putting on your heart?

*It is inspiring and motivating to be around people who are pursuing a vision. Who do you know and respect that is pursuing a vision? How can you be around this person?

Spend some time telling God what is on your mind and asking for Him to enable you to dream, dig and dive into what He has specifically, uniquely built you to do to display Who He is.

"How is never a problem with God. When He puts something in your heart to do, He goes to work behind the scenes to ensure that it happens. In the meantime, we are to remain faithful to Him and focused on the vision." Andy Stanley

Revealing

Week 7

Day 5

Master of our soul and Commander of our destiny, Thank You for creating us in Your image. Thank You for the opportunity to reveal Your heart and character to those around us by the individual uniqueness You have given us. Continue to convince us that our life is for Your glory.

Reflecting on the week:

We are greatly blessed by the people who have dreamed big, dug deep to get wisdom and dove in to accomplish what we are uniquely built to do. My step-dad, Pete, comes to mind. He is gifted with landscape design and took a large back yard with a grassy hill and made it into a refreshing escape. My worship leader, Ryan, is gifted at arranging music. Each Sunday morning as we sing to the Lord, the music provides a way for me to meet with the Lord. My neighbor, Carrie, who is a stay at home mom, is continually finding ways to serve the neighbors in practical ways like pulling weeds, shoveling driveways, or helping clean and organize. There are others like Howard Hendricks who is a gifted teacher, and Mozart who brings healing and inspiration to hearts through his music. All of these people let us see an aspect of God's character and bring joy to the lives around them. *"There will always be a correlation between what God has put in an individual's heart to do and what He is up to in the world at large... Like a good father, our heavenly Father has a vision for each of His children, a vision that lends support to His work in this world."* Andy Stanley

*Sum up what we talked about this week.

*What stood out most to you about this week? Why do you think it stood out to you?

*What anxieties or thoughts surfaced? How have you responded to them? Take some time now to address them and respond in action-oriented faith.

Spend the rest of your time praying and taking your dream and passion to Him like Nehemiah did. (It might be helpful to re-read Nehemiah's prayer and response 1:5-11.) Talk to Him about every aspect of your hopes. Tell Him how much you need Him to come through, and ask Him to give you courage, enablement, consistent vision, a pure heart, and whatever else you are going to need to keep walking by faith.

Emmanuel

Week 8

Day 1

God with us, what a privilege to get to walk with You, to get to live life with You. How amazing that You, the God of Abraham, Isaac and Jacob Who was and is and is to come chooses to be intimately involved in our lives.

Page Jumpers

Read 1 Samuel 14:24-16:23
List things that jump off the page (verses that stand out to you):

-

-

-

-

-

Cloud of Witnesses

When Austin was a sophomore in high school, his older sister, Heather, went on a mission trip to Africa. Austin's parents thought it would be a good experience for him to experience a different culture so they let him take two weeks off of school to go join Heather after her mission trip to travel around the country a bit. Austin was not a believer at the time, so he was more interested in seeing Mount Kilimanjaro and gorillas than being a part of what God was doing there. While they were driving through the vast country of Tanzania, the military truck they were riding in the back of got in an accident and tipped over. It was dark and they were in the middle of nowhere with no one who spoke

English. Native Africans had heard the impact noise and were coming out of the woods. There were no cell phones, no 911, so there is no help on the way. Amidst the chaos, a truck pulls up and in a rough translation of Swahili, a man says he will take the worst injured to the nearest doctor. Austin's arm and leg were bleeding and Heather had a bump on her forehead the size of half a golf ball. They jumped in the truck with two other African guys. One of the guys had his foot hanging on by only a bit of skin, and the other was bleeding from his mouth.

As they are in this truck Heather starts talking about how it could be possible that this guy could be taking them away to beat them up and take their money, or that this doctor they are going to could be a witch doctor. She goes on to tell of what she has seen in African hospitals and how even if it was a good doctor, most African hospitals are not sanitary. They will stick a needle in one person and then in someone else.

At that time Austin was looking up at the stars and a peace which he had never experienced washed over him. He knew they would be ok. He said to Heather, "We are going to be ok." She said, "Yeah, I think so." "No, I know we are."

After a short 15 minute drive, they pulled up to a one story building. Austin jumped out and knocked on the door. A white guy opened the door and had an Indiana shirt on. Austin was shocked and asked if they spoke English. The guy answered, "Yes," so Austin rushed through the story of the accident and injuries. The guy said, "Wait a minute, sit down. It looks like you have a broken leg." Austin asked how he knew and the guys said, "We are missionary doctors from Indiana, if you were to get in an accident in this country, this is the best place you could be."

Impossible situations have a way of giving God a chance to shine, to show off for that matter. Just when we think there is no way out, or no way for things to work out or no rescue coming, God steps in and comes through to save the day.

This week we are going to see how God has come through in situations where He feels far away, in situations caused by our own sin, and in unlikely situations.

Here Am I

Spend some time asking God to show you times when He has come through for you and make notes of them below. (Think mentally, physically, spiritually, circumstantially, financially, emotionally, and relationally.)

Emmanuel

Week 8

Day 2

Oh Lord, Thank You for this time with You, to get to meet with You and hear from You. Thank You for Your Word that You have made so available to us. Thank You that it is alive and active and able to convict us where we need convicting, as well as to motivate, comfort and inspire us. Today as we meet with You, please give us eyes to see, ears to hear, and hearts to understand what You want us to get out of today. We long to hear from You, for from You are the words of life. Thank You for making Yourself available to us, and for coming to dwell among us.

Eyes to See

Read 1 Samuel 14:24-52

*How would you tell this story? What details would you be sure to not leave out?

*By looking at Jonathan's actions and the things he said to people, what do you think he cared about?

*Looking at Saul's actions and the things he said to people, what do you think he cared most about?

*What are some possibilities of why the other men didn't tell Jonathan about the vow before he started eating?

*What were some of the results of the vow?

*Describe the physical and mental condition of the men in the army.

Ears to Hear

Each time I read this section of scripture I am struck by a few phrases. In verse 35, it is revealed that Saul is doing his own thing and is not really living to please God. The author finds it important to show us this when he says, "Then Saul built and altar to the Lord; **it was the first time he had done this**." In verse 36 we see that the priest has to be the one to initiating dependence on God. "But **the priest** said, "Let us inquire of God here." The third verse that always jumps out at me is "But God did not answer him that day." This is the one that sparks my curiosity. This is the verse that gets me asking why. Why did God not answer him?

I believe there are many reasons God may feel far away sometimes, and today we are going to look at three of them. 1. Sin 2. To test us 3. To display His glory

1. Sin.

Fill in Isaiah 59:2 "But your iniquities have separated you from your God; your sins have _____ _____ _____from you, so that He will not hear."

Eye contact is an important thing in our culture. Without it, we tend to feel distant and uncared for. When I am talking to Austin and he is looking at me instead of his phone or computer, I feel like he is really listening, like he is cares about me and what I am saying. When I am trying to tell my two year old son that he can't take toys away from other kids, I want him to look at me. It communicates to me that he is hearing me. Our sin cuts off this kind of connection with God. In this case of sin, when we feel distant from God it can be used as an indicator to us that something is wrong with our heart and needs to change.

In verse 42, we are told that the reason that God did not respond to Saul was because Jonathan had sinned by breaking the law and eating the honey. His sin made a separation between him and God, and between Saul and God. Though Scripture does not tell us that Saul's sin had hidden his face from God as well, it is obvious through what has been written.

"When you read King Saul's words recorded in Scripture, they often reveal a heart controlled by pride, foolishness, and deceit. He would say foolish things just to impress people with his 'spirituality,' when in reality he was walking far from the Lord...Saul's heart was not right with God and he foolishly forced his army to agree to a vow of fasting until evening (v. 24). He didn't impose this fast because it was the will of God but because he wanted his soldiers to think he was a man wholly dedicated to the Lord. But this command was only more evidence of Saul's confused and superstitious faith. He thought that their fasting plus the presence of the ark would impress the Lord and He would give them victory."[42]

2. To test us.

I think of the story of the gentile lady we talked about in week one, who was asking Jesus to heal her demon possessed daughter. I remember how Jesus wooed her to pursue Him. Sometimes God lets us experience dry times, times where we don't feel as connected to Him to challenge our faith, to give us a glimpse of our heart of what it would take to get us to stop pursuing Him. Sometimes God tests us, not so He can find out new information, but so that we can. What a smart thing! Think about it: if you were feeling like God was far away, like you weren't hearing from Him, perhaps even like He wasn't even there, would you still seek out consistent, extended quality time with Him?

So sometimes when we feel distant from God, it is not a result of sin but rather it is a gracious gift from Him to grow us, to stretch us, to help us be able to persevere in pursuing Him even when it hurts and we don't feel like it.

3. For His glory.

I love that God does stuff just to show us Who He is and what He is like.

> "As Jesus was walking along, He saw a man who had been blind from birth. 'Rabbi,' His disciples asked Him, 'Why was this man born blind? Was it because of his own sins or his parents' sins?' 'It was not because of his sins or his parents' sins,' Jesus answered. 'This happened so the power of God could be seen in him" John 9:1-3.

> "A man named Lazarus was sick. He lived in Bethany with his sisters, Mary and Martha. This is the Mary who later poured the expensive perfume on the Lord's feet and wiped them with her hair. Her brother, Lazarus, was sick. So the two sisters sent a message to Jesus telling him, 'Lord, your dear friend is very sick.' But when Jesus heard about it he said, 'Lazarus's sickness will not end in death. No, it happened for the glory of God so that the Son of God will receive glory from this" (John 11:1-4).

Like the blind man who experienced hardship so that God could come through and show Himself as the Healer and like Lazarus who God used to show Himself as the God who raised the dead, God sometimes chooses to let us experience feeling distant from Him so that He can better reveal Who He is to us and the people around us, to show us His glory! What a gift!

Heart to Understand

Self-reliance and impulsiveness can keep us from receiving God's blessing and protection. When the entire army had gone into the woods and found honey, they were gazing at a blessing and the provision

---

42 Wiersbe, Warren (2007). *The Wiersbe Bible Commentary: Old Testament*. Colorado Springs, CO: David C.

of God. They were exhausted, and honey has every nutrient they would need to be able to press on in a healthy way. But Saul's impulsive law kept them from receiving this blessing.

*Can you think of any situations from the last week where you experienced the consequence of impulsiveness?

*Describe the last time you felt disconnected or distant from God. How did you react to your feelings?

*The next time you feel like God is not there or uninvolved, what do you hope your reaction will be? Is there anything you can do to prepare yourself for that time?

Emmanuel

Week 8

Day 3

Oh Lord, You are so amazing! How You are outside of time and see the beginning from the end, and yet You still provide for us. You still are able to orchestrate details to reveal Yourself to us, still able to burst onto the scene and save the day. Lord, as we study Your Word today, would You help us see You. Help us not get stuck seeing things from our limited understanding of the world and from our personal time period. Please speak to us today.

Eyes to See

Read 1 Samuel 15:1-35

*Describe this scene the way Saul sees it.

*Tell this story the way Samuel would perhaps tell it.

*Describe this story from God's perspective.

Ears to Hear

Today we are going to see how God has come through in situations caused by our own sin, and see that we can't get away with sin.

The Amalakites were known for coming against weak and defenseless people. Think of the people who steal young girls and keep and sell them as sex slaves. In chapter 30 in verses 1-4 we read about how they ransacked a town, set it on fire destroying everything and took all of the women "young and old". This image makes me think of the soldiers in the movie *Braveheart*, who would treat the women miserably. I imagine that when the Amalakites took the women, it wasn't because they wanted to be nice and give them a warm cozy place to live. I suspect it was to make them their personal slaves and I imagine that involved forced sex "young and old".

We also know that Haman from the book of Esther was a descendant of the Amalakites. He was the fruit of Saul's disobedience to the Lord. Haman is the man who wanted to holocaust the Jews. "Haman looked for a way to destroy all the Jews throughout the entire empire of Xerxes" (Esther 3:6)

On a side note, it fascinates me to think about God knowing the end from the beginning. He saw all the consequences of Saul's sin. But He also knows all the blessings that would have happened if Saul had done what God had told him to do. Nothing is hidden from God.

We cannot sin and get away with it. There will always be consequences, whether we see them or not. Saul and even Samuel had no idea the consequences of a descendant setting a plot to kill them years and years later because of this act of disobedience. I find it scary to think that even your sin and my sin has the potential to bring devastation to others as well.

Heart to Understand

We can see that Saul's sin had huge consequences, and what for? What did he think was worth disobeying God for? The best of the sheep and goats, the cattle, the fat calves, and the lambs, everything, in fact, that appealed to them. They destroyed only what was worthless or of poor quality.

> "You have shown contempt by offering defiled sacrifices on my altar. Then you ask, 'How have we defiled the sacrifices?' 'You defile them by saying the altar of the Lord deserves no respect. When you give blind animals as sacrifices, isn't that wrong? And isn't it wrong to offer animals that are crippled and diseased? Try giving gifts like that to your governor, and see how pleased he is!' says the Lord of Heaven's armies. 'Go ahead, beg God to be merciful to you! But when you bring that kind of offering, why should He show you any favor at all?' asks the Lord of Heaven's armies. 'How I wish one of you would shut the temple doors so that these worthless sacrifices could not be offered! I am not pleased with you,' says the Lord of Heaven's armies, 'and I will not accept your offerings. But My name is honored by people of other nations from morning till night. All around the world they offered sweet incense and pure offerings in honor of My name. For My name is great among the nations,' says the Lord of Heaven's armies. But you dishonor My name with your actions. By bringing contemptible food, you are saying it's all right to defile the Lord's table" (Malachi 1:7-12).

"When they grew up, Abel became a shepherd, while Cain cultivated the ground. When it was time for the harvest, Cain presented some of his crops as a gift to the Lord. Abel also brought a gift-the best of the firstborn lambs from his flock. The Lord accepted Abel and his gift, but he did not accept Cain and his gift. This made Cain very angry, and he looked dejected. 'Why are you so angry?' the Lord asked Cain. 'Why do you look so dejected? You will be accepted if you do what is right. But if you refuse to do what is right, then watch out! Sin is crouching at your door, eager to control you. But you must subdue it and be its master" (Genesis 4:1-7).

I wonder how often we do the same thing, save the best for ourselves and then justify our action, choosing to say yes to our desires over saying yes to what God has told us to do. It strikes me that God is asking questions hundreds of years later to different people from different cultures about the same matter: the matter of taking what we want from what is rightfully His. He sees the hearts of mankind and sees that we can be incredibly greedy and self-pleasers above God- pleasers.

Isn't it interesting that in all three of our instances of people (Saul, the people Malachi was talking to and Cain) who withhold from God what was rightfully His, God responded in anger. Not only are these people called out on their sin, but they are being told what they are clinging onto is not really theirs to have. Can you see where the anger comes from?

But before Saul is called out on his sin, he is totally unaware of it.

*How do we know Saul is unaware of his sin?

*Give a detailed description of how Saul responds when Samuel brings his sin to his attention.

*Explain if you think Saul ever evidenced true repentance.

Man, does this expose our need for people in our life that walk with God to tell us the truth about the things in our life! We can be incredibly blind sometimes. We need people who will be like Samuel, who when they are faced with our sin and what God thinks about it, will spend huge chunks of sacrificial time praying about it and then will confront us. Samuel was so deeply moved when he heard this that he cried out to the Lord all night. Early the next morning Samuel went to find Saul. 15:10-11

*Who have you allowed to be a Samuel in your life who can call you out on sin?

*Who would you like to give permission to be a Samuel in your life? How can you talk to them about this?

Read Esther chapter 7 and describe how God came through for the Jews.

"God will save the day, and all will say, my glorious, my glorious, my glorious, my glorious." David Crowder

Emmanuel

Week 8

Day 4

My glorious, You have told us so many times that You will be with us. Would you explain to us? Would you give me a glimpse of Your glory, of what You mean when You say that You are with us? Let it move me to the depth of my being. Let it push me to action, to surrender, to love. Let Your Spirit teach me today and open my mind to understand.

Eyes to See

Read 1 Samuel 16:1-23

*In verses 1-13, what stands out to you and why?

*Which important details in this chapter do you think might be the easiest to overlook?

*If you were to write a discussion question to help your group examine and understand something in this chapter, what question would you ask?

*After re-reading verses 14-23, come up with as many questions as you can about this section.

*Choose two of your questions above and do some research to come up with the best answer you can. (If you don't own any commentaries Bible helps, www.biblestudytools.com has some available.)

Ears to Hear

Psalm 22:1-2 show us David sometimes felt abandoned, and that God was not with him. "My God, my God! Why have You forsaken me? Why do You remain so distant? Why do You ignore my cries for help? Every day I call to You, my God, but You do not answer." Though David felt abandoned, he continually put his trust in what was true and his feelings soon followed. "Yet You brought me safely from my mother's womb and led me to trust You when I was a nursing infant. I was thrust upon You at my birth. You have been my God from the moment I was born…Praise the Lord, all you who fear Him! For He has not ignored the suffering of the needy. He has not turned and walked away. He has listened to their cries for help" (22:9, 23, 24).

When God is with us, it means that the fullness and totality of God's attributes are completely present with us. Bill Bright says it this way: "It means that there is not a sliver of space anywhere in the universe where He is not dynamically and powerfully present with all of His wonderful personal attributes. Everywhere throughout the world, to the utmost reaches of the universe and in heaven, God is always and immediately present with all of Who He is."[43]

For some reason, I have always had an irrational fear of sharks. When I was little, I did not want to go in the deep end of the pool thinking that a shark would eat me. When I was about ten, my dad took me with him and some of his friends to go water skiing. I wish there were words to describe how scared I was when he went in the water. I thought for sure I would never see him again and that a shark was going to snatch him from the end of that line. Well, many years later I got married to my incredibly wise husband, Austin, and his parents gave us a trip to Saint Thomas Island for a honeymoon. My fear of sharks was still present in my life but not as dominating, so we decided to go snorkeling. As I had my face in the water (which made me feel like I was totally submersed) God spoke to me. "If I go up to the heavens, You are there; if I make my bed in the depths, You are there" (Ps 139:8). As He brought those words to my mind, a light bulb clicked. "He is even here!" He was even, there in my fear, in the depths of the ocean, He was there, right there with me. He had never left me or forsaken me.

Describe the situation of each of these instances where God said, "I will be with you".
Exodus 3:11-12

Joshua 1:5-6

---

43   Bill Bright, *God Discover His Character* pg. 62

Judges 6:12-14

Isaiah 41:10

Isaiah 43:1-2

Jeremiah 1:7-9

Jeremiah 42:11-12

Matthew 28:18-20

Acts 18:9-11

Each of these people were sent. They were commissioned. When God said He would be with them, He was saying He was going to come through for them. Go back through each passage above and either circle in what you have already written or write down how God coming through in each of these situations relates to the mission He gave them.

Heart to Understand

"God saved you by His grace when you believed. And you can't take credit for this; it is a gift from God. Salvation is not a reward for the good things we have done, so none of us can boast about it. For we are God's masterpiece. He has created us anew in Christ Jesus, so we can do the good things He planned for us long ago" (Ephesians 2:10). God has plans for our life, "plans for good and not for disaster, to give you a future and a hope" (Jeremiah 29:11). but apart from Christ, when we were separated from Him, we could not experience or walk out the plans He had for us. What a gift that when we surrendered our lives to Christ He gave us the ability through His Holy Spirit to live for the reason He created us. To think that God says about you "I knew you before I formed you in your mother's womb. Before you were born I set you apart" (Jeremiah 1:5). To meditate on the reality that while you were just a group of cells implanting on the walls of your mother's womb, God had plans for you. By letting His Spirit enable you, you can actually live out the plans God desired long ago.

*What are some things God has commissioned, you to do? What has He called and sent you to do? (For help, use the verses above and think through if this was a timeless and universal call. Was it meant for you as well, or just the person in the verse?)

*How does God's promise to come through for you in these situations affect you?

*If you lived your daily life believing God was with you, what would change?

"None of us has a long time here on planet Earth. It's kind of a staging ground. It's our split second in eternity when we have an opportunity to invest our lives, our time, our talent and our treasure to fulfill what our Lord came to do and commissioned us to do." -Bill Bright

Emmanuel

Week 8

Day 5

Our God who promises to come through for us, Your servant Ravi Zacharias tells us "Meaninglessness doesn't come from being weary in pain; meaninglessness comes from being weary with pleasure." Thank you for this reminder. Help us be about what You have called us to during our short time on this earth.

Reflecting on the week:

Glance back at days 1-4 and write down the things God highlighted to you.

Is there a theme? If so, what?

Why do you suppose He is saying these things to you?

What is a step you can take in obedience to Him? How does the Holy Spirit relate in this step?

It is not by force nor by strength, but by my Spirit, says the Lord of Heaven's armies. Zechariah 4:6

Victorious

Week 9

Day 1

Lord, You are the ultimate Victor, the winner, our hero. What a joy to be on Your side, knowing that You will come through and show Yourself mighty. We love that You can never fail and that nothing is too difficult for You! To You belongs the victor's crown, and to You belongs our hearts and lives.

Page Jumpers

Read 1 Samuel 17:1-19:24
List things that jump off the page (verses that stand out to you):

-
-
-
-
-

Cloud of Witnesses

Here are some of my friends who have taken risks for the Lord. They are everyday people just like you and me. I hope you are encouraged by their stories.

Sara McNutt

In the last class of my senior year in college the professor had opened up the class to share our beliefs and experiences (at my request). I came ready to share my testimony and to tell an entire class of relativist mystics that there is only ONE truth and it's found in the life and teachings of Jesus Christ, Who came to forgive our sins; that there is no other way to God but through Him, and that we are without excuse because of the testimony of His truth that He's given us through His creation. I literally sat shaking in my chair, feeling sick to my stomach, but the moment I began to speak it was as if the Lord laid a veil of His presence and protection over that place. Every face was riveted to mine and not one person spoke. When I finished speaking, there must have been at least 10 seconds of complete silence, and then a few asked genuine questions, desiring to know more. The Lord truly anointed that time and place and it will always be a remembrance "stone" for me in my walk with the Lord.

Ali Kushniroff

I started going to Metro State not because I dreamed of going or because I loved the location, but because I had no other choice. My grades were not good enough to go somewhere else. I felt completely stuck at Metro, without a choice and without hope. As my grades became progressively better during my first year in college I stared looking at options for the next semester. I looked at Arkansas State, California, North Carolina, and even the option of taking a semester off. I hated school, living arrangements, and the location. I kept thinking, *What do I want? What do I need?* It was all about me. When I finally asked God, *What do You want?* I was surprised to find that He wanted me to stay right where I was. About a week later I was presented with the opportunity to go to Russia for a summer. I had always wanted to go there and see that side of the world. But if I went to Russia all summer I could not go out of state. My options were staying in Colorado for the summer and working to pay for out-of-state tuition, or going to Russia and staying at Metro. After much prayer I decided to go to Russia on a mission trip with Campus Crusade and stay at Metro. This was a huge risk, I was having to trust God with coming up with the money to go to Russia, where and who I was going to live with when I got home, and had to trust God would provide community when I returned to Metro in the fall. God did measurably more than I could have dreamed of. I love school and Metro now more than ever before. He is amazing.

Brittany Ralston

I guess the riskiest moment of stepping out in faith so far has to do with a friend that I have shared Jesus with over my last four years. His name is Henry. I met him in the dorms my freshmen year and because we are in the same major, our sophomore and junior year we had tons of classes together. He is really smart and so we started studying for all of our tests and classes together. Through those times the Lord continued to put him on my heart to pray for and to share with. Sophomore year he was very hard hearted towards everything but I continued to trust in the Lord and be bold for him. I tried to meet Henry's needs where he was at and share with him as much as I could. I often would pick him up at two in the morning drunk at parties and other similar situations. Through those times I was able to continually share the love of Christ with him. The second semester of my junior year we were studying one night and talking about the end of the world and I was telling him there is so much more to live for in life than this world and that without Jesus we have nothing. It was a great conversation and lasted for about two hours.

A couple months later he was diagnosed with gout and all summer was stuck in bed because of his pain and inability to do anything. I continued to pray that the Lord would use it in his life to draw Henry to Himself. Henry went to this natural doctor who ended up being a very strong Christian and throughout this whole last summer the gout continued to spread through his whole body and he was stuck in bed, so he ended up reading his Bible constantly. He came down during the summer and we had a really long talk one night about his "new life". He told me that the night back at the beginning of the semester when we had had the end the world talk, he went home that night and asked the Lord to come into his life. His life has completely changed and he is constantly telling his friends about Jesus and is now thinking about doing an internship with Campus Crusade so that he can tell people about Jesus. I have never seen the Lord work so greatly in someone's life that I had trusted Him so much with and constantly been taking risks of sharing my faith and not knowing how he would respond as my friend. Henry's new found faith has impacted so many people already and it's amazing to see how much he is willing to let the Lord work through him.

Caley Patterson

Trusting God is not "safe" in the sense that you know the end result, because, well you never do. I was terrified to say yes to start dating. Don't get me wrong, I was so ready but I was scared to death! I had all these fears and all these ideas in my head about what I wanted it to look like and expectations that I had. It was the risk that scared me. Relationships can be incredibly risky. My fears obviously guided my decisions at first but then realized that the Lord was putting this in my path in order to maybe teach me about Himself in a new way. I know my relationship with David has taught me so many things about myself and about the man I want to marry and more about God than anything I can remember. I have grown immensely and even though David and I aren't together anymore, in past year and a half my eyes have been opened to how wonderful the Lord has created man and women to be partners and move through life together as a team. Yes, relationships are risky. Yes, there is always room for hurt and pain and heartbreak. There is no doubt about that but the Lord had a purpose for David and me being together. After time invested, heart and emotion invested there will always be risk involved. But I think that is what the Lord wants us to do. Take risks. If we take risks-or let's call them- steps of faith- the Lord will and can grow and stretch us in ways we could never imagine. Isn't that what trusting Christ is? A risk? Yes, of course--it is something we can never know the end result but hey that is the fun of it! We can learn to enjoy and be glad in the things we have.

Melanie Coffman

The most risky thing I have ever done for the kingdom was to quit all of MY life plans and follow after God. I was in Russia in 2007 on a mission trip with Campus Crusade and I knew that God was telling me that I should be doing something like this with my life. However, I had plans. I had a boyfriend of over 4 years whom I was planning to marry. I had plans to get a Doctorate and was in the process of applying to graduate school for that. Plus, I had a family and a life and friends. Surely God wouldn't call me away from all that, would He? I realized that God doesn't call me to leave everything I love, but He was calling me to love Him more fully and completely, with my whole heart. I am still at the front end of this journey, but I have learned that God's plans for me are far better than anything I could ever dream up. So, I am striving to love Him more, and seek only His will for my life. This has involved leaving behind much that I once thought was very valuable, but I have found treasure beyond compare.

Jennifer Hepp

I think the riskiest thing I've done for God's kingdom was going to Albania my junior year of college on a CCC summer project (Jesus film). I went b/c I felt like God was calling me to, even though I had to travel there alone, didn't know anyone there or anyone going. A group (the Traveling Team) had come to my campus and talked about unreached people groups and I felt like God was calling me to go, specifically to go to Albania. It felt really risky because I had to travel there alone, didn't know anyone going. It was a little over a year after 911, so my family didn't want me to go; they felt like it was too dangerous. But God continued to put Albania on my heart. One night after I was praying about going, I was reading in Romans where Paul was talking about Illyricum, I looked down and my Bible study notes said that it was present-day Albania. I felt torn whether God would call me to do something that my parents were not happy about, but I had a conversation with my aunt that really stuck out to me. She told me that this sounded like the Holy Spirit guiding me, not like something Satan would be trying to convince me to do. So, I decided to go. A travel agent helped me book my four-stop flight there. This was my first time flying and my first time in foreign airports. When I finally got to the Albanian airport, it was an adventure just finding the man picking me up (who did not speak English) and traveling seven hours by bumpy road to the city where we were staying.

We had a couple of days at the base. I was one of the few Americans there on the summer project mission trip and I was the only American on my team. They taught us how to use the *Jesus* film equipment, how to meet and invite the villagers to the *Jesus* film and sent us out. Two of the Albanians on my team spoke English while the other 3 did not. They dropped us off in one village, telling us that they would pick us up in a couple days and that we should get ourselves to three nearby villages to show the *Jesus* Film. We had no food and no place to sleep, but God provided. The first night we slept in one lady's shop on the floor and the people who we invited to the *Jesus* film fed us from the meager food they had. We showed the film, had a pretty good turn out and moved on to the next village.

While we were walking to the next village, a car stopped to give us a ride. Later on, when that car broke down, they asked us all to pray to God and God allowed their car to start and we made it to the next village. At this village, we invited the townspeople to the *Jesus* film and so many people came! But right after the film started, an angry Orthodox priest came yelling across the yard and ripped the Jesus film. He was shouting, as were many of the townspeople. Because everyone was speaking Albanian, I had no idea what was going on and I just prayed. Even though we didn't get to show all of the film, one young man came up to our team members after the priest left and said, "I can tell that you are real Christians; I want what you have" and he prayed to receive Christ. That night an older couple invited us to sleep with them at their house. We got to sleep on real beds and eat fried chicken—it was a real treat!

We made our way to the third village, where a large crowd was gathered to watch the Jesus film. Nearby a few Muslim people in the town were upset about showing the film about Jesus and so they got some young men riled up and those young men began throwing stones and firecrackers at us. Again, this was all in Albanian, so I had no idea what was going on, but I began to pray and we quickly packed up and all piled into a vehicle made for only half of us. It was very scary, but God was at work.

We spent the second half of the trip going back to those villages to meet with those who were new believers and do Bible studies with them. It was an amazing adventure. It felt like I was in the book of Acts. I'm so glad I trusted God and went, even though it was so risky! I got to be a part of unreached people hearing the gospel of Jesus Christ for the first time!

Lindy Allen

I think one of the biggest leaps of faith I have taken in terms of trusting God was when I went on Young Life staff. I had just had a baby and Will had just finished his student teaching and gotten his teaching license. It was August and Will still didn't have a teaching job. I was the main breadwinner for our little family. I had felt God pulling on my heart for years about going into youth ministry, but it never felt like the right time. After I had Whitney I felt the call very strongly. (maybe it was hormones....ha!) So, I took a $20,000/year pay cut, left my job with the National Park Service and took a position with Young Life. Our total family income would be $15,000/year if Will didn't get a job. That is below poverty level. And, we had just purchased our townhome so there was a mortgage to pay!

But, I did it. I took a leap of faith, accepted the position and 2 weeks later Will got a teaching position. The story surely goes on from there, but that was a big step for us.

There truly are some incredibly beautiful women out there that are willing to risk it all for Jesus! This week we are going to look at the power of God in the face of the Goliaths many of us face; giants of connecting with the lost, communication, and comfort zones.

Here Am I

What risks have you taken to display God's heart and passion?

What is something that feels risky to you?

What would help you do it?

Who are the risk takers in your life?

At age 95, what do you suppose you would have wished you risked more of?

What fears keep you from action?

Victorious

Week 9

Day 2

King of Kings, thank You for rescuing us from ourselves and from the eternity that we were destined for. Thank You for sending someone into our life that was courageous enough to talk to us about You. Thank You for interrupting our lives and setting us free from the bondage of sin. Make us into agents of rescue for others.

Eyes to See

Read 1 Samuel 17

*Describe every aspect of intimidation and manipulation tactic you see Goliath using toward the children of Israel.

*Why do you suspect God waited forty days before He provided David to fight against Goliath?

*Put yourself in this scene (as whoever you want-a fighter, a feeder, an overseer-use your imagination). Describe a scene you would likely see. Describe the feelings and conversations you encounter.

*What is the difference between the motivation of the soldiers and David, and how did those motivations come about?

*Verse 17 is one of the places we see David run to the battle lines. Why do you think he did this?

*What feelings arise as you read how Eliab responded to David?

*What does the way David responds to Eliab show us about his character?

*What does the way David responds to Saul show us about his character, faith and identity?

*What thoughts come to your mind as you read about David's three choice weapons? (v.40)

*How do you feel about David's confidence in God giving him success?

Ears to Hear

Korina is a student leader involved in our ministry. She said she wanted to be more involved and strategic in the Great Commission but said, "I feel like I've been given all these tools already but am not yet comfortable with actually using them... but I want to, I guess I'm just scared of messing up." The other day Korina put herself out there at the risk of failing and got into spiritual conversations with other students. God came through and gave her an opportunity to share the gospel with three girls who were very open and all three girls surrendered their lives to Christ!

Not long after that Angi, another student leader, told us that a friend of hers brought a friend to church on Sunday and that she, Angi took the initiative to walk through the gospel with him and he gave his life to Christ. Angi just gave her life to Christ in April and is taking giant steps of faith in co-leading an introductory Bible study and in discipling a new Christian.

Hannah is another student leader who surrendered her life to Christ a couple of years ago, went to Russia with us, and is now leading a Bible study and discipling girls. Last week she and a friend went to the mall to get into spiritual conversations and ended up talking with a guy who had been reading the Bible for 10 months trying to get to know God. They shared the gospel with him and he gave his life to Christ right there in the mall!

God is at work in the lives of people around us, but it seems so often that our fears keep us from even getting into conversations with them to find out. Bill Bright, the founder of Campus Crusade said, "Successful witnessing is taking initiative to share Christ in the power of the Holy Spirit and leaving the results up to Him." Really that is all we can do. God is the One that changes hearts, but He has called us to be part of the adventure of telling them His story.

For ten years I did not share my faith. I would invite my friends to church and youth group hoping someone else would share the actual gospel with them. Ten years is a long time to not be obedient to what God calls us to do. Romans 1, says that when we disobey God, our hearts become hardened. This is what happened to me.

I went to college wanting to be involved in ministry. I liked the idea of girls coming to know Jesus and I wanted to be the one who would help them grow into strong disciples after they had given their lives to Him. Whenever the topic of evangelism would come up, I had a very arrogant attitude and would get angry at anyone who disagreed with me. I distorted the verse "Always be prepared to give an answer to everyone who asks you to give the reason for the hope that you have" (1 Pet. 3:15) and made that out to mean that you don't go to people, you let them come to you. As a result I would get very angry at people who were taking initiative to share the gospel. I honestly thought, *They are just making my job harder, because now the non-believer is offended and I have to win them back.* When I think about this, I am embarrassed by my self-centeredness and sad about all the opportunities wasted because of my arrogance. But praise God that He is able to soften even the hardest of hearts.

I hope you are wondering what happened. How did God change my hard heart? Well, God blessed me with Austin. We met after I had returned from a mission trip and we hit it off. (It's an incredible story of God orchestrating divine appointment after divine appointment). Austin and I were both student leaders for Master Plan Ministries in Durango. (The ministry we now lead in Denver) Austin and our friend, John, were constantly sharing their faith. At first it bothered me, but I couldn't argue with the fruit they were seeing, people were giving their lives to Christ. I couldn't believe it! When I looked back on my Christian life, not one person had ever come up to me and asked me to share the gospel with them. Who knew? Sure, there were people that came to Christ because I invited them somewhere, but it was not because I took the initiative to start the conversation with them. So one day I said to Austin, "Ok, walk through with me what you say to people when you are sharing the gospel." I was going to see if it would be something I would get offended at if I were a non-believer. God used that conversation to change my heart and attitude for life. Austin used the Four Spiritual

Laws developed by Bill Bright in a conversational way. He was not cramming anything, it wasn't a canned presentation, just a simple conversation. I thought, *I can do this.* So I tried it out. It felt totally normal (once I could get enough guts up to get into the conversation) and God blessed me with being able to see eternal fruit born for His kingdom by girls surrendering their lives to Christ because of our conversation.

I am not sure where your heart attitude is regarding sharing your faith, but I am pretty sure that you are probably not as hard hearted about it as I was. Even if you are, will you be willing to let God shape your opinions about it today?

*Describe similarities between 1 Samuel 17:47 and 1 Corinthians 2:1-5.

*Describe similarities between 1 Samuel 17:47-49 and Acts 8:26-30.

*Describe the result of the Lord's victory through David. (v. 51-53)

*Describe a story of someone who shared her faith which resulted in incredible courage in the lives of the people who heard about it.

Heart to Understand

To help us talk about many of the different aspects of evangelism, let's use a MAP. M.A.P. stands for Methods, Avenues, and Point

The Method

There are numerous means available to communicate the unchanging gospel message. Some tools are better fit for specific situations. So we need to have a well-supplied toolbox so we can pull out what is needed in the time we need it. I recommend working with one tool until you are completely confident with it and then move on to another. Shoot for mastery.

Some methods of sharing the gospel:

- Biblical presentations
  *Romans Road (Walking through Romans 3:23, 6:23, 5:8, 10:9-10)
  *The Four Spiritual Laws/Would You Like to Know God Personally? Booklet. (Ordered at http://www.campuscrusade.com)
  *The Bridge illustration (Training to draw it at http://www.evangelismcoach.org/2008/how-to-use-the-bridge-illustration or order booklet at http://www.navpress.com)

- Testimonial presentations
  *The story of how you came to surrender your life to Christ.
  *Stories of how God came through for you and how you better saw His character (with the gospel (the why you needed Jesus to forgive you and the how you surrendered to Him put in the story)

- Philosophical arguments
  *Apologetics
  *Who is Jesus Bible study
  *Trilema (Explanation found at http://www.greatcom.org/resources/areadydefense/ch21/default.htm)

But in order to use these tools, you have to break four **Sound Barriers** which were developed by Campus Crusade.

1. Getting into a simple conversation. What's your name, how are you etc..

2. Swinging the conversation to spiritual things.

3. Sharing the Gospel.

4. Asking them to respond to the Gospel/asking for a decision.

Questions are a great tool to help you break through each sound barrier. Here are a couple of examples.

- Do you have any kind of spiritual beliefs?

- If you died right now and were standing before God and He said, "Why should I let you into heaven," what would you say?

- If what you were believing is not true, would you want to know?

Come up with a question you would feel comfortable asking to help you break each barrier.

1.

2.

3.

4.

The Avenues

As God works through believers in seeking to save the lost, there are three different types of relational avenues which give us opportunity to use our tools. These avenues are determined by the nature of the relationship between the believer and the unbeliever.

1. **Organic**: Getting into conversations with others in the normal course of life.

   Read some of the examples below and write down a few key words or a sentence reminding you what it says.
   John 1:40-51
   John 4:1-42
   Colossians 4:5-6
   1 Peter 3:15

   *Describe a modern day example.

   *What are some pro's and con's of this avenue?

2. **Communal**: Inviting non-believers to be part of your believing community. Letting them see how believers interact and using this to get into a spiritual conversation with them.

   Read some of the examples below and write down a few key words or a sentence reminding you what it says.
   John 17:21-23
   John 13:34-35
   Acts 2:42-47

   *Describe a modern day example.

   *What are some pros and cons of this avenue?

3. **Missional**: Intentionally taking the gospel to an individual you have not met.

   Read some of the examples below and write down a few key words or a sentence reminding you what it says.
   2 Timothy 4:2
   Mark 1:38-39
   Luke 9:1-6, 10:1-17
   Acts 8
   Acts 11:19-24

   *Describe a modern day example.

   *What are some pros and cons of this avenue?

   *Through which of these avenues did you come to Christ?

   *Which of these does your community emphasizes?

   *Which one of these avenues is the most challenging for you personally? Why?

   *Are all three of these avenues necessary to saturate our culture? Why?

The Point

The way of salvation.

   *This might seem elementary, but if we get this wrong, we totally miss it. So, what is the gospel message? What things does someone have to understand to be transferred from the kingdom of darkness to the kingdom of light?

*What does Colossians 1:21-23 say the gospel is? What key points does someone need to understand the full gospel?

*What would be the result if someone trying to understand the gospel did not understand each of the following truths?

Romans 3:23

Romans 6:23

Romans 5:8

Romans 10:9-10, 13

"Each time I am with someone for five minutes or more, I consider it a God-given opportunity to testify of God's mercy and grace in my life. You may be thinking: Bill Bright is the president of a worldwide organization dedicated to introducing people to Christ. Surely, proclaiming the gospel is easier for him than for me. I could never witness like that. I am naturally a shy and reserved person, so sharing my faith is sometimes difficult for me. I must continually rely on the power of the Holy Spirit to be a fruitful witness."[44]

You are in the most strategic time in your entire life for setting yourself up for courageously living for God's kingdom. The decisions you are making right now are becoming the foundation stones your life is going to be built on. The habits you are making now are the very things that will make you who you are, and the people you are allowing to influence you (whether real or fictional) are the very people you will become like, and what you are neglecting now is being set up in your life as a lifelong habit. "I pray that you may be active in sharing your faith, so that you will have a full understanding of every good thing we have in Christ" (Philemon 6). When we share our faith we get to experience God and see His mighty hand working in people's lives and "What's done in this life echoes for eternity." Russell Crowe from Gladiator

---

Bright, Bill (2002). God: Discover His Character. Orlando, FL: New Life Publications

Victorious

Week 9

Day 3

Oh Lord, We only see a glimpse of You and yearn to see You as You truly are. Lord, we know that we have such a small view of You, we sometimes think You are powerless and careless. Open our eyes to how powerful You really are. Please don't let our small view of You stay as it is. Let us see Your glory today.

Eyes to See

Read 1 Samuel 18-19

*Describe the favor David was receiving. Do you find anything odd about this?

*What would the temptation of experiencing all the success and favor David did? What is David's attitude in the midst of these temptations?

*Describe the progression that takes place in Saul's thoughts, attitudes and actions.

*What the enemy intends for evil, God uses for good. Describe the different scenarios where you see this happen with David.

*If you were to paint a picture of one of the scenes in these chapters, which one would you choose and why?

*Put yourself in David's shoes. What would be your first reaction to your boss and best friend throwing a spear at you? What would you think and feel?

*By the time Michal helps David flee, what would you guess David was thinking and feeling?

Ears to Hear

Read Psalm 59. David wrote this Psalm when Saul had sent men to watch David's house in order to kill him, before Michal helped him to escape. Write down what stands out to you.

Psalm 59 lets us see what David was thinking and feeling. Is it different than you guessed? It is different than I would have thought. I am encouraged that even in this horrible time of being passionately hated, he is thinking about God's glory being seen and known to the ends of the earth. Rather than having a "poor me" attitude, he is relying on who God says He is. There is so much hope in this kind of perspective.

In verse 5 we see exactly what attribute of God David is relying on. He calls God "Lord of Hosts", and he also called God "Lord of Hosts" in his response to Goliath. So what does Lord of Hosts mean? Why is it significant that he was relying on this characteristic of God in these times? "Lord of Hosts", also known as Jehovah-Tsebaoth is "cited 282 times in Scripture and is a military word meaning "God of Battles." Our God is a Warrior. He is a Fighter, and we are in His army. As children of the Lord of Hosts, we are following after the One Who wins every battle…God wants warriors who stand up for Him in the face of the enemy so that the lost may be saved. That is the most important battle we face… David trusted in God's ability to fight his enemies and win his battles for him." (The Names of God, pg. 150-151, Lester Sumrall)

Everything Saul used for evil, God used for David's advantage and in this we get a glimpse of the power of God. Nothing can hinder Him from doing as He pleases. No one can thwart His plans.

*How do you see the power of Jesus in the following verses?
Mark 5:1-13

*A Roman legion was made up of 6,000 men. What does Isaiah 37:36 show us what just one angel is capable of doing?
John 18:1-5

Just at the sound of His name, 500 non-believing soldiers are knocked to the ground. This is the power underneath our Maker's finger. "It takes no more effort for God to create a universe than it does for Him to create and ant."[45]

Heart to Understand

"Have you considered that God wants us to reflect His power on earth? As we begin to understand our God's vast and magnificent power, our lives cannot help but be transformed. Everything about us will change-our attitudes, actions, motives, desire, our lifestyle, and even our view of God. As we are transformed, we light up the world around us. Our society which was once darkened by fear, ignorance, and hopelessness will become lightened without witness of God's power, care, and intervention in our lives."[46]

*When Bill Bright says everything about us will change-our attitudes, actions, motives, desire, our lifestyle, and even our view of God as we understand His power, what is an example of this happening in your life?

*What is an example of something in your life that needs to be changed from understanding the power of God?

*For each aspect of who you are, describe what it would look like to rely on God as your Lord of Hosts.

• Emotionally

---

45 Evans, Tony (1994). *Our God is Awesome.* Chicago, IL: Moody Press.
46 Bright, Bill (2002). God: Discover His Character. Orlando, FL: New Life Publications

- Spiritually

- Mentally

- Socially

- Physically

Write out a prayer expressing your desires in these areas.

Victorious

Week 9
Day 4

God, You are perfect: perfect in holiness, perfect in beauty, perfect in love, perfect in power and perfect in communicating. What a privilege to get to worship You and be loved by You. Oh Lord, make us more like You, make us peace-makers, people who are willing to trust You in conversations and willing to purse and even initiate talking about hard things like You do.

Eyes to See

Review 1 Samuel 18-19 and use the space below to draw out the scenes, explain the scenes as a movie or write a poem about the scenes.

Ears to Hear

In 19:18 David goes to see Samuel at Ramah, then they both head off to Naioth, which was likely a section in Ramah home of the school of the prophets. This was a place where Samuel and David could devote time to worship and prayer, asking God for wisdom and having others pray for them.

When Saul's men come to Ramah and start prophesying, they begin to sing songs and praises to God. They did not become prophets but were declaring things true about God. God's protection of David and Samuel in this event was not through a battle but through the changing of hearts and attitudes. The Holy Spirit turned these warriors into worshippers.

From this event we see that people can experience an amazing encounter with the Holy Spirit and yet have no change in character. This happened to Saul two times, where people even said, "Is Saul also among the prophets?" Yet, Saul remained unchanged. Special manifestations are not evidence that a person is a true believer and follower of Jesus. In the last days, the anti-Christ will perform many miracles and deceive many. Judas preached sermons and even performed miracles and yet he was not a believer. Saul, like Judas, had many opportunities to see the Lord's hand at work, but chose to deny Him and not surrender his life to Him. Saul's life is a tragedy. Because he would not surrender to the Lord, he became obsessed with destroying David until he ended his own life, lacking the help of the One Who could have given him victory. Saul was not open and authentic with his thoughts and feelings, so healing did not come. Instead Saul's jealousy turned to bitterness, and it has been said that bitterness is like drinking poison and expecting someone else to die.

Read 1 Samuel 18:6-8 and describe Saul's attitude.

When Saul should have been praising God with the ladies, he had his eyes fixed on himself. As much as I hate it, I can relate to this. I understand being frustrated when others get credit I feel I deserve or when I don't get as much respect as I want or think I deserve. In fact I was just feeling thing way last weekend. Multiple times I felt overlooked and unvalued when students went to Austin for help instead of me. *"What am I, chopped liver?" is* a phrase that was internally repeated throughout the span of the weekend. This dissatisfaction and focus on myself instead of God lead to comparing myself to others and that led to jealousy which moved me to feel defeated, thinking, *"I wasn't uniquely good at anything, so why even try"*. I was not living in light of the truth of Who God is, Jehovah-Nissi, the Lord my Banner, the Lord my Conqueror. Instead of being focused on Him being my strength, I was discouraged by the reality that apart from Him I can do nothing as John 15:5 says. When I confessed my bad attitude and communicated with the Lord about it and discussed it with Austin, God brought healing. In fact, He opened my eyes to some pretty neat things about Who He is and what He thinks of me. If I would not have communicated, I would have forfeited seeing God's glory.

It is so easy to not communicate out of fear of what people will think, or fear of rejection. I have noticed how common-place it is to disguise this lack of communicating as holy with comments like *"I don't want to defend myself."* But we need to take every thought and compare it to Scripture and make it obedient to the truth. So let's see what God has to say about communicating, also known as peace-making since peace will not come any other way except through healthy relating through communicating.

Describe how communicating relates to the following verses
Hebrews 12:14-15

1 Peter 3:8-12

2 Corinthians 13:11

2 Timothy 2:22-26

In 1 Samuel 19:1-6, describe the communication that takes place and the result.

Some important aspects of communicating are to stick to one issue at a time, to be clear about what you saw or heard and what your thoughts and feelings were about it. If you have ever overheard people arguing, there tends to be blame-shifting, accusing and attacking. It is important to take responsibility for your thoughts, feelings and actions. This is done by using "I" statements. *"When _____ happened, I felt_____"* and end by making sure to share what you would like to happen or to be different in the future. Most conflicts are resolved when you understand one another, so seek to understand them and their perspective and not be the fool who does not delight in understanding, only in revealing his own mind. (Proverbs 18:2)

Heart to Understand

"People march under different 'banners' today. They put their trust in different things; they give credit for their success to different things. What do you credit for making you who you are today?" Perhaps you credit your brains or physical abilities, money or knowing the right people. These are banners you hold up as you march on to your personal victories. But all these things will fail you someday. Advancing age will weaken your brain and rob your muscles of strength. Inflation will suck your money out of the bank. Fickle human nature will turn your friends against you. Repeated failures will give a hollow ring to your arrogance. March under any of these banners, and you will follow it to defeat."[47] When we are putting our trust in our own abilities, we are not putting our trust in God and His ability. When we are crediting ourselves for our great achievements, we are not giving God the credit He deserves. When we are comparing ourselves to other people, not only does the Bible call us unwise, but we are forfeiting seeing the glory of God and starting the downward spiral of being self-focused leading to defeat, jealousy and bitterness.

*Can you relate to Saul or me in any of these attitudes?

*What is your natural response to conflict?

*What are your default banners (the things you tend to give credit to for your successes)?

When Austin and I took students to Russia for a mission trip, God provided an amazing place for us to live. It had everything we needed to take care of Asher and it was within walking distance of the grocery store and the campus we were ministering on. The only down side of this apartment was that it was on the 6th floor and the elevator was broken. Multiple times a day I had to figure out how to carry a baby, all my stuff and a stroller up six flights of stairs. I definitely did not have a shortage of exercise during those six weeks in Russia.

---

47 Stone, Nathan (2009). The Names of God. Wheaton, IL :Moody Publishers.

One day Austin had a discipleship appointment during Asher's nap time at our apartment since I was on campus. The student was talking about some things he was wrestling with and Austin had him write down and confess his sin before the Lord and talked to him about his identity in Christ. Austin took the paper with all this student's confessed sin on it and lit it on fire as a visual of what Jesus had done through His death on the cross, removing his sin from him completely. Being on the 6th floor, they threw the burning piece of paper out the widow assuming it would completely burn by the time it hit the sidewalk. As Austin dropped the burning paper, he realized the window of the apartment directly below was open. Just then the wind blew the paper into the open widow. Scared of setting the building on fire, Austin ran to the apartment and began to frantically pound on the door. Nobody answered so he tried the door to see if it was open. It was. He walks in, and then comes face to face with two Russian ladies who don't speak English. Through excited motions, Austin tries to tell them a burning piece of paper flew into their apartment. I'm sure they were freaked out thinking a crazy man speaking a different language broke into their house. He sees the paper (which had not touched anything that could catch on fire) and runs to it, picks it up and leaves. Who knew confessing our sin, could be such an adventure. But I guess the reality is, when we communicate with the Lord and confess our sins to one another we are healed like James says. We are free to see the glory of God - what better adventure in life is there!

Take some time to bring your heart and thoughts before our Jehovah-Nissi. If you have been letting other things be your banner, admit it as sin and bring true repentance (a change of mind followed by a change of action) to the Lord. Fix your eyes on Jesus, the Author and Perfecter of your faith. If you have been more focused on getting credit or respect rather than on giving Him credit and respect, admit it and let God deal with it. Throw off the sin that so easily entangles and run with perseverance the race marked out for you. Feel free to use the space below.

Victorious

Week 9

Day 5

Our powerful and victorious God, What a privilege to serve You, to get to see You show off Your great strength in our lives. Open our Eyes to See You do this more and more that our entire life is filled with stories of You showing Your greatness to and through us.

Reflecting on the week:

Go back and look at the things you wrote and underlined this week. Jot down the things below that stuck out to you or that God spoke to you about.

Lee Strobel and Mark Mittelberg wrote an inspiring book called The Unexpected Adventure, which I highly recommend. They conclude their story of adventures sharing the gospel with people and how God showed up by saying this. "We all love the idea of adventure, but here's the truth: adventure inevitably involves risk, which in turn always entails some measure of anxiety or nervousness. So if you're feeling apprehensive about an outreach opportunity, it's probably a good sign. It means you're well on your way to experiencing real adventure…It is interesting that the apostle Paul summed up the biblical understanding of the life of God's people by quoting a verse in the Old Testament and making it part of the New Testament as well: 'The righteous will live by faith' (Habakkuk 2:4 and Romans 1:17).

Notice these verses do not say, 'The righteous will initially receive salvation by faith, and then they will huddle in safe, predictable, and comfortable places.' Rather, we *live* - present tense - by faith. What is biblical faith? It's 'God-directed risk.' It's embracing God's unseen salvation, trusting in His unseen protection, obeying His unseen Spirit, following His unseen leadings, building His unseen kingdom, and preparing ourselves and others for His as-of-yet unseen home in heaven. It's the risk of taking Him at His word in our daily actions… So a good paraphrase of these hallmark Old and New Testament verses might be, 'The righteous will pursue lives marked by obedient, God-honoring risk taking.'

The ministry of Jesus was attractive and exciting in part because it was filled with God-honoring danger, culminating in His risking everything for the redemption of the world. I could add the examples of the exhilarating excursions of Paul and the other apostles, the risk-taking leaders of the early church, and the courageous missionaries who have taken the gospel to the ends of the earth, often in settings brimming with trouble and treachery.

These heroes of our faith have set the pattern. The course is laid out, and today's exciting journey is waiting to begin: if you want more adventure in your spiritual life, then you've got to start taking some spiritual risks.

Whose door is God telling *you* to knock on? What phone call do you need to make, or what email do you know you ought to send? Which neighbor should you invite over for a backyard barbeque? What relative could you reach out to? Who is the old friend you need to reestablish contact with? Ask the Holy Spirit to show you the steps you need to take – big or small – to engage in the unexpected adventure. Then step out and follow his lead *today*. There's no doubt: it will be a foray into a life of spiritual rewards both in this life and the one yet to come."[48]

Take some time to let the Holy Spirit lead your thoughts. Write down things that come to mind.

*How do you think God wants to demonstrate and display His power in and through your life?

*What areas in your life need His power to be transformed?

*What risks can you take to share the gospel? Have a hard conversation?

Austin and I feel privileged to be called to the mission of making multiplying disciples through the process of evangelism and discipleship, and are overwhelmed with joy as we see God working through us. But as we only have 1-4 years to invest in each student, we wonder what happens after they graduate. Recently God reminded me that our labor in Him is not in vain (1 Corinthians 15:58) by showing us He bears fruit that remains. (John 15:16) When Austin and I were on staff at the University of Northern Colorado three years ago, I discipled (helping her walk by faith, communicate her faith and multiply her faith) Stephanie, who was eager to grow. One thing we focused on was stepping out of her comfort zone to share the gospel. She overcame her fear and

---

48 Strobel, Lee and Mittelberg, Mark (2009). *The Unexpected Adventure: Taking Everyday Risks to Talk with People about Jesus.* Grand Rapids, MI: Zondervan

shared with her friend Sarah, who surrendered her life to Christ and began to grow. A couple weeks ago I was contacted by Hilary, a Denver student wanting to get involved in our ministry. It turns out that Sarah and another friend had shared the gospel with Hilary last year and she gave her life to Christ. The adventure of God-honoring risk taking is one that bears eternal fruit and will forever be worth it!

Elohim

Week 10

Day 1

Elohim, the only supreme and true God full of power and might, this week would You open our Eyes to See Your power and might in very real ways in our lives and in Your Word. We can have such a small view of You sometimes, please enlarge our perspective. Let us see You as You truly are that our desires and thoughts would not be small. Oh to know You, to truly know You, that we may reflect You by the power of Your Spirit. We lay our time, our distractions and our discouragements down before You as a fragrant offering, desiring to be pleasing to You.

Page Jumpers

Read 1 Samuel 20-22
List things that jump off the page (verses that stand out to you):

-
-
-
-
-

Cloud of Witnesses

"KOLKATA, INDIA – On 3 May, 2010, two men and one woman from Kolkata were sentenced to 10 years in prison for the trafficking and commercial sexual exploitation of three minor girls. Over the course of one year, the victims had been forced to provide sexual services for the commercial gain of their captors. The perpetrators were arrested by the Criminal Investigation Department (CID) on

February 16, 2007, while attempting to sell three minor girls for the purpose of sex. International Justice Mission (IJM), a human rights agency, assisted CID throughout the case, including in locating the three victims and providing vital evidence on the basis of which the three victims were rescued and the perpetrators arrested.

The girls, 12, 14 and 16 years old, had been lured by traffickers from their rural villages in Nepal and West Bengal with the prospect of legitimate work in Kolkata. Instead, they were "sold" to the accused persons, who in turn forced them to provide sexual services to as many as 12 customers a day.

The convictions are a milestone in sex trafficking casework in India. According to a 2009 report by the United States Department of State, 1,970 traffickers have been arrested within the states of Andhra Pradesh, Bihar, Maharashtra, Goa and West Bengal, resulting in just 30 convictions – a mere 1.5% of trafficking-related arrests.

'The courageous testimonies of the three girls, along with the compelling evidence that was seized by the CID at the time of the arrests in February 2007, convinced the Kolkata court to hold the perpetrators in custody throughout the trial,' said IJM advocate Saptarshi Biswas. 'The conviction of all three perpetrators today sends a clear message to traffickers that their crimes will not be tolerated and demonstrates the state of West Bengal's determination to ensure that access to justice is not denied to the most vulnerable and marginalized.'

Immediately after their rescue, the minors were placed in aftercares homes where they have been receiving counseling and schooling. "The girls have been completely transformed since their rescue," reports IJM social worker Rupa Chetri, who has worked closely with all three former victims. "They are thriving in their studies and are hopeful for their futures."

This week we are going to reflect on how to deal with suffering in our broken world, why Jesus came, and how to push each other on toward displaying God's heart".[49]

Here Am I

To prepare your heart for this weeks study, spend some time thinking about and writing down the suffering you see around you, local and global. Write down how it makes you feel and what thoughts come up as you think about it.

---

49   International Justice Mission. *Human Traffickers Receive Landmark Convictions In Kolkata*. Retrieved from http://www.ijm.org/newsfromthefield/humantraffickersreceivelandmarkconvictionsinkolkata

Elohim

Week 10

Day 2

Oh Lord, Who sees the affliction of the righteous and Who is slow to anger but will not leave the guilty unpunished, give us Your perspective of suffering today. Let us feel what You feel and see the way You see. We need You to expand our vision from our own limited culture, emotions and time period. Lord, please explain to us how You see this situation at Nob and how You view the suffering around us today. Enable our thinking and feeling to be lined up with Yours.

Eyes to See

This week we are going to work through our section of chapters backwards, dealing with the tragedy at Nob first. Please reread 1 Samuel 21-22 again and answer the following questions. Most of the questions will not be able to be answered by chapters 21 and 22, so you will need to get out some commentaries to help. (Again, please google online Bible commentaries or go to www.biblegateway.com or www.biblestudytools.com)

*Why did David go to Ahimelek the priest? How far away was Nob from Gibeah?

*What was the bread situation about?

*Do you think it was coincidence that God provided David with Goliath's sword? What is the significance of this?

*Why was David afraid of King Achish?

*What are your thoughts about David having courage to fight Goliath and remaining with Saul for so long dodging swords as he tried to kill him, but now being afraid of a King? What do you suppose led up to or contributed to this fear?

*Read Psalm 56. This psalm is said to refer to 21:10-15. Thinking of David acting like a crazy person, do you believe he was acting in faith or fear? Explain your thoughts and explain what commentators have to say.

Ears to Hear

How do we deal with this broken world? An honest view of God has to be our foundation. If we are tempted to curse God and walk away like Job's wife did, it is because our view of God is too small or perhaps distorted.

Who is this that obscures My plans with words without knowledge? (Job 38:2) God says Job's complaining and raging against Him are unjustified and are a result of limited understanding of Who He is. So God goes on to blow Job away showing His glory. Read Job 38:1-39:1, 40:1-14 and write down how it makes you feel.

When we live unholy lives and God allows the consequences of our choices to catch up with us, it is easy to blame Him. Is this not a higher view of ourselves than we ought to have? Is this not putting our opinion above our Maker's? Shall we accept good from God, and not trouble? (Job 40:8) The Lord gave and the Lord has taken away; may the name of the Lord be praised. (Job 2:10) Are you willing to see God's involvement, Who He truly is and praise Him even in the midst of suffering? (Job 1:21) Job 42:1-7 shows us that a low and improper view of God is something that we actually need to repent of and is recognized by how we view suffering.

My heart breaks, and my anger is fired up when I hear stories about girls who have been sold into the human trafficking industry. To hear that they will be tortured if they do not meet their quota of 10-20 clients a day makes me sick to my stomach. My anger can quickly give way to discouragement when the solution does not seem to be as extravagant as the problem. I want it all to stop right now, which causes me to cry, "Lord, come quickly, and do not delay any longer!" I cannot avoid the questions of "God, how can you allow this to continue?", "How can you allow little five year old girls to be raped twenty times a day!?", "When are you going to do something about it!?"

Perhaps you have posed the same questions to God. His answer, The Lord isn't really being slow about His promise, as some people think. No, He is being patient for your sake. He does not want anyone to be destroyed, but wants everyone to repent. (2 Pet. 3:9) Yes, Lot was a righteous man who was tormented by the wickedness he saw and heard day after day. So you see, the Lord knows how to rescue the godly people from their trials, even while keeping the wicked under punishment until the day of final judgment. He is especially hard on those who follow their own twisted sexual desire, and who despise authority. (2 Pet. 2:8-10) This truly expands my small view of God. He allows these grotesque acts to continue because it is far better than people experiencing hell for all eternity. He feels the pain, more than you or I could ever imagine, but it pales in comparison to the pain of hell that people will experience who choose not to turn to Him in repentance. How great is His love! But yet, He will not leave the guilty unpunished. If God were to judge all evil today He would do a complete job. If God stamped out evil today, none of us would be left. It is of the Lord's mercies that we are not consumed because His compassions fail not (Lamentations 3:22).

Jesus promised us that Here on earth you will have many trials and sorrows. But take heart, because I have overcome the world (John 16:33). We will be opposed by our own flesh and the flesh of other people, even Christians, by circumstances and the ways and culture of this world and our enemy the Deceiver.

Nate, a friend of Austin and I, put together a list of how we can see this opposition in the early church in almost every chapter in the book of Acts:

Chapter 2 – Peter and the Apostles made fun of by the Gentiles
Chapter 4 – Peter and John arrested and imprisoned
Chapter 5 – Apostles arrested, imprisoned and flogged
Chapter 6 – Stephen arrested, falsely accused
Chapter 7 – Stephen stoned to death
Chapter 8 – The Church persecuted
Chapter 9 – The Church continued to be persecuted by Saul and after his conversion, Grecian Jews tried to kill him also
Chapter 11 – Opposed by legalistic Christians
Chapter 12 – Christians persecuted by Herod, Peter imprisoned
Chapter 13 – Paul and Barnabus opposed by Elymas the sorcerer, talked bad about and persecuted by the Jews
Chapter 14 – Paul stoned and left for dead
Chapter 15 – Opposed by legalistic Christians, disagreement between Paul and Barnabus
Chapter 16 – Paul and Silas imprisoned and beaten in Phillipi
Chapter 17 – A rioting mob ran them out of Thesalonika, the Bereans were initially receptive towards them but became agitated and stirred up against them – they escaped to Athens, where they were better received but were also scorned
Chapter 18 – Opposed, abused and arrested by the Jews in Corinth
Chapter 19 – Opposed by a rioting mob in Ephesus
Chapter 20 – Plotted against by the Jews in Greece
Chapter 21 – Paul was arrested and the Jews attempted to kill him in Jerusalem

Chapter 22 – The Jews chanted, "Rid the earth of him. He's not fit to live!" about Paul while he was imprisoned

Chapter 23 – Paul put on trial, struck, and the Jews again plotted to kill him vowing, "Not to eat anything until we have killed Paul."

Chapters 24 – though 26 – Paul put on trial before Felix, Festus and Agrippa

Chapter 27 – Paul shipwrecked

Chapter 28 – Paul bitten by a snake and imprisoned in Rome.

Paul described it this way, "I have worked much harder, been in prison more frequently, been flogged more severely, and been exposed to death again and again. Five times I received from the Jews the forty lashes minus one. Three times I was beaten with rods, once I was stoned, three times I was shipwrecked, I spent a night and a day in the open sea, I have been constantly on the move. I have been in danger from rivers, in danger from bandits, in danger from my own countrymen, in danger from Gentiles; in danger in the city, in danger in the country, in danger at sea; and in danger from false brothers. I have labored and toiled and have often gone without sleep; I have known hunger and thirst and have often gone without food; I have been cold and naked" (2 Cor.11:23-27). And yet he says, "For our light and momentary troubles are achieving for us an eternal glory that far outweighs them all" (2 Cor. 4:17).

There is a very godly man who lives in a Middle Eastern country that my husband Austin and friend Nate got to meet. He cries over the country he lives to tell about Jesus and told Austin, "the soil of this country has to be broken up by the blood of martyrs" This was after he told Austin about his two friends that were killed. This is their story.

> "On April 18, 2007, five Muslims entered a Christian publishing company and killed three believers in the southeastern province of Malatya. The 3 believers, Tilmann Geske (a German missionary), Turkish Pastor Necati Aydin and Ugur Yuksel (also Turkish) were having a Bible study and prayer meeting. Five young Muslim men who they had been sharing with for quite a while were also present. After Pastor Necati read one chapter the Muslim men tied each of them up and began torturing them for 3 hours. Tilman was stabbed 156 times, Necati 99 times...They were disemboweled, and their intestines sliced up in front of their eyes. They were emasculated and watched as those body parts were destroyed. Fingers were chopped off, their noses, mouths and anuses were sliced open...Finally, their throats were slit from ear to ear. In an act that hit front pages in the largest newspapers in Turkey, Tilman's wife Susanne Geske in a television interview expressed her forgiveness. She did not want revenge, she told reporters. "Oh God, forgive them for they know not what they do," wholeheartedly agreeing with the words of Christ on Calvary (Luke 23:34). Turkish Pastor Fikret Bocek urged, "Don't pray against persecution, pray for perseverance."[50]

"I have no pleasure in the death of the wicked... turn back from your evil ways; for why will you die, O house of Israel?" (Ezekiel 33:11) Goethe, the German poet and novelist said, "If I were God, the suffering of the world would break my heart." It did! In a Messianic Psalm, Christ speaks through the prophet and says, "Their insults have broken my heart, and I am in despair" (Psalms 69:20). Jesus wept over the fallen condition of man (Luke 19:41). God Himself is the great Sufferer and has fully met the problem of evil in giving His only Son, Jesus Christ, at infinite cost to Himself. The suffering

---

50   Consolidated from a report by Voice of the Martyrs.

of the world broke God's heart, at the cross. "But He was pierced for our transgressions, He was crushed for our iniquities; the punishment that brought us peace was upon Him and by His stripes we are healed" (Isaiah 53:5). C.S Lewis said, "Pain is God's megaphone to a dying world."

The origin of evil is an academic question. The question we should ask is, "What can be done about the present fact of evil?" Christ is the answer for evil. He alone can change men's lives. Trusting Christ as Savior will not eliminate evil from our lives or the world. But it will change our desires to do evil and our perspective concerning evil. The initial question, "How can a loving God allow evil and suffering?" will then be restated, "Why does a loving God allow evil and suffering?" We will think often on this question. As we trust God, we will get some insights into its answer, but with our finite minds, we will never have all the answers. God is God, and we must have the same trust that Job had when he said, "Though He slay me, yet will I trust in Him" (Job 13:15).

Heart to Understand

The story of the eighty five priests being killed for no reason is very sad. It is an injustice, and yet God was not surprised about it but had told Samuel of this very event years earlier. This is the fulfillment of the prophecy spoken against Eli in chapter 2, verse 31. Even when pain and suffering is part of our life or the lives around us, or when people seem to be conspiring against us who like Saul, are manipulative and assume our motives are evil, God is still very involved and is working the situation for our good and His glory.

*How has your view of suffering been encouraged or challenged today?

Read Psalm 52 which reads between 1 Samuel chapter 22 and 23.
*David is talking about Saul. Describe his perspective and hope.

*Think of a couple situations of suffering that arouse your anger. If you were to have the same hope and perspective of David, what would it sound like? Write your own psalm about it.

Elohim

Week 10

Day 3

Our Lord, the God of David and Samuel, .we submit ourselves to You today and desire for you to glorify Yourself through us. Thank You for Your Word and Your Spirit to explain it to us. You are such an incredible and generous God. We admit that we can do nothing apart from You, Please come be on the throne of our hearts. Make us teachable and receptive to the things You want to show us today.

Eyes to See

Yesterday we looked at suffering and one of the reasons that God allows it, because He does not want anyone to live without Him for eternity. Today we are going to dive into that more, taking a break from 1ˢᵗ Samuel and looking at the implications of that desire. Write down the verses below.

John 3:17

John 12:44-46

John 17:24

John 20:30-31

Luke 5:31

John 20:21

> *According to these verses, what was Jesus' mission on earth?

We have talked a lot about how we exist to glorify God. There is no more clear way to make God known than through the Great Commission, Through the proclamation of Who God is to non-believers, which is called evangelism, and to help believers walk by faith, communicate their faith, and multiply their faith, which is called discipleship. The Great Commission is not the only way to glorify God but it is the most obvious and clear way.

"God's purpose in creating the universe and redeeming fallen mankind is to display His glory through the manifestation of His divine attributes. God created the human race and has so orchestrated the events of human history including the fall, the flood, the formation of the nation of Israel, the incarnation and atonement of Christ, the creation of the church, and the coming end times events of judgment and restoration of creation all for the purpose of demonstrating His attributes. Through the fall and redemption of man, God has manifested His righteousness and His love. In the one act of Christ dying on the cross, God demonstrated His justice and His mercy. It was all in God's infinite wisdom that He has orchestrated all of the events of history and it was all done to the 'praise of His glory.' All of history is moving to the day when "the earth will be filled with the knowledge of the glory of the Lord, as the waters cover the sea" (Hab. 2:14, Isa. 11:9). God is so glorious and He finds so much joy in His own glory that He wants others to behold Him and rejoice in Him as well. He doesn't need His creatures, but He created man to take part in His only perfect happiness. It was out of the overflow of the joy that the Triune God possesses in His own being that He wanted others to participate in it and rejoice in it with Him... The great commission is the greatest priority in this present age. If we believe that, then we should make it *our* greatest priority"[51]

Ears to Hear

Sometimes we can hear all these things about our purpose being to glorify God, and how we are supposed to be sharing our faith and be serving the people around us and be a good steward of our gifts, and get overwhelmed. Hopefully the following diagram with help to bring all of this into practicality.

Life Direction Circles
Our Purpose answers the question, "Why do we exist?" This will be the same for all people of all time periods.

Our Mission answers the question, "What are we here to do?" This is the same for all of us.

Our Uniqueness is how God has built us. (In week 7, we used the INVEST acronym to get a picture of this) This is different for everyone.

Our Vision is a picture of the desired future. A mental image of a possible and desirable future state. This is different for everyone.

---

51   Massimo Lorenzini A Passion for the Great Commission www.frontlinemin.org pg 8, 10

Life Direction Circles

Purpose: Answers "Why do we exist?"
Mission: Answers "What are we here to do?"
Uniqueness: INVEST Acronym
Vision: Picture of the desired future. A mental image of a
possible and desirable future state.

Purpose*: To glorify God.
To know God and make Him known.*

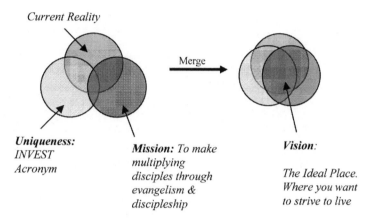

Current Reality

Merge

Uniqueness:
*INVEST
Acronym*

Mission: *To make
multiplying
disciples through
evangelism &
discipleship*

Vision*:*

*The Ideal Place.
Where you want
to strive to live*

So our purpose, our reason for existing, is to glorify God. Our mission is to make multiplying disciples through the process of evangelism and discipleship. Believe it or not, we are in the most exciting time in history to be involved in His Great Commission. "The harvest is plentiful but the workers are few" (Mt 9:37). Do you believe that about the people around you?

Austin's good friend Nate (who I have mentioned a few times before and is an excellent teacher. If you want to hear him speak or get resources on evangelism and discipleship check out his website www. eternityimpact.com) worked at a snowboard and skateboard shop while he was in college. After the store closed and the employees went home they had to do a pocket check where they would show each other what was in their pockets before they left to make sure no one was stealing anything. Nate consistently carried around a pocket Bible with him and his co-worker Kelly had seen it. One night while they were closing, Kelly asked Nate if he was a Christian and then went on to explain that she was beyond forgiveness because of the sexual lifestyle she lived. Nate shared the gospel with Kelly telling her that nothing could be further from the truth, and how God desperately wanted to forgive her and could forgive her. After an hour of talking, and through many tears, Kelly surrendered her life to Jesus and received forgiveness that she thought was impossible.

The following Sunday, Kelly met up with Nate at church introducing him to her boyfriend, Wally. Wally owned his own company and was incredibly wealthy. He seemed like he had it all together, enjoying life being a ski bum in Durango, Colorado. How easy it would be to think he had it all together and didn't need Jesus. But the first thing he said to Nate was, "If I can't find out how to have Christ in my life and how to get forgiveness, I'll kill myself." After church they went out to lunch and then back to his condo where Nate share the gospel with him and Wally gave his life to Christ.

God is working on the people around you. "I will draw all men to Myself" (John 12:32-33). The harvest is ripe.

In The Faith Equation, Dr. Marvin Bittinger, Professor of Mathematics at Purdue University and author of over 175 college math textbooks, claims that by 2033 every person on the planet capable of understanding the gospel will have been presented the gospel, according to modern evangelism trends.

Here are some of those trends:
34,000 people are coming to Christ each day in South America
28,000-37,000 Chinese people are turning to Jesus daily
23,000-25,000 people in Africa are surrendering their lives to Christ.
Every hour, 667 Muslims convert to Christianity, which is 16,000 every day.

Egypt – some reports say 1 million Egyptians have trusted Christ over the past decade or so. The largest Christian congregation in the Middle East, meets in an enormous cave on the outskirts of Cairo. Some 10,000 believers worship there every weekend.

Afghanistan – only 17 Muslims came to Christ before 9/11/01, but now more than 10,000

Kazakstan – there were only 3 known Christians in 1990, but now more than 15,000

Sudan – more than 1 million Sudanese have converted to Christianity just since 2000 despite a radical Islamic regime and an on-going genocide that has killed more than 200,000. Seminaries are being held in caves to train pastors to shepherd the huge numbers of people coming to Christ.

Iran – in 1979, there were only 500 known Muslim converts to Christianity, but today Iranian pastors and evangelical leaders say there are more than 1 million Iranian believers in Jesus Christ, most of whom meet in underground house churches. One of the most dramatic developments is that many Muslims are seeing dreams and visions of Jesus and thus coming into churches explaining that they have already converted and now need a Bible and guidance on how to follow Jesus.

So worldwide there are 174,000 people turning to Christ every day.[52]

The opportunity has never been more dramatic and the need has never been so huge. We can even have a global impact in our hometown through organizations such as Global Media Outreach who share the gospel with people online. We can travel and communicate with people all over the world. You have been placed strategically in this very place, for this very time. "From one man he made every nation of men, that they should inhabit the whole earth; and he determined the times set for them and the exact places where they should live" (Acts 17:26). Worldwide, massive revival is occurring, except here in America where less than 2% of Christians share their faith.

We can be a part of this amazing revival, through the power of the Holy Spirit leaving results to God. But it takes strategy. How will you personally reach the people God puts in your sphere of influence?

Here's Paul's strategy:
"As his custom was, Paul went into the synagogue, and on three Sabbath days he reasoned with them from the Scriptures" (Acts 17:2) In Phillipi, he went to the place of prayer and began sharing the gospel. They were arrested, beaten and imprisoned. In Thesalonika, he went to the synagogue and began sharing the gospel and a rioting mob drove them out of town. In Berea, he went to the synagogue and began sharing the gospel where they were received initially but run out of town by the same people that had run them out of town in Thesalonika. In Athens, he went to the synagogue and began sharing the gospel where some sneered but he was mostly well received. In Corinth, he went to the synagogue and began sharing the gospel. The Jews opposed him and became abusive. In Ephesus, he went to the synagogue and shared the gospel for 3 months. The whole city became a rioting mob and ran him out.

52 Barret, David B. and Johnson, Todd M. The Global Evangelism Movement.

179

What is your strategy? Because of your God given purpose and mission, it has to include evangelism and discipling those that come to Christ, and helping them become disciple makers. Believe it or not, reaching this world is very possible. Starting with 45 of us, multiplying once annually the whole world could be reached in 29 years. But to strategically be about God's mission for our lives we have to be focused and generally there are three kinds of Christians described by Steve Shadrach in his book The Fuel and the Flame.

1. Busy: This describes someone who has filled up his calendar with all kinds of activities, even spiritual ones. For her, maturity equals "Christian busyness," that is, heading to a Bible study now, then a concert, afterward a fellowship, over to the soup kitchen next, etc. As great as these things might be, many times they are packed into people's schedules out of boredom, insecurity, not being able to say no, or because they have no life objective they're committed to.

2. Effective: This person can say not too many glorious opportunities, but she's not really sure what to say yes to. She's narrowed down her priorities to a few important things that relate to evangelism and discipleship, but she has no specific Great Commission plan. Using a shot gun, rather than rifle, she sees God using her in the lives of a number of people, but deep down she knows she isn't making disciples.

3. Strategic: We have a lot of busy Christians, some effective ones, but precious few who are truly strategic. This person looks at her area of influence from God's perspective and has singled out the group she will reach and disciple for the Lord. This person will leave an eternal legacy behind.

We have our purpose, mission, uniqueness and current reality. But if these remain separate, we begin to feel like we are going crazy. The goal is to merge these together as much as possible. Jesus was of courser perfect at this, and expert. He used His uniqueness of being able to heal (so people would know He was God) to preach, and his current reality was traveling around to do it. In Mark 1:35, we see that His uniqueness was getting a little more attention, so He said "come let us go to the towns nearby so I may preach there also, for that is what I came for". We need to merge these circles as much as we can and live as much as we can in the ideal place.

Steve Shadrach in his book Fuel and the Flame, tells of a college student named Amber who understood this and went about her mission with great strategy. "Amber was a little shy at first, but she really wanted to represent Christ in her dormitory. She had just returned from a summer training program her ministry had sponsored, and their 'back to campus' emphasis helped give her the direction and boldness to plan her work, and then work her plan! She decided that she was going to try to meet every new freshman girl in her dorm as well as each student on her floor. Not only did she always keep her door open with a welcome sign on it, but she made it a point to introduce herself to anyone in the dorm she had not met. She arrived early to help girls move in, made posters for each of the girls' doors with their names on it, sponsored a popcorn and movie night the first weekend, and took three carloads of girls to her church that first Sunday.

Even though most of the other juniors had moved out of the dorm into their own apartments, Amber chose to stay put, and lay her life down for these young freshmen. It wasn't long until she was the ring leader of the entire dorm. Every girl liked and respected Amber, came to her with questions and problems, and wondered what it was that made her such a happy and sacrificial person. Amber started floating the idea of having a Bible study on each of the dorm's three floors. Girl after girl responded enthusiastically, even though Amber did not know where many of them stood spiritually. She identified the two most influential girls on each floor and asked them to host the study in one of their rooms and to help recruit the girls from their floor. Feeling honored to be chosen by Amber, the 'dorm mama,' they each went to work making posters, spreading the word, cooking up some munchies, and even starting competitions to see who could recruit the most girls to their floor study!

By late September, Amber had three full-blown, investigative Bible studies started, averaging eight to twelve girls in each one. Amber recruited Sara, a Christian friend from off campus, to help her round up the girls a few minutes before nine each night, bring in a load of New Testaments to pass out, and then launch everyone into a fascinating discussion on a chapter of John, each week trying to answer two questions: (1) Who is Jesus Christ? And (2) What does He want with me? Amber and Sara worked hard on preparing lead-in questions, involving each girl in the discussion, and pouring out their love and attention on one and all. As she and Sara interceded for each girl every morning, it was obvious the Holy Spirit was penetrating the hearts of many of them by using three powerful tools: (1) the truth of the Word, (2) the prayers of Amber and Sara, and (3) the girls observing the unconditional love Amber and Sara had for them and each other.

Three or four times a week Amber and Sara would treat a different girl whom they sensed God was working in to a cup of coffee, some chit chat, and a chance to hear and understand the gospel message. Over the course of the semester, the two leaders promised each girl the chance to get a customize presentation of how to have a personal relationship with God, and, miraculously, over thirty girls jumped at the opportunity. Amber had taken a step of faith, opened the funnel up very wide by meeting and serving over one hundred girls in her dorm, asked almost forty of them to join small-group studies, shared the gospel with over thirty of them, and was now seeing girl after girl open up her heart to the Lord Jesus Christ. It was the most exciting, satisfying experience Amber and Sara had ever had in their entire lives. The Lord was on His way to transforming that campus because a shy little college student decided to put her trust in a big God, walk toward her fears, and pray, share, and love a bunch of young freshmen into the kingdom."[53]

Your weaknesses, inabilities and failures present no challenge to God's plan for your life; your willingness does. Are you willing? What's keeping you from giving priority in your life to the Great Commission? Most of us would probably say we lack time for investing in other people. Our days and weeks are too full to take the time to get acquainted with a stranger or to disciple a new believer.

Heart to Understand

Looking back at week 7, fill in your Uniqueness. Then also fill in your Current Reality and Vision. (I've already filled in your purpose and mission for you)

Purpose *To glorify God, to know God and make Him known*

Mission *To make multiplying disciples through the process of evangelism and discipleship*

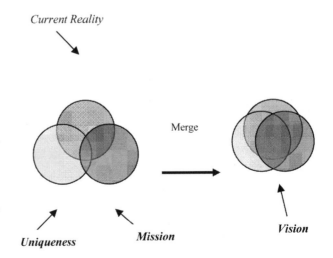

Current Reality

Merge

Uniqueness *Mission* *Vision*

53 Shadrach, Steve (2003). *The Fuel and the Flame*. Tyrone, GA: Authentic

Uniqueness (INVEST acronym from Week 7 Day 2)

Current Reality (circumstances of life)

Vision (Desired picture of the future, where your Current Reality, Uniqueness and Mission align.)

*How can you use your uniqueness to carry out the mission Jesus gave you of making multiplying disciples through the process of evangelism and discipleship in your sphere of influence?

Strategizing:

*What group of people do you want to focus on in your ministry to make multiplying disciples?

*Where would you consider to be the most strategic place to reach them? Where are they already gathered?

*Describe the situation where this group is gathered.
- What are the people like? (Needs, interests…)

- What ministry has (or has not) taken place in recent years?

- Who are the key people that will help give you access to this group?

- What are some possible problems or barriers that you may face in exposing this group to the gospel?

*Given the above information, what are all the possible evangelistic strategies that would be appropriate for this group?

*Come up with a plan of action (what will you do, when, who needs to help, what tools or resources do you need, where will it take place, etc.) Put these on a calendar and to-do list.

*What is God's part? What are the things that only He can do? Add these to your prayer list.

*After you lead someone to Christ, what will be your first next step with them? What kind of follow up will you use?

Here are some things Jesus did with and for His disciples to help them walk by faith, communicate their faith and multiply their faith.

Matthew 5:1-2

Matthew 14:16-21

Matthew 16:13-20

Mark 3:4

Mark 3:7

Mark 3:14, 6:7

Mark 3:23, 4:1

Mark 4:40

Luke 8:1

John 13:1-17

John 17:9-12

John 17:18

When we think about the way Jesus trained the twelve or the way Paul mentored Timothy, it wasn't just a formal program of teaching like we do today in schools and classrooms. Jesus said to His disciples, "Come follow Me and I will make you fishers of men" (Mark 1:17). Someone said, "Christianity is more caught than taught." Teaching is absolutely necessary, but won't fully impact a person's life without the action. How can someone do something they have never seen?

Elohim

Week 10

Day 4

Lord of the harvest, the fields truly are ready for harvest. Would You send out workers into the harvest fields? Would you use us to bear fruit that remains? Put people in our lives to push us on toward living for the purpose and mission You have given us. Would You teach us to number our days that we may present to You a heart of wisdom and would you make us into people that push others on toward love and good deeds, the works that You prepared for us before time began?.

Eyes to See

Re-read 1 Samuel 19:1-17, 20:1-42

*Sum up these verses in a few sentences.

*How would you describe Jonathan?

*Put yourself in Jonathan's shoes. What would you be thinking and feeling? What would be some temptations for you?

*Describe the relationship between Jonathan and David.

David and Jonathan are a good example of true fellowship. The word "fellowship" is from the Greek word "koinonia" meaning "belonging in common to." The idea that is conveyed is the bond of common purpose, a partnership to accomplish God's kingdom mission. Partnership carries responsibility and acting on the benefit of others before self. It can only be accomplished in purity when there is a foundation of Christ. Personally, I think the word fellowship causes people to think of hanging out with believers and having potlucks, which is not the real meaning of the word. So I will use the word community from now on.

"Do not be bound together with unbelievers; for what partnership has righteousness and lawlessness, or what fellowship has light with darkness?" (2 Cor. 6:14) There is no partnership between Christians and non-Christians because the Christian has been given a new purpose which the non-Christian does not have. They are going two different directions and therefore it is impossible to have fellowship.

*Read Hebrews 10:24-25. What does it tell us about a God honoring community?

Read Acts 2:42-47 The early church gives us a great example of what fellowship practically looks like. They were partnering together for the good of their brothers and sisters in Christ and were about the mission God had given them.

*How would you describe the difference between Christian get-togethers and real fellowship?

Ears to Hear

Though Christian groups abound, it is more of a rarity to find groups that truly are pushing each other to be about God's mission.

*Why do you think that is?

Let's look at some of the benefits of a community pushing and encouraging each other to accomplish things for God's kingdom.

Write out Hebrews 3:13

What is a benefit of the godly community seen in this verse?

Write out John 17:20-23

What is a benefit of the godly community seen in this verse?

Write out James 5:16

What is a benefit of the godly community seen in this verse?

REAPS is an acronym that shows some benefits of being involved in a community of believers who are pushing each other toward a mission.

R- Rescues us from a hard and deceived heart.

E- Eternal decisions are made

A- Allows the two basic needs of mankind to be met. To love and be loved, and to feel worthwhile to self and others.

P- Personal maturity comes as a result of the ability to bond, communicate, and accept self and others even when they fail.

S- Sets up an atmosphere for healing.

When we are around others who are continually pushing us to engage in the mission we talked about yesterday, of making multiplying disciples through the process of evangelism and discipleship, we will experience the abundant life God has for us.

Healthy disciples, like healthy cells, reproduce themselves. Reproduction and multiplication is something that God has ordained as a natural part of the life cycle. God's plan in the Great Commission is for believers to reproduce in a manner that is significantly similar to human reproduction. The world's population is exploding. God's plan, as set forth in the Great Commission, is for explosive reproduction of believers by discipling each new believer to reproductive maturity.

Let's say for example that a gifted evangelist is able to lead 1,000 people to Christ every day. Each year he will have reached 365,000 people, a phenomenal ministry indeed. Let's compare him with a disciple who leads not 1,000 people a day to Christ, but only one person a year. At the end of the year, the disciple has one convert; the evangelist, 365,000. But suppose the disciple has not only led this man to Christ, but has also discipled him. He has prayed with him, taught him how to feed himself from the Word of God, gotten him into fellowship with like-minded believers, taken him out on evangelism opportunities, and has shown him how to present the Gospel to other people. At the end of that first year, this new convert is able to lead another man to Christ and follow him up as he himself has been followed up.

At the start of the second year, the disciple has doubled his ministry—the one has become two. During the second year, each man goes out and leads not 1,000 people per day to Christ, but one person per year. At the end of the second year, we have four people. You can see how slow our process is. But note, too, that we do not have only converts, but disciples who are able to reproduce themselves. At this rate of doubling every year, the disciple leading one man per year to Christ, will overtake the evangelist numerically somewhere in the 19th year. From then on, the disciple and his multiplying ministry will be propagating faster than the combined ministry of dozens of gifted evangelists (Walter Henrichsen, Disciples Are Made Not Born, 141-42)."

Describe what this looked like in the New Testament.

2 Timothy 2:2

1 Corinthians 4:17

1 Thessalonians 3:2

1 Thessalonians 2:1-8

What immediately strikes you about the previous passages? Did you get the impression Paul was very involved in Timothy's life? If so, then you're getting the picture. To walk out the mission God has given us to make disciples, we have to be firmly rooted in a community that is pushing us on toward the mission, a community where new believers can also belong, and catch the vision to reach the world for Christ. When we share the gospel, we are inviting folks to the greatest adventure of their life, we are inviting them to be part of God's mission, which is the means He is going to use to reach the world.

Heart to Understand

"In his devotional book Quiet Talks with World Winners, S.D. Gordon recounted a story of a group of amateur climbers who planned to ascend Mount Blanc in the Swiss Alps. On the evening before the climb, the guides outlined the prerequisite for success. They said that due to the difficulty of the climb, one could reach the top by taking only the necessary equipment for climbing, leaving all unnecessary accessories behind.

A young Englishman didn't listen and proceeded up the mountain with a blanket, a small case of wine, a camera, a set of notebooks, and a pocketful of snacks. On the way to the summit the other climbers began to notice various items left along the path—first the snacks and the wine, a short while later the notebooks and camera, and finally the blanket. The young man managed to reach the peak, but, just as the guides had predicted, he did so only after discarding all his unnecessary paraphernalia.

Gordon made this application to the Christian life: "Many of us, when we find we can't make it to the top with our loads, let the top go, and pitch our tents in the plain, and settle down with our small plans and accessories. The plain seems to be quite full of tents."

Fellow Christian, where is your tent pitched? Have you settled on the plain? Or, are you still following Christ in obedience to the Great Commission? What changes do you need to make to follow Christ in this area? The church is the bride of Christ. The church is of infinite value to Him because He paid an infinite price to redeem her. He willingly endured the pain and shame of the cross to redeem us. How much it must grieve Jesus when we don't esteem the value of the church and the Great Commission. Let's not insult our Lord by living as if our goals and plans are more important than His. Let's follow His example by living sacrificially in order to carry out the work of disciple-making. Let's recommit ourselves to the great task of making disciples by evangelizing, edifying, and equipping the people around us."[54]

　　　*Who do you know that has a passion for the Great Commission? Who is her community?

54　Lorenzini, Massimo. Retrieved from www.frontlinemin.org

*If you don't already have a group of believers pushing you toward living for the Great Commission, where can you find one?

*Who is someone with whom you can share your insights from this week?

*What things in your life are keeping you from making the Great Commission a priority?

*Are there two believers in your life that would be willing to have a regular time of fellowship/ community where you mutually encourage and hold each other accountable in the mission? Talk to them about setting up a regular time together. (Tomorrow I will refer to these as your Community Girls.)

Elohim is a name for God that is plural, portraying the connectedness of Father, Son, and Holy Spirit. When we partner with other believers in the mission, we are beautifully displaying God's character, revealing His glory. What a privilege!

Elohim

Week 10

Day 5

Elohim, what a privilege to partner with other believers in the mission beautifully displaying Your character, revealing Your glory. Apart from You we can do nothing of eternal worth, so would You please enable us to spur one another one toward love and good deeds.

Reflecting on the week:

True fellowship is partnering with another Christian to be about God's mission. It REAPS (**R**escues from a hard heart, **E**ternal decisions are made, **A**llows for our greatest needs to be met, **P**ersonal maturity is grown and it **S**ets up and atmosphere for healing) .

But in order for us to really experience true fellowship or community, we need to be willing to open up to people. We have to bring our fears, confidences and insecurities out in the open. We have to honestly communicate with where we are right now and where we want to be. The only things that grow in the dark are lies. When we keep things hidden trying to save face, then truth and healing can never come to those places of our hearts.

Look back at your notes through the week and jot down some of the things you were thinking and feeling.

Make it a priority to communicate these things with your Community Girls.

I AM

Week 11

Day 1

The Great I Am, Who is totally self-existent, from You, to You and through You are all things. You are truly gracious. Here we are, not totally put together desiring to know You. We are desperate for You to help us see You, that we would continue to be changed by You and reflect You to those around us. Lord, please empower us to submit and yield to You today and to come to You with a willing heart.

Page Jumpers

Read 1 Samuel 23 and summarize.
List things that jump off the page (verses that stand out to you):

-

-

Read 1 Samuel 24 and summarize.
List things that jump off the page (verses that stand out to you):

-

-

Read 1 Samuel 25 and summarize.
List things that jump off the page (verses that stand out to you):

-

-

Read 1 Samuel 26 and summarize.

List things that jump off the page (verses that stand out to you):

-

-

-

Cloud of Witnesses

Francis Chan tells some incredible stories of people who sought to live their lives fully surrendered to God in his book Crazy Love. One of them is Jamie Lang. Here is her inspiring story.

> When Jamie was twenty-three years old, she flew from the United States to Tanzania with $2,000 from her savings account. She planned to stay until she ran out of money, at which point she would come home.

> Jamie was overwhelmed by all of the need that she encountered, so she started praying that God would allow her to make a radical difference in one person's life. After about six months, she met an eight-year old girl at church who was carrying a baby on her back. Jamie learned that the baby's mother was dying from AIDS and that she was too weak to care for him. Jamie began to buy formula for the little boy, Junio, to provide him with the nutrition he desperately needed. At the time, he was half the size of a healthy baby.

> Jamie fell in love with baby Junio. She wondered if she was being foolish-a barely twenty-four-year-old, single, white American entertaining thoughts of adopting a baby. Besides, she didn't even know if Tanzania allowed international adoptions. Eventually, she discovered that the country *didn't* allow international adoptions; however, because she had lived there for over six months, she could establish residency.

> Before Junio's mom died from AIDS, she came to Jamie and said, "I have heard how you are taking care of my son, and I have never known such a love. I want to be saved." Just before she died, she said, "I know that my son is taken care of, and I will see him in heaven someday."

> Jamie spent six months going through the adoption process and then five months working with the American embassy to get Junio a visa. When she finally came home, she had been gone for a year and a half.

> Junio is now five years old, totally healthy, and HIV negative. When Junio's mom was pregnant with him, she took a "morning-after pill" late in her pregnancy in order to abort him. But instead it induced premature labor, and because Junio was so small, no bleeding occurred during his birth. Thus, he did not contract HIV from his mother. What was intended to end his life, God used to save it.

Since adopting Junio, Jamie has gotten married, has had a little girl, and is moving back to Tanzania with her family to work with Wycliffe to translate the Bible for a group that has never heard it before.[55]

This week we are going to look at the role of honoring God and others in our life, and what it means to live for and to be willing to die for righteousness.

Here am I

Spend some time writing out a prayer to God telling Him what's on your mind and heart and asking Him to prepare your heart for what He wants you to act on this week.

55   Chan, Francis (2008). *Crazy Love: Overwhelmed by a Relentless God*. Colorado Spring, CO: David C. Cook.

I AM

Week 11

Day 2

Great and Mighty God Who is able to do all things, the great I AM, who is totally self-sufficient and in need of nothing, what a privilege to know You, to serve You and to be loved by You. We come to You, the Author and Perfecter of our faith Who endured the cross so that we could love You and be loved by You. We want to offer ourselves again to You today, to do as You please in our lives.

Eyes to See

Skim through 1 Samuel, chapters 23-24 reminding yourself of each of the stories, and read through the insights you recorded under yesterday's Page Jumpers.

> *If you were to make a movie about one of the characters you read about, who would you choose and why? What would be the main focus of the movie?

> *From 23:7-12, what can you see to be capabilities of our desires apart from Christ, (our human nature)?

> *In 23:16-17 we see Jonathan risk his life to help him find strength in God. What difficulties might Jonathan have faced in doing this (physically, emotionally, mentally, spiritually, and relationally)?

*Look at 24:8-15. What stands out to you about David's character and attitude?

*Look at 24:16-21. What are your thoughts about what Saul says?

Ears to Hear

The little mountain town of Durango that I have mentioned before has a river running through it. It really is a wonderful river with gold medal water, so it has great fishing and mid-sized rapids that make it very family friendly. But my favorite thing about the river is the sidewalk that runs alongside of it through the entire town. It has charming lamp posts and is always full of people walking and riding their bikes. Austin and I began our friendship on long walks on along the river. Sometimes I would go on walks with God, just talking to Him about all kinds of stuff. On one of these walks my most embarrassing moment happened. I even get embarrassed thinking about it now. There is this one spot on the river where there are a lot of trees along the edge of the river and it creates a secluded place. It's beautiful. I decided to stop there for a while, right on the edge of the river with the trees behind me separating me from the sidewalk. I decided to sing to God. I felt certain I was far enough away from the path that no one could hear me. Believe me, I made sure, because it takes a lot for me to sing in front of people. There I was singing, with my eyes closed and my hands raised, praising God with everything I had. After singing a couple of songs I opened my eyes, only to discover three rafts full of people had floated down the river right in front of me, not more than 10-15 feet away from me! . Seriously, how embarrassing! They had not made a peep. Why would a whole boat full of people not say anything?! Not even a throat clearing or something just to let me know that I was exposing my heart in their presence.

If singing in front of people is not too difficult for you, then I am not sure you can feel the real weight of this. I was so embarrassed, but that soon gave way to anger at God. I said to Him, "How could You!?" I thought, "Here I am opening up my heart to You in a very vulnerable way and You let everyone see me."

I still wonder what the people in those boats thought. I mean seriously, what would you have thought? Wacko comes to mind. Once I got embarrassed, it quickly became about me, rather than about God. Here I was, wanting to offer Him a sacrifice of praise. He gave me the opportunity and the first thing I did was get mad at Him and throw a little fit. Something that started as a pure offering ended in a fleshly response.

Max Lucado is one of my favorite authors and his book, It's Not About Me, is one of my favorite books. He has such an incredible way with words. He describes our quickness to turn to a self-focus in this way.

> We've been demanding our way and stamping our feet since infancy. Aren't we all born with a default drive set on selfishness? *I want a spouse who makes me happy*

and coworkers who always ask my opinion. I want weather that suits me and traffic that helps me and a government that serves me. It's all about me. …But what chaos this philosophy creates.

What if a symphony orchestra followed such an approach? Can you imagine an orchestra with an "It's all about me" outlook? Each artist would be clamoring for self-expression: tubas blasting nonstop, percussionists pounding to get attention, the cellist shoving the flutiest out of the center-stage chair, the trumpeter standing atop the conductor's stool tooting his horn, sheet music disregarded, conductor ignored. What do you have but an endless tune-up session! Harmony? Hardly. Happiness?... Not at all… What if we played the music the Maestro gave us to play? What if we made His song our highest priority? Would we see a change in families? We'd certainly hear a change. Less "Here is what I want!" More "What do you suppose God wants?"

But how do we make the shift? How can we be bumped off self-center?...We move from me-focus to God-focus by pondering Him, witnessing Him. We are changed by following the counsel of the apostle Paul: "Beholding as in a glass the glory of the Lord, [we] are changed into the same image from glory to glory, even as by the Spirit of the Lord" (2 Corinthians 3:18 KJV).

Heart to Understand

Saul was much like a little kid who desperately wanted something and stomped his feet and threw a fit when he didn't get it. He was obsessed with finding and killing David and when his plan went wrong he would erupt in a fit of rage. In chapter 23 we hear that he told his troops he was sending them to Keilah to rescue the people, whereas his real motive was to capture David and execute his vengeance. Saul's anger not only moved him to slaughter the priests of Nob as we read last week, but his anger drove him to even stake the lives of his own people in the city of Keilah to destroy David.

On the contrary, David's incredible mercy was displayed in the cave when he restrained himself and his men from killing Saul. We can be sure (as seen in Psalm 54) that David was angry at Saul for abusing the authority God had given him and for seeking to kill David for no legitimate reason. Even David's men saw it as an opportunity for revenge, while David saw it as an opportunity to show mercy and prove that his heart was right. God was giving him an opportunity to answer his own prayer for vindication. He who is slow to anger is better than the mighty, and he who rules his spirit than he who takes a city" (Prov. 16:32 NKJV).

Perhaps many Christians today would have agreed with David's men. It seems that over and over I hear people say, such and such happened; therefore it must be God's will. Would you have been one to agree with David's men? Would you see the reality that Saul was right there in front of you, defenseless, as a situation that God had set up so you could destroy him? Sometimes when we see things from our own perspective we can make up our own, *Well of course that means_____.* David saw the same situation that his men did, but what he thought should be done was very different. Sometimes it is difficult to see what is right and true in the midst of confusing circumstances. But that does not mean there is no truth, or that one thing is right for one person and something else is right for another. God does have an absolute truth and it can be found in His Word.

This specific situation is a bit hard for us to relate to, since most of us are not in the military and most likely have a very different view of killing than these men did. God tells us that murder is wrong. (Just so we are on the same page, murder is taking the life of someone without authority to do so). Killing is not always murder. When God told Saul to kill the Amakites, He gave them the authority to do so, and therefore this act was not murder. God is the only One able to give the authority to take a life, since He is the One that created life.

1st Samuel 24:8-15 shows the incredible courage David had. He confronted the evil Saul was doing. As you probably noted earlier, David must have been terrified to call out to the one hunting him and broadcast his confrontation of sin.

> Read Acts 13:4-12.
> *What similarities do you see to 1 Sam. 24:8-15?

> *Would you find it difficult to say this to this man? Why or why not?

> *What values and beliefs about God does someone have to have in order to confront evil like this?

> *Are there situations in your life right now where an evil act needs to be spoken against?

Spend some time talking to God about these situations. Share your fear and anxieties with Him. Ask Him to give you courage to respond the way that David did. Ask him to give you His boldness and perspective and then spend some time praising Him for Who He is and what He is like.

I AM

Week 11

Day 3

Oh Great and Mighty One, with one desire we come, that You would reign in us. We're offering up our lives, a living sacrifice, that You would reign in us. We want to give You the honor You deserve. Please teach us how. Open our eyes to what it means to honor You.

Eyes to See

Read 1 Samuel 25

> *Get ready to use your imagination. Put yourself in the house of Nabal and Abigail. Imagine what you see. What does it look like? Describe the atmosphere.

> *What observations about Abigail's passions, character, and values can you make?

> *If you sat down with Abigail for coffee in heaven and she asked you what was most helpful about her story, what would you say?

> *Try to describe this story as though it were set in modern times.

"David hoped that Nabal would reward him and his men for their service. David's expectation was logical. Any man with 3,000 sheep and 1,000 goats could easily spare a few animals to feed 600 men who had risked their own lives to guard part of his wealth. Common courtesy would certainly dictate that Nabal invite David and his men to share his food at a festive season when hospitality was the order of the day. It wouldn't be easy to feed 600 men in the wilderness, so David sent ten of his young men to explain the situation and to ask to be invited to the feast."[56]

Ears to Hear

Read Luke 7:36-50

This is such a beautiful picture of worship. The prostitute saw who Jesus was and was moved to action. She made a choice to give Him something incredibly precious and valuable to her, her perfume, her livelihood. The most important thing to a prostitute was her perfume, which this lady held in this alabaster jar. Her devotion was sacrificial, intentional, and courageous. What is your alabaster jar?

When Jesus entered Simon's house, Simon did not give Jesus a basin to wash His feet and did not greet Him with a kiss. This would be like bringing a special guest into your home and not opening the door for him, taking his coat and saying hello. What Simon did was very offensive. I wonder if he was slightly jealous of Jesus and that is why he went out of his way to try to show Jesus was not anything special. Perhaps this is why the prostitute is crying, wondering, *Don't they know Who He is? Why are they treating Him this way?*

I love how Jesus doesn't just sweep things under the carpet, but addresses attitudes and actions. He brings this offense to Simon's attention at the same time that He brings truth to the lies he was believing. A humble man at this point would apologize for his lack of respect and thank the woman for compensating for his rudeness. But Simon is not able to recognize his faults, and is only able to point the finger at the woman.

Still talking to Simon, Jesus turns to the woman. How beautiful! He is looking right into her eyes and starts bragging on her in front of the entire roomful of people. Who in these men's worlds would be the most undeserving of honor? A prostitute woman. But Jesus seizes the opportunity to brag on her because of her faith.

This story is incredibly shocking to the men in that room because not only does Jesus praise and honor a despised women, but He goes on to make her the noble hero. His honoring of her brings with it the benefit of restoring her to community.

This was a common habit of Jesus. He bragged on John the Baptist, the paralytic's friends, Mary, the woman with a demon possessed daughter, the centurion man "Turning to the crowd following Him, he said, "I tell you, I have not found such great faith even in Israel" (Luke 7:9). And why? Why would God of the universe, Who is able to see our hearts, stop what He is doing and honor flawed people? One reason is because He values life and wants to give dignity.

---

56 Wiersbe, Warren (1993). *The Bible Exposition Commentary (Volume 1)*. Colorado Springs, CO: Victor Books/ SP Publications, Inc.

Simon was caught up with how he was being perceived by other people. But when we are focused on the thoughts and opinions of others, we can't be concerned with honoring them or God. As we have seen in 1st Samuel so far, David is also very honoring. I've heard it said the most important thing about you is what you believe about God, and by David's actions, it is obvious he thought very highly of God and recognized His authority in life. If there was someone in my life that hated me so deeply that she spent a lot of her life chasing me down to kill me, someone who whole-heartedly devoted herself to destroying my life, I don't think I would have had the attitude that David had. In 2nd Samuel we see how he bragged about Saul when he died - the very guy who tried to destroy him! He did not say a bad thing about him but rather wrote a song and had the army sing about how great Saul was. CRAZY WOW! That is honor!

Sometimes it is easy to think there is nothing good about someone, so how in the world can I brag about them to others? If David can honor his worst enemy, someone who tried to destroy his life, someone devoted to kill him. Surely I can honor those who are hard to honor.

I find it interesting that David is characteristically very honoring of others. At this point, however, he lets his anger get the best of him. He didn't stop to talk to God about the situation, which was also out of character for David but rather he impulsively rushed out to satisfy his desire for revenge. What a great reminder that at all times we need to "Stay Alert! Watch out for your great enemy, the devil. He prowls around like a roaring lion, looking for someone to devour" (1 Peter 5:8). But after Abigail spoke with him and honored him in front of his men, he began to calm down and began to realize he was in the presence of a remarkable woman. She helped him recognize it was the Lord who stopped David from giving in to his flesh. David listened to godly counsel and admitted he was wrong and God forgave him.

Read 2nd Samuel 1:17-27

*Describe how David honors Saul and describe your thoughts and feelings about it.

*Saul obviously did some things that were not pleasing to the Lord. What can you learn about honoring people in truth? Does honoring someone mean you can't stand up against the evil things they do? Why or why not?

*Describe how Abigail honored/bragged on David.

*What was the result in David's heart and attitude?

Heart to Understand

Austin and I have a friend we met in Durango who now does college ministry with his beautiful wife down in Texas. Eli and Mandy both love the Lord and want their lives to please Him in every way. God has gifted Eli with musical abilities and in teaching. Every time you get in a conversation with Eli, he wants to share with you something the Lord has taught him. We invited Eli to come to Denver and put on a concert and speak to our students. The week he came, we were dealing with a gossip problem going on with some of our students. You know how it goes: so and so told so and so this, and then they told so and so that. But God orchestrated things so beautifully to have Eli come at that exact point. Eli is the most honoring person I know. He uses every opportunity he can get to honor people. So, he spoke to our students about honor. He taught them what honor was using examples of bragging on Austin and I, interwoven throughout his teaching. It was beautiful. The next day, I overheard some of the girls that were involved in the gossip bragging on other people!

While he was teaching our students about honor, he told a story that happened to him.
When Eli lived in Durango, God challenged him to be a man of honor, to not speak against his leaders but instead be a warrior, a defender for them isn't it interesting that it is most tempting to speak poorly about our authorities, when they are the exact ones God calls us to honor). He overheard his friend talking badly about the leader of their ministry, and Eli actually went up and punched the guy. After that, the gossip stopped as this group of guys started bragging on the leader and on others.

Awhile later the ministry quadrupled in size and the enemy got people gossiping and talking badly about each other instead of honoring each other. That year within a few months the group had gone back down to the size it was before. Honoring others has incredibly rewarding fruit, whereas gossip has incredibly destructive fruit.

> *Describe a few instances you have seen of someone honoring someone else and the effects it had.

> *Who in your life has a consistent track record of honoring people? What opportunities do they use to honor people?

For some reason God has not given me a good memory, in fact He has not given me even a satisfactory memory. It can be very discouraging at times but He reassures me that His grace is sufficient for me and that His power is make perfect in my weakness. One of the implications of having a bad memory is that I have a hard time remembering the previous week. So I have to be proactive. At the end of each week I try to sit down and reflect on the week. Using my schedule to help jog my memory, I think about how I saw God work in people's lives and who He used to do it. Then when someone asks me how my week was, I use those stories to brag on God and on the people He used.

Perhaps you are like me, and have to make an effort to honor people. But don't let that stop you, the reward is well worth it!!

*How are you at honoring people? What aspects of it do you find hard? What do you find easy?

*What situations are most conducive for you to honor others?

*What is something you can start doing this week to help you make honoring others a habit in your life?

I AM

Week 11

Day 4

Jehovah, our God Who was and is and is to come. All glory, honor and power belong to You. Would You allow us to more fully understand that? You are the God Who never fails and always does everything perfectly, Who perfectly knows truth from error and Who has perfect courage. By Your Spirit, would You make us people who reflect You in this way, people who love You so deeply that we will do what You say is right no matter what it costs us. Lord, give us Your courage.

Eyes to See

Read 1 Samuel 26

> *Do you think David's interaction with Abigail had an effect on how David acted toward Saul in this second confrontation? If so, why and how?

> *Describe what David does and why he does it.

Saul had driven David out of his own land, the very inheritance that the Lord had given his family. David pursued doing what was right by trying to reason with Saul, bringing to light his wrong thinking and action. If David had sinned, he was willing to admit it and seek forgiveness from the Lord. But if Saul was treating David like a criminal because of the lies his officers had told him, he wanted Saul to recognize they were the offenders, not him. David took some great risks in doing what was right in this situation.

*What were some of the risks David faced in this chapter?

*How does David deal with these risks?

Ears to Hear

In Pakistan, police arrested Hector Aleem, 51, husband and father of two, on charges of sending a text message that insulted Muhammad. At his court hearing, a crowd of 100 or more began chanting death threats to him. Police raided Aleem's house at 1:30 in the morning and assaulted him, his wife, and two daughters. They stole his money and valuables, and broke pictures of Jesus hanging on their walls. While in jail, the police denied him adequate food and access to medicine for his heart condition. At the hearing, the man who set Aleem up was implicated but crowds were yelling, "If you release him, then we will kill him outside." Sources said they believed Aleem was framed because of his social activism as director of a small non-governmental organization that lobbies for the rights of Pakistani Christians in Islamabad.

Aleem is an example of someone who is taking great risks for the sake of doing what is right. But the risks don't deter him, and one day he will get to stand before his Maker and hear Him say, *Well done, good and faithful servant.* (Matthew 25:21)

I love the movie *Valkyrie*. It is a true story of men who took a stand against Hitler and tried to overthrow him. They came up with an elaborate plan that would stop the killing of the Jews. However the plan involved murdering Hitler (which God had not given them the authority to do). The reason I love the movie so much is that these men risked their lives to do what was right. The first time I watched the movie I sobbed because their plan failed. I was so sad that they staked their life on their plan, and it failed. But what my emotions showed me was that I valued success more than I valued doing what was right. God used it to help me value from the core of my being that doing what is right is worth doing, even if you are going to lose the battle.

In these last days, we are going to need to fight many battles, battles that will seem like losing battles. But that doesn't mean they are not worth fighting for. It is worth standing up for what is right, because it is the right thing to do. In the end we will win. We will win the war. It is worth fighting because it displays the glory of God. It will be painful and we will be hated and attacked like our Pakistani brother, but it will be worth it. Yet what we suffer now is nothing compared to the glory he will reveal to us later. (Romans 8:18)

Torrey's new topical textbook defines *martyrdom* as "death endured for the Word of God and testimony of Christ". That means being killed for saying and doing what God's Word says is right and true. I use to think that being a martyr was someone who died because they wouldn't renounce they believed in Jesus. Though that is also part of it, it is not the whole definition. Truly understanding what a martyr is should expand our perspective of how highly God values people standing up for what

He says is right and true. He values it so much that He, the God of the universe, will honor them. That shows how much He values standing up for what He says is right, righteousness.

*How does Revelation 6:9 and Revelation 20:4 define *martyrdom*?

"Then you will be handed over to be persecuted and put to death, and you will be hated by all nations because of Me. At that time many will turn away from the faith and will betray and hate each other, and many false prophets will appear and deceive many people. Because of the increase of wickedness, the love of most will grow cold" (Matt 24:9-13).

It makes sense that in the last days many will turn away and not be willing to endure persecution. Persecution for standing up for what God's Word says is right, things like not killing babies and not condoning sexual immorality (homosexuality). I can see many not willing to endure persecution for those things.

Read these instances of martyrdom and write down who was martyred and what strikes you about it.
Genesis 4:3-8

2 Chronicles 24:20-22

Jeremiah 26:20-23

Mark 6:18-28

Acts 7:51-60

Hebrews 11:32-40

What do these verses have to say about hope in the face of suffering?
Jeremiah 46:25-28

Philippians 3:10

James 1:2-3

1 Peter 1:3-7, 13

1 Peter 4:12-14

Heart to Understand

I am struck by the reality that pain and fear can easily deter us from what God has "called" us to do. Austin and I heard about snowflake adoption (adopting an embryo that was made through couples doing in-vitro fertilization. There are over 500,000 babies in freezers waiting for a warm womb to continue to grow in, and only 200 people have adopted one.) About a year ago, Austin and I sensed God leading us to adopt a snowflake baby in the future. Well, now it's the future and God is showing us now is the time. Galatians 6:10 says, "As we have opportunity, let us do good to all people". We believe God has given us "opportunity" to provide a womb for a baby to grow in. We believe the right thing to do is to adopt a baby that has no hope for the future.

So, we started the process. But then, how do I explain what happened? Well, after three doctor's appointments, each worse than the one before, things came into perspective. It was going to be twice as much money as we had thought. The drive to the doctor was very far away, and I was going to have to give myself shots every day for 3 months, and I hate needles! The list goes on and on of inconveniences. On my first drive home from the doctor, as I was crying and telling God I wasn't sure if I could do it, He reminded me of something my friends Dusti and Elizabeth had said before, "*I will not bow to the idol of convenience!*" He reminded me that life was worth it, that life is always worth the inconvenience. So, I, too, determined not to bow to the idol of convenience.

After doctor appointment number two, when I heard about the one-and-a-half-inch long needle Austin would have to put in me every day, and not being able to have coffee, and having to be on bed rest for two days, and not being able to lift my boys for two weeks, I really thought *God, I really don't think I can do this.* After doctor appointment number three, where some tests didn't work and some even more invasive procedures were going to have to be done, through tears, I started questioning the "calling" and hoping and praying for God to give me some *sign* that He *really* wanted us to do this. How crazy! I actually turned to a mystical experience or circumstance when it got hard, rather than trusting God's Word, believing it was the right thing to do.

I love God's Word, and that is why I was so shocked later that my default when things got hard was to put my trust in mysticism and circumstances. Yuck! Why in the world does it seem like circumstances (which can totally be set up by Satan sometimes) and mystical experiences or feelings would be more reliable that God's Word when things get hard? Austin said it's our faith bumping up against our flesh, exposing our tendency to look for other life lines.

What an eye opener to even the word "calling". Most of the time when we use the word "calling," we are meaning we experienced a mystical feeling or an interpreted circumstance that we believe meant God wanted us to do something. Instead of reading His Word and realizing that He truly wants us to do something whether we "feel" like it or not. God has "called" us to do what's right, to share our faith, to take the gospel to those who haven't heard, to pray, etc.

But how His grace is sufficient! The next day He spoke verse after verse to me and gave me strength to trust Him and His Word more than anything else. Here are the verses He spoke to me regarding moving forward with this adoption. "But rejoice inasmuch as you participate in the sufferings of Christ, so that you may be overjoyed when His glory is revealed" (1 Peter 4:13). "Let us not become weary in doing good" (Galatians 6:9). "Therefore, I urge you, brothers and sisters, in view of God's mercy, to **offer your bodies as a living sacrifice**, holy and **pleasing to God-this is true worship**" (Romans 12:1). "I consider that our present sufferings are not worth comparing with the glory that will be revealed in us" (Romans 8:18). "Whatever you do for the least of these you do for me"

(Matthew 25:40). "For I have the desire to do what is good, but I cannot carry it out... who will rescue me from this body of death? Thanks be to God, Who delivers me through Jesus Christ our Lord" (Romans 7:18, 24, 25). "You see, at just the right time, when we were still powerless, Christ died for the ungodly" (He took on physical infliction for the benefit of those who couldn't do anything about their condition. Through His suffering He freed us from what held us back from doing what were created to do-glorify Him. Carrying this baby would give it life and give it opportunity to do what we were created to do, glorify God) "My grace is sufficient for you" (2 Corinthians 12:9).

Austin and I were confident that God wanted us to adopt an embryo, we were not sure of when. We did the best we could using Spirit-filled reasoning and decided on doing the transfer in March of 2010. The month before we were hoping to have the baby transferred we were told our finger prints got mixed up and they had to start the entire process over and were also told the embryos we wanted to adopt were adopted by another couple. Things were starting to look dismal of offering a baby a womb in March. As we kept praying and doing what we could to move forward, we were told our finger prints had been rushed and were completed and needed to be matched with a baby. But the next week we found out that we were pregnant. The shock of all shocks. No wonder God wasn't clear with us about the timing, it wouldn't be March or anytime in the year 2010. He had another little life planned before this embryo baby comes into our family.

So how do we endure? How do we press on to do what is right in the face of suffering for it? "We do this by keeping our eyes on Jesus, the Champion who initiates and perfects our faith. Because of the joy awaiting Him, He endured the cross, disregarding its shame. Now He is seated in the place of honor beside God's throne. Think of all the hostility He endured from sinful people, then you won't become weary and give up. After all, you have not yet given your lives in your struggle against sin" (Hebrews 12:2-4). "So then, since Christ suffered physical pain, you must arm yourselves with the same attitude He had and be ready to suffer, too" (1 Peter 4:1).

Abel, the first martyr, did what was right in giving his best to God, and was killed for it. What are you willing to endure for the sake of doing what is right according to God's Word? Are you willing to have people talk badly about you? Lose a tax exemption? Go to prison? What would it take to stop you from doing what is right?

    *Spend some time really thinking about this and journaling your thoughts.

    *What are some situations in your life that are opportunities for you to do what is right even though it might be difficult?

    *What is the right thing to do in these situations? Practically, what does God want you to do?

I AM

Week 11

Day 5

God, can we accept good from You and not bad? Can we tell You, the Potter, what to do with our lives? No. Help us be people that are willing to submit to You no matter the cost and take a stand for what Your Word says is right, no matter how much it might hurt. Increase our faith, that we might be a fragrant offering to You, holy and pleasing.

Reflecting on the week:

Read a young girl's journal written in the face of persecution.

June 18

Dear God, Tapan got a job with a Christian organization. He is so excited. They do medical work to help prevent AIDS, and also share the "Jesus Film" with others and tell them about Christ. People say that the Muslim extremists in our village have a "hit list" and that if you work for a church or Christian group, that you are put on that list. I hope that does not happen to Tapan!

July 23

Today, when I was walking by the madrassa *(Islamic school), one of the boys told me that if my brother keeps showing the "Jesus Film" that they're going to do something to him. I told Tapan this, but he just calmly replied, "God is protecting me. Every day that I am alive, it is because of His mercy, and if I am hurt or killed, it will be for His glory." God, I wish that I could just hold onto my brother and tell him that he must stay at home, or hide somewhere. But I know that is not what You want him to be doing. Please help me to be able to let him go.*

July 29

God, no! No, no, no, NO!! Men broke into Tapan's room. While Tapan and his friend Liplal were sleeping, they began to stab them over and over until they were practically hacked to death. As soon as we heard their cries, we tried to get into the room, but they had chained all of our doors and the neighbor's doors closed. We could do nothing but bang on our doors and listen to Tapan and Liplal's screams. One of the neighbors finally broke through their door and the murderers ran off. Someone got a car and we all piled in to drive them to the hospital, but—but it was too late.

October 26
Dear God, I have doubted You so much over these last few months. It has been so hard having Tapan gone. I want to blame You for his death. Sometimes I think to myself, "If only Tapan had not been a Christian, than he would not have been killed!" But then I think, "If Tapan had not been a Christian then he would have been dead in his sins. How much better is it that he was free from guilt and sin and now is alive in heaven." Yes, I know that is true. But often times a message is harder to cling to than the real, fleshly body of Tapan.

July 29
Dear God, One year ago today, Muslim men martyred my brother because he was a Christian. Because of that I have struggled with hatred, bitterness, and depression, but, I have also seen Your love, strength, and compassion. It would be easy to say, "I do not believe in the Christian God anymore," but it would not be better. I can honestly say that I have felt Your presence this year. You are not the God of easy answers, magical fixes, or painless lives, but You are the God Who meets us in the middle of it.[57]

Ask God to speak to you as you meditate on Psalm 23:4-5. Take this slowly, try not to rush through it. Think through each word and then try emphasizing different words in the passage. Write down the things He brings to your mind.

---

57   Retrieved from www.opendoorsusa.org

Alpha and Omega

Week 12

Day 1

Oh how we love You and are amazed by You, the Beginning and the End, the Alpha and Omega. How wonderful it is to think about how You have always existed and will continue to forever. Thinking about your eternal character helps us recognize that we, along with the nations of all time, are but a drop in a bucket. Our life is but a vapor, here for a little while and then gone. Help us see and delight in Your eternalness this week.

Page Jumpers

Read 1 Samuel 27:1-28:2
List things that jump off the page (verses that stand out to you):

-
-
-
-
-

Do you think David did these things out of reliance on God and having a proper view of Him, or do you think he got tired of fighting the good fight? Explain your reasoning.

In this chapter it seems David got tired of pressing on in fighting the good fight. Instead, he deceived Achish about his request for a city, the raids he was making, and the desire to fight the king's battles.

David led Achish to believe he was attacking cities and towns in Judah, when he was really raiding the towns and camps of the allies of Achish. "David was wiping out the people that Joshua and his successors failed to exterminate when they entered the land, following the orders given by Moses in Deuteronomy 20:16–18."[58]

Cloud of Witnesses

I just got a letter from my aunt and uncle. They send this letter out to friends and family recounting the year. This last year for them was not filled with wonderful rewards of their faithfulness to Jesus but rather full of pain and suffering. My aunt and uncle love Jesus so much and live lives of intimacy with him. I admire them greatly. This last summer we were having a conversation about the things we won't get to do in heaven, one of which is sharing the gospel and how important it is to do right now. My uncle said, "Ya know another thing we won't get to do in heaven is suffer." He actually used the words "get to do" in the same sentence as "suffer". Coming from him of all people, it was awe inspiring. About six years ago my aunt and uncle had a baby named Gabe. Gabe was ten pounds when he was born and had very broad shoulders, therefore on his journey out of the womb he got stuck which cut off his oxygen. He survived but now has cerebral palsy. Bruce and Brooklyn feed him with a feeding tube three times a day and have to do almost everything for him. This last year their daughter had a baby who arrived on the scene at twenty four weeks. The doctors did the best they could to keep the baby alive, but were not able to. Not long after their son got in a terrible car accident that almost took his life, shattering his skull and breaking many of his bones. In their letter they said they count it all joy because their hearts are set on heaven. They are filled with hope, knowing the pain and suffering is not all there is. It makes me think of the verse, Oh death, where is your sting? Brooklyn said, "It is my great honor and joy to serve my 8 year old son Gabriel, who endures great physical challenges secondary to cerebral palsy. His courageous and happy outlook on life is incredible. I am a better Christian, mother, and friend because of him"

This week we are going to look at heaven, Jesus' return, and reflect on whether we are ready.

Here am I

Our battles come from our flesh, the world and the enemy. Satan is the father of lies, the deceiver, the tempter, an accuser of Christians, the evil one, the arch traitor of God; he kills, steals, wants to destroy our testimony and tries to make us ineffective in our Christian life. Satan as a lion does for sick, young or straggling victims. When we are feeling alone, weak, helpless, and cut off from other believers and are so focused on our troubles that we forget to keep Christ on the throne, we are especially vulnerable to Satan's attacks, which, along with the world's and the flesh's attacks come in the form of lies. Satan deceives by misquoting Scripture, uses a mixture of lies and truth, and injects suspicion, intolerance, discouragement, doubt and so on. The world attacks us with lies telling us a different standard to measure up to rather than God's. Our flesh is deceitful above all things and also tries to get us to believe lies that will benefit itself.

"We are human, but we don't wage war as humans do. We use God's might weapons, not worldly weapons, to knock down the strongholds of human reasoning and to destroy false argument. We

---

58   Wiersbe, Warren (2007). *The Wiersbe Bible Commentary: Old Testament.* Colorado Springs, CO: David C. Cook

destroy every proud obstacle that keeps people from knowing God. We capture their rebellious thoughts and teach them to obey Christ" (2 Corinthians 10:3-5).

Our strength and ability to fight against the attack of lies only comes as we are surrendered to our Father. The only way to fight and win the battle to live the Christian life is by living in the power of the Holy Spirit (Christ on the throne). Walking with a surrendered lifestyle to the Holy Spirit is the empowerment, the source, and Ephesians 6:14-18 explains the tools that God has given us to defeat all lies.

"Stand firm then, with the belt of truth buckled around your waist, with the breastplate of righteousness in place, and with your feet fitted with the readiness that comes from the gospel of peace. In addition to all this, take up the shield of faith, with which you can extinguish all the flaming arrows of the evil one. Take the helmet of salvation and the sword of the Sprit, which is the word of God. And pray in the Spirit on all occasions with all kinds of prayers and request. With this in mind, be alert and always keep on praying for all the Lord's people" (Ephesians 6:14-18).

Brief overview of the tools God has given us:

The belt of truth- Knowing the truth of God and His Word and walking it out, resulting in living a life of integrity, honesty and sincerity.

>   *What does integrity, honesty and sincerity look like in action?

The breastplate of righteousness- Walking out the righteousness (right standing before God) that God has already declared us to be and, as a result, making right choices and disciplining ourselves to live out who God says we are.

>   *How can believers walk out their righteousness?

>   *How can someone prepare to share the gospel?

Shield of faith- Actively putting your trust in the Word of God. The ability to do this comes from "eating and exercising" (studying God's Word and applying it).

>   *What is an example of actively putting trust in Christ?

Helmet of Salvation- Putting our confidence in Jesus Christ and keeping Him on the throne, walking in the Spirit.

> *How do you get Christ on the throne? (If you are having a hard time remembering or putting it into words, look back at Week 2 Day 4. If you do remember, please check your answer)

Sword of the Spirit- This is God's Word. Knowing it, hoping in it and using it. Jesus gave us a perfect example of how to use this offensive weapon when Satan was feeding Him lies in Matthew 4.

> *What are some lies you've heard recently?

> *Using the above lies, evaluate your battle skills. What weapons did you use to fight against those lies? Which ones did you not use and perhaps need some sharpening?

Spend some talking to God about your preparedness for battle and ask Him to show you what action He wants you to take

Alpha and Omega

Week 12

Day 2

Lord of heaven and earth, give us hearts that yearn for the new earth You are preparing. Give us eyes to see and hearts to understand what You are preparing for us. Thank You for Your promise that You will reveal it to us. Thank You for Your incredible grace to show us the deep things of Your heart.

Eyes to See

Read 1 Samuel 28:3-25

> *Why do you speculate God did not answer Saul right then? (Look at Proverbs 1:28-31 and explain if you think it applies to Saul)

> *What things does this incident expose in Saul's heart?

> *God had outlawed consulting with mediums and spiritists (Leviticus 19:31, 20:6, 27, Deuteronomy 18:11) Why do you suppose He did that?

"When someone tells you to consult mediums and spiritists, who whisper and mutter, should not a people inquire of their God? Why consult the dead on behalf of the living? Consult God's instruction and the testimony of warning" (Isaiah 8:19-20).

> *Do some research using commentaries and other resources about this incident and write down your findings.

Unlike believers who immediately go to heaven and are in the presence of God when they die (2 Corinthians 5:8, Phil. 1:19-23), when an unbeliever dies, his spirit goes to a place called *Hades,* which means "the unseen world"—that is, the realm of the dead. Hades will one day be emptied of its dead (Revelation 20:13), who will then be cast into hell to join Satan, the beast, and the false prophet. The picture we see here of this supposed Samuel and the place he comes from looks like a better picture of Hades than heaven.

Ears to Hear

Austin told me of a time when he was in high school and a friend of his said he would rather have fun in hell than be bored in heaven. What other opinions or cultural ideas have you heard about heaven?

When you think of heaven, what do you think of? It is common for people to think of a place in the clouds where you sing all day long. Last week we looked at the hope that gets us through suffering. That hope is heaven. If we have a distorted or small view of it, it will probably make it pretty hard to look to as a source of hope.

"He opened his mouth to blaspheme God, and to slander His name and His dwelling place and those who live in heaven" (Revelation 13:6). Satan, the father of lies, wants to get us to believe lies not only about God, but also about heaven. If Christians aren't sure if they want to go there, how much more difficult it will be to encourage someone else to go there.

Maybe you have been told to not ask too many questions about what heaven will be like because "No eye has seen, no ear has heard, no mind has conceived what God has prepared for those who love Him" (1 Corinthians 2:9 NIV). But look at the very next verse "But God has revealed it to us by his Spirit. The Spirit searches all things, even the deep things of God" (vs. 10).

"Then I saw a new heaven and a new earth, for the first earth had passed away" (Revelation 21:1). If the word earth in this passage means anything, it means that we can expect to find earthly things there, including atmosphere, mountains, water, trees, people, houses, even buildings and streets. All of these features are mentioned in Revelation 21 and 22.

For each of the following verses describe what heaven is described as

Hebrews 11:10

When we hear the word city, we don't need to scratch our heads and think *I wonder what that means.* We understand cities. They have buildings, culture, arts, goods and services. They are filled with all kinds of events, people who are engaged in activities, gathering, conversations and work.

Hebrews 11:16

Countries have territories, rulers, national interests, pride in their identity, citizens who are diverse and unified.

1 Corinthians 15:42-43

Again when God speaks of our having bodies, we don't need to shrug and say "I just can't imagine what having a new body would be like". We've had bodies our entire lives and even longed for a better one. When Jesus was raised from the dead, H told His disciples, "Touch Me and see, a ghost does not have flesh and bones as you see I have" (Luke 24:38). The Bible has a lot to say about heaven, but we tend to overlook it. When we start to think about heaven in tangible terms, our desire for it grows. The more we desire it, the more we will be motivated to walk out the things God is calling us to do like Abraham's descendants who were longing for a better country, a heavenly one. (Hebrews 11:16) The earth as we know it now has been damaged by our sin and is now under a curse. You and I have never known a world without sin, suffering and death, yet we yearn for that very world.

> *What amazing things do you see that make you think that this world was meant to be your home?

> *What terrible things do you see that lead you to think this is not your home?

"Look! I am creating a new heavens and a new earth and no one will even think about the old ones anymore. Be glad; rejoice forever in My creation! And look! I will create Jerusalem as a place of happiness. Her people will be a source of joy. I will rejoice over Jerusalem and delight in My people. And the sound of weeping and crying will be heard in it no more. No longer will babies die when only a few days old... In those days people will live in the houses they build and eat the fruit of their own vineyards... They will not work in vain, and their children will not be doomed to misfortune... I will answer them before they even call to Me. While they are still talking about their needs, I will go ahead and answer their prayers! The wolf and the lamb will feed together. The lion will eat hay like a cow" (Isaiah 65:17-25). Do you get the sense like I do that God is pretty psyched about the new place and wants us to see it, understand it, long for it and enjoy it?

Randy Alcorn is the man who is leading the charge for expanding our view of heaven. He wrote a great book on heaven and even paints a clear picture of heaven in his fictions books that increases your desire for it.

Here are 21 brief observations he made about heaven from Revelation 6:9-11:

"When [the Lamb] opened the fifth seal, I saw under the altar the souls of those who had been slain because of the word of God and the testimony they had maintained. They called out in a loud voice, 'How long, Sovereign Lord, holy and true, until You judge the inhabitants of the earth and avenge our blood?' Then each of them was given a white robe, and they were told to wait a little longer, until the number of their fellow servants and brothers who were to be killed as they had been was completed" (Revelation 6:9-11).

1. When these people died on Earth, they relocated to Heaven (v. 9).

2. These people in Heaven were the same ones killed for Christ while on earth (v. 9). This demonstrates direct continuity between our identity on earth and our identity in heaven. The martyrs' personal history extends directly back to their lives on earth. Those in the intermediate heaven are not different people; they are the same people relocated—"righteous men made perfect" (Hebrews 12:23).

3. People in heaven will be remembered for their lives on earth. These were known and identified as ones slain "because of…the testimony they had maintained" (v. 9).

4. "They called out" (v. 10) means they are able to express themselves audibly. This could suggest they exist in physical form, with vocal cords or other tangible means to express themselves.

5. People in the intermediate heaven can raise their voices (v. 10). This indicates that they are rational, communicative, and emotional—even passionate—beings, like people on earth.

6. They called out in "a loud voice," not "loud voices." Individuals speaking with one voice indicate that heaven is a place of unity and shared perspective.

7. The martyrs are fully conscious, rational, and aware of each other, God, and the situation on earth.

8. They ask God to intervene on earth and to act on their behalf: "How long…until you judge the inhabitants of the earth and avenge our blood?"(v. 10).

9. Those in heaven are free to ask God questions, which means they have an audience with God. It also means they need to learn. In heaven, people desire understanding and pursue it.

10. People in the intermediate heaven know what's happening on earth (v. 10). The martyrs know enough to realize that those who killed them have not yet been judged.

11. Heaven dwellers have a deep concern for justice and retribution (v. 10). When we go to heaven, we won't adopt a passive disinterest in what happens on the earth. On the contrary, our concerns will be more passionate and our thirst for justice greater. Neither God nor we will be satisfied until His enemies are judged, our bodies raised, sin and Satan defeated, earth restored, and Christ exalted over all.

12. The martyrs clearly remember their lives on earth (v. 10). They remember at least some of the bad things from earth, since they even remember that they were murdered. (Heaven's joys are not rooted in ignorance, but perspective.)

13. The martyrs in heaven pray for judgment on their persecutors who are still at work hurting others. They are acting in solidarity with, and in effect interceding for, the suffering saints on earth. This suggests that saints in heaven are both seeing and praying for saints on earth.

14. Those in heaven see God's attributes ("Sovereign…holy and true") in a way that makes his judgment of sin more understandable.

15. Those in heaven are distinct individuals: "Then each of them was given a white robe" (v. 11). There isn't one merged identity (aka Nirvana) that obliterates uniqueness, but a distinct "each of them."

16. The martyrs' wearing white robes suggests the possibility of actual physical forms, because disembodied spirits presumably don't wear robes. The robes may well have symbolic meaning, but it doesn't mean they couldn't also be physical. The martyrs appear to have physical forms that John could actually see.

17. God answers their question (v. 11), indicating communication and process in heaven. It also demonstrates that we won't know everything in heaven—if we did, we would have no questions. The martyrs knew more after God answered their question than before they asked it. There is learning in the present heaven.

18. God promises to fulfill the martyrs' requests, but says they will have to "wait a little longer" (v. 11). Those in the intermediate heaven live in anticipation of the future fulfillment of God's promises. Unlike the eternal heaven—where there will be no more sin, curse, or suffering on the new Earth (Revelation 21:4)—the present heaven coexists with and watches over an earth under sin, the Curse, and suffering.

19. There is time in the intermediate heaven (vv. 10-11). The white-robed martyrs ask God a time-dependent question: "How long, Sovereign Lord…until You judge the inhabitants of the earth and avenge our blood?" (v. 10). They are aware of time's passing and are eager for the coming day of the Lord's judgment. God answers that they must "wait a little longer" until certain events transpire on earth. Waiting requires the passing of time. (This seems to refute the "no time in heaven/ instantaneous resurrection" theory, as well as soul sleep.)

20. The people of God in heaven have a strong familial connection with those on earth, who are called their "fellow servants and brothers" (v. 11). We share the same Father, "from Whom every family in heaven and on earth is named" (Ephesians 3:15, ESV). There is not a wall of separation within the bride of Christ. We are one family with those who've gone to heaven ahead of us. After we go to heaven, we'll still be one family with those yet on earth. These verses demonstrate a vital connection between the events and people in heaven and the events and people on earth.

21. Our sovereign God knows down to the last detail all that is happening and will happen on earth (v. 11), including every drop of blood shed and every bit of suffering undergone

by His children. Voice of the Martyrs estimates that more than 150,000 people die for Christ each year, an average of more than four hundred per day. God knows the name and story of each one.[59]

If the universe will be renewed and the heavens will be in existence, why would we not continue to explore them for all eternity, to the glory of God? If under the curse we landed on the moon, and have the capabilities to land on Mars, what would keep us from really seeing what is across our galaxy?

Heart to Understand

"Then I saw a new heaven and a new earth, for the first heaven and the first earth had passed away, and the sea was no more. And I saw the holy city, New Jerusalem, coming down out of heaven from God, prepared as a bride adorned for her husband. And I heard a loud voice from the throe saying, 'Behold, the dwelling place for God is with man. He will dwell with them, and they will be His people, and God Himself will be with them as their God. He will wipe away ever tear from their eyes, and death shall be no more, neither shall there be mourning, nor crying, nor pain anymore, for the former things have passed away.' ...Then came one of the serve angels how had the seven bowls full of the seven last plagues ad spoke to me, saying, 'Come, I will show you the Bride, the wife of the Lamb.' And he carried me away in the Spirit to a great, high mountain, and showed me the holy city Jerusalem coming down out of heaven from God, having the glory of God, its radiance like a most rare jewel, like jasper, clear as crystal... The wall was built of jasper, while the city was pure gold, clear as glass. The foundations of the wall of the city were adorned with every kind of jewel. The first was jasper, the second sapphire, the third agate, the fourth emerald, the fifth onyx, the sixth carnelian, the seventh chrysolite, the eighth beryl, the ninth topaz, the tenth chrysoprase, the eleventh jacinth, the twelfth amethyst. And the twelve gates were twelve pearls, each of the gates made of a single pearl, and the street of the city was pure gold, transparent as glass... Then the angel showed me the river of the water of life, bright as crystal, flowing from the throne of god ad of the Lamb through the middle of the street of the city; also, on either side of the river, the tree of life with its twelve kinds of fruit, yielding its fruit each month. The leaves of the tree were for the healing of the nations. No longer will there be anything accursed, but the throne of God and of the Lamb will be it, and His servants will worship him. They will see his face, and his name will be on their foreheads. And night will be no more. They will need no light of lamp or sun, for the Lord God will be their light, and they will reign forever and ever" (Revelation 21-22 TNIV).

Since this doesn't say "like" or "as," we know this city that will be brought down from heaven will be a literal Jerusalem. Jesus will come dwell on earth, the new earth, with man. Generally, when I read this I skip over the whole ruby, topaz, jasper stuff since I can't picture it. But, recently I was again reminded of how insufficient and uninspiring a view of heaven people have. Really, if our view of heaven is singing all the time or sitting in a church service or being alone on fluffy clouds, how can we set our hearts and minds on something and actually long for and greatly anticipate if it seems dull? Like 1 Corinthians 2:10 says, we can think about the reality of heaven and its awesome-ness because God's Spirit actually leads us into understanding. Awesome.

---

59 Randy Alcorn, Eternal Perspective Ministries, 39085 Pioneer Blvd., Suite 206, Sandy, OR 97055, 503-668-5200, www.epm.org, **www.randyalcorn.blogspot.com**, **www.facebook.com/randyalcorn**, **www.twitter.com/randyalcorn**

While thinking about these buildings. I was wondering, 'Why in the world would God have these details written down about architecture and not about any other part of the new earth culture?". But this is so cool! From what I can think of, everything that is created is made of the natural resources we have. But what if there were different natural resources, or maybe just a little different, better. What if someone used their gifts to glorify God by discovering out how to build things out of jasper and gold and other precious metals? So, instead of seeing the buildings we have now made out of steel, how beautiful would it be if the actual material the building was made out of was beautiful. Everything we make comes from our natural resources, cars, musical instruments, pictures, everything. So perhaps in describing the details of what the buildings are made of gives us a glimpse of everything else that is there. How beautiful heaven is going to be. Not only will the natural setting be beautiful but everything created by us will be beautiful. No cement! Woohoo. I bet the people in Russia are going to be thrilled.

*How has your picture of heaven changed today?

*Who can you share this with this week?

Alpha and Omega

Week 12

Day 3

Lord, You are so faithful and gracious to show us Your heart. Thank You for this time with You. What a privilege! This week would you enlarge our perspective of You and of Your dwelling place? Let us see Your glory and be taken with You. Soften us where we need softening and strengthen us where we strengthening.

Eyes to See

Read 1 Samuel 29-30

*From what you know of David, what do you think were his real intentions in this battle?

*Describe what you would be feeling if you were David's wife, Abigail. David has pretended to be part of the Philistine army for over a year now, the very army of Goliath that hated God so long ago and now are going to battle against your people. What would you be encouraging David to do?

*1 Samuel 30:6 says that David was greatly distressed because the men were talking of stoning him because they were so bitter. Who in this story do you sympathize with and why?

*Do a little comparison between David and the bitter men. What was the heart condition, what did it lead them to do, and what was the result? (Do you think the verse 22 guys are part of the bitter men?)

David-

Bitter men-

Someone once said bitterness is like drinking poison and expecting someone else to die.

*What do these chapters show you about God's character?

Ears to Hear

Our enemy, the devil is prowling around seeking someone to devour. He wants to destroy our lives the way the Amalekites burned and destroyed Ziklag, stealing the blessings God had given. But our Savior wants to redeem our past and save us from our future. He wants to establish a new place where the enemy cannot destroy and steal, a place where there is no bitterness, envy, jealousy and fighting with people that are on your same side. The beautiful scroll talked about in Revelation 5 is the way this will be established.

Read Revelation 5 and focus on the scroll. John is in heaven, seeing a scroll sealed with 7 seals. He sees an angel proclaiming, "Who is worthy to break the seals and open the scroll?" John cries because there is no one who can open the scroll, but then an elder tells him he doesn't need to cry because Jesus is worthy. Our sacrificial Lamb is worthy to open the scroll. I don't know about you, but this got me saying, *"What in the world is on that scroll? Why in the world is it so traumatic if it is not opened? Why do the 7 seals (the beginning of the tribulation) have to be broken in order to read it?"* Whatever is on that scroll causes the angels to fall down before Christ because of His worthiness to open it saying, "You are worthy to take the scroll and to open its seals, because You were slain, and with Your blood You purchased for God members of every tribe and language and people and nation. You have made them to be a kingdom and priests to serve our God, and they will reign on the earth" (Revelation 5:9-10 TNIV).

On a side note, the seals are broken and 7th seal is when our prayers are poured on the altar and then the censer hurled at the earth bringing a crazy earthquake. Sometimes I think it takes forever for God to answer some of my prayers. I have only been alive for a very short amount of time compared to the grand scheme of things. Night and day people have been praying the same things as me for generations and generations-for God to reveal Himself as Judge and King. The angels have seen people praying this for generations and generations. They see that He "Is not slow concerning His promise toward us but patient, not willing that any should perish" (2 Peter 3:9). What a day that will be when everyone's prayers will be fulfilled. It motivates me to pray more, to be among those whose prayers are an offering and powerfully come into reality.

Renald Showers who is widely recognized as one of the most distinguished theologians in America today talks for a long time about significant principles that were involved in God's land redemption program for Israel under the Mosaic Law. Read what he says about the meaning of the scroll.

"It seems apparent that the sealed scroll Christ took from the right hand of God in heaven (Revelation 5) is the deed of purchase for mankind's tenant possession or administration of the earth. He will thereby assert His right to recover mankind's forfeited inheritance. He declared that Christ will do this amidst demonstrations of judgment, affecting every department of nature, as though to shake it from the enemy's grasp.

The unique, eternal God created the universe for His own benefit and sovereign purpose; therefore, only He has the right to rule the entire universe, and that right includes the right to crush any enemy who challenges His rule. God gave mankind tenant possession of the earth as an inheritance with the intention that mankind function as God's representative, administering God's rule over the earth in accordance with His will. This was a theocratic arrangement. Mankind forfeited their tenant possession of the earth by following Satan's lead and rebelling against God. As a result, the theocracy was lost. Satan usurped the tenant possession of the earth and has continued to rule the world system ever since mankind's fall.

God purposed to restore the theocracy, which would require the redemption of mankind's forfeited inheritance. To do so, God sent His Son, Jesus Christ, into the world to become a man so that, as a kinsman, He could redeem mankind's tenant possession of the earth. Christ paid the redemption price for mankind and their inheritance by shedding His blood on the cross, thereby fulfilling the first responsibility of the Kinsman-Redeemer. When Christ paid the redemption price, a scroll deed of purchase for mankind's tenant possession of the earth was prepared, sealed with seven seals (to guarantee its security against change, so that it could serve as irrefutable evidence in the future), and placed in a safe location-God's right hand.

Seven years before His coming to the earth, Christ will take the sealed scroll deed of purchase from God's hand in preparation for the fulfillment of the second responsibility of the Kinsman-Redeemer-the eviction of Satan and his forces and the taking of the earth's tenant possession. In order to give refutable evidence of His right as the Kinsman-Redeemer, Christ will take the scroll, break its seals, open it, and read it. As He breaks the seven seals, Christ will instigate a tremendous seven year bombardment of divine wrath or judgment against the domain of Satan and his forces in preparation for His coming invasion to evict these enemies. This seven-year bombardment is described in Revelation 6-18. Through this bombardment Christ will prove that He has the power and authority to fulfill the second responsibility of the Kinsman-Redeemer. After Christ has read the scroll deed, He will evict Satan and his forces from the earth (Revelation 19:20-20:3). Then He will take tenant possession of the earth and, together with redeemed mankind, will rule the earth in accordance with God's will as the last Adam, God's representative, for a thousand years."[60]

No wonder John would weep and the angels would fall down and worship when Jesus took the scroll. He is the only hope for our earth and life to be restored and redeemed.

*Does this expand your view of the cross? How?

---

60   Showers, Renald (1995). *Maranatha -- Our Lord, Come!: A Definitive Study of the Rapture of the Church* Bellmawr, NJ; The Friends of Israel Gospel Ministry, Inc.

Jesus tells us there will be specific events will proceed His coming to redeem and restore the earth and everything in it; those events prior to His return are known as the Tribulation. I won't talk a lot about it but I just can't resist telling you how Jesus has and will fulfill the Jewish feasts that were set up to showcase His story. The Jewish feasts are celebrations, holidays, to help parents communicate to their children in a clear and dramatic way Who God is and what He can do. The Hebrew word translated "feasts" means *appointed times*. "The idea is that the sequence and timing of each of these feasts has been carefully orchestrated by God Himself. Each is part of a comprehensive whole. Collectively, they tell a story."[61] There are seven feasts outlined in Leviticus 23 that are called "the feasts of the Lord". Four of the seven holidays occur in the spring of the year and have been fulfilled by Jesus' first coming. The final three feasts occur in the fall and depict specific events associated with His second coming. The beauty of these feasts is the clear symbolism that points to Jesus and the fact that each of the first four holidays occurred on the exact day of the feast celebration! Wow, God's timing truly is perfect! Here is a brief overview of each feast:

1. **Passover**

    The Messiah was crucified on Passover as our Passover Lamb. This feast is celebrated with food where each item specifically points to Christ and how He took the wrath of the Father on Himself so we would have a way to be forgiven for not being perfect.

2. **The Feast of Unleavened Bread**

    God appointed this holiday to occur the day after Passover and to last seven days. On the first and the seventh day the people gather together to meet with God and present an offering to Him. This week was to be a time of remembering of how God brought the Israelites out of slavery and of cleansing from sin that so easily entangles. This is the feast that was being celebrated at the time that Hannah prayed and is also the feast that was being celebrated when the angel led Peter out of prison.

3. **The Feast of Firstfruits**

    This feast occurs on the second day of the feast of Unleavened Bread. Before Christ it pointed to the resurrection and reminds us that death could not hold Jesus as He triumphantly rose from the dead. In celebrating the resurrection of Jesus we are celebrating Him as our firstfruit Who enables, frees and motivates us to look forward to the new earth and our being fully redeemed. What a great hope Jesus has given us! He beat death and is coming again to claim the earth as His own, to destroy everything raised up against Him, and to redeem the earth and His people fully.

4. **The Feast of Weeks (Shavout)**

    This holiday is celebrated seven weeks from Firstfruits. This feast is also called Pentecost. No wonder Jesus told the disciples to wait for the Holy Spirit; He was going to give them His gift of the Holy Spirit on this holiday. "In celebrating the feast of weeks, two loaves were brought to the Temple. They represented Jew and Gentile, now one in the Messiah with the coming of the Holy Spirit."[62]

---

61 Howard, Kevin and Rosenthal, Marvin (1997), *The Feasts of the Lord*. Nashville, TN: Thomas Nelson Inc.

62 Howard, Kevin and Rosenthal, Marvin (1997), *The Feasts of the Lord*. Nashville, TN: Thomas Nelson Inc.

5. **The Feast of Trumpets (Rosh Hashanah)**

This first day of the New Year is a one day holiday celebrated as a day of rest commemorated with blowing trumpets and offering sacrifices to God. The only observance of this feast is recorded in Ezra 3:1-6 when the temple was rebuilt and the sacrifices were reinstituted. Nehemiah 7:73-8:13 tells us that revival took place in Israel as God's word was read to the people during this feast. 1 Corinthians 15:51-52 and 1 Thessalonians 4:16-17 both tell us that believers will be caught up in the clouds to meet the Lord when the trumpet is blown.

6. **The Day of Atonement (Yom Kippur)**

Kippur is from the Hebrew word kaphar meaning "to cover." On Yom Kippur, atonement was made for the previous year's sins through the shedding of an innocent animals blood. This was a day devoted to fasting and repenting. Yom Kippur points to Jesus' future work in the nation of Israel in recognizing Him as Messiah and bringing them to repentance.

7. **The Feast of Tabernacles (Sukkot)**

This was the last feast given by the Lord. It is most festive and joyous holiday for it celebrates the Messiah coming to dwell with men. It is celebrated by building booths or huts to live in for a week. It was also a reminder of God's past provision during the forty years they were in the wilderness. It is celebrated five days after the Day of Atonement and there are is to be no working on days 1 and 8 of the week-long celebration. During the festival there were to be daily sacrifices and the law was to be read. Tabernacles was one of the pilgrimage feasts, meaning that people from all over were to travel to Jerusalem and "not appear before the Lord empty-handed" (Deuteronomy 16:16) It was at the feast of Tabernacles that the glory of the Lord appeared as Solomon dedicated the newly built Temple to the Lord and filled the Holy of Holies. What a great picture of the final act of God in the story of redemption of mankind. The King coming down to make His dwelling with man.

Heart to Understand

"For the Lord Himself will come down from heaven, with a loud command, with the voice of the archangel and with the trumpet call of God, and the dead in Christ will rise first. After that, we who are still alive and are left will be caught up together with them in the clouds to meet the Lord in the air. And so we will be with the Lord forever. **Therefore encourage one another with these words**. Now, brothers and sisters, about times and dates we do not need to write you, for you know very well that the day of the Lord will come like a thief in the night. While people are saying, "Peace and safety," destruction will come on them suddenly, as labor pains or a pregnant woman, and they will not escape. **But you, brothers and sisters, are not in darkness so that this day should surprise you like a thief"** (1 Thessalonians 4:16-5:4 TNIV).

Many times when people talk about the very last days, they say that the Lord will come like a thief in the night and therefore we shouldn't think about such things. But Paul tells us that as believers we should be thinking and talking about it, dreaming about it, planning for it. Though we will not know the day or the hour, we will know the season. (Matt. 24:32-34)

Read 1 Peter 1:3-14

> *What were the prophets intently trying to learn about? What thoughts does that lead you to think?

> *What stands out to you about these verses?

Read 2 Peter 3:11-14

> *What is emphasized over and over? Why?

> *How does God want us to live in light of His return?

> *Practically what would your above answer look like in your life?

"By setting our focus on that day, we can remember the importance of living according to God's agenda instead of ours. William McDonald said, "The only way to have a successful life is to project yourself forward to that glorious time, decide what will be really important then, and then go after that with all your strength."[63]

63 *A passion for the great commission.* Retrieved from www.frontlinemin.org

Alpha and Omega

Week 12

Day 4

Lord, we really want to live in a way that pleases You and brings about the most fruit for Your kingdom and glory for Your name. Would You continue to refine us like gold and cause us to see You more clearly and our sin more clearly that we would be able to surrender more and reflect You more. We long to hear from You today. Here we are, at Your feet; speak for Your servants are listening.

Eyes to See

Read the last chapter of 1 Samuel, chapter 31.

>   *As you read verse 7, put yourself in these people's shoes. What would you be thinking and feeling?

>   *As you read verses 2-6, put yourself in Saul's shoes. What would you be thinking and feeling?

>   *Now put yourself in Saul's armor-bearers shoes and describe your thoughts and feelings.

*Read Revelation 19:11-21. Picture yourself in the army following Jesus. Describe your thoughts and feelings.

*Are you living your life right now with thoughts and feelings more like that of Saul's people, Saul, Saul's armor-bearer or the army of Jesus? Explain your answer.

Ears to Hear

"Satan came to steal, kill, and destroy; and since he can't destroy you, [Christians] he will discourage you, take away your courage. If he can't discourage you, he'll distract you!"[64] Therefore, "Our greatest fear as individuals and as a church should not be of failure but of succeeding at the things in life that don't really matter,"[65] because, like G.K. Chesterton says, "Meaninglessness doesn't come from being weary with pain; meaninglessness comes from being weary with pleasure."

One second before you die, if you could look back over your life, would you be satisfied with what you did with it? Here are the three most common things people at age 95 people say they would change about their lives, if they could:

1. They would have risked more

2. They would have reflected more

3. They would have done more that outlived them.

    *If you were to answer that question right now about your life, would you agree with any of the above answers?

A.W. Tozer said that "The reason why many are still troubled, still seeking making little forward progress is because they haven't yet come to the end of themselves. We're still trying to give orders, and interfering with God's work within us." Surrender is not passive resignation, fatalism or an excuse for laziness. It is not accepting the status quo, giving up rational thinking or repressing your personality. God wants to use your unique personality for investing in eternity!

Fully surrendering to God is best demonstrated in obedience. Everybody eventually surrenders to something or someone. If not to God, you will surrender to the opinions or expectations of others, to money, resentment, fear or your own pride, lusts or ego. The greatest hindrance to God's blessing in your life is not others; it is yourself, your self-will, stubborn pride, and personal

---

64 Comfort, Ray (1989). *Hell's Best Kept Secret*. New Kensington, PA: Anchor Distributors.

65 Chan, Francis (2008). *Crazy Love: Overwhelmed by a Relentless God*. Colorado Springs, CO; David C. Cook.

ambition. You cannot fulfill God's purposes for your life while focusing on your own plans. We are called to live as investors in eternity. Your task if you choose to accept it and continue to walk in it, is to actively love God by surrendering your life to a life of obedience, investing in eternity through evangelism and discipleship. Your Christian life will never be an exciting adventure unless you are actively willing to get out on a limb of faith and humbly watch God fulfill His promises to guide, protect, and use you in His kingdom expansion efforts. In response to His love, work as though it is all up to you, but trust knowing that it really is all up to Him. Make a great commitment to the Great Commandment and the Great Commission and then at the age of 95 (or however long you have left) look back and see you had a life that was full and satisfying, that you risked all that you had for His glory, and that you did things that outlived you having an impact on eternity.

Saul did not finish strong, he did not discipline himself and make his flesh his slave, but rather was disqualified from the race (1 Corinthians 9:27) Oh, the joy of not suffering the fate of Saul but being able to say at the end of our lives, "I have fought the good fight, I have finished the race, and I have remained faithful. And now the prize awaits me-the crown of righteousness, which the Lord, the righteous Judge, will give me on that day of His return. And the prize is not just for me but for all who eagerly look forward to His appearing" (2 Timothy 4:7-8).

Heart to Understand

Revelation 2-3 can help us get a pulse on where our hearts are as compared to where they need to be to be prepared for our King to come and establish His throne on earth. As you read each of these descriptions of the churches, underline the things that are characteristic of your life. Ask the Lord to give you clarity to see what is true about your life, not what you would like it to be; to see accurately, not higher or lower.

Ephesus
The Ephesus church was independent. They endured hardship and persevered and brought truth where there were lies. But they were not walking with God. They did these things in their own strength. They tried hard to be good Christians, but by their own will power and therefore lost intimacy with God.

Smyrna
This church is worthy of praise. They would not give in to what the world wanted them to do and suffered for it. They lost jobs because they had been discriminated against because they would not deny Christ and what His Word said was true. They were slandered. Jesus commended them and told them not to be afraid.

Pergamum
This church was without backbone. They would not deny Christ verbally, but they compromised their actions to avoid what people would think of them and do to them. They would not take a stand for what was right and true.

Thyatira
This corrupted church did many good deeds but they tolerated people teaching and believing things about God that were not true, and they did not stand up against sin.

Sardis

This deceived church had a reputation not based in reality. They gloried in the past, of how much God had done through them in the past, but ignored the reality that they were doing nothing today. They were not engaged in the battle. They had no doctrinal problems but there was also no persecution because they were not invading the Enemy's territory.

Philadelphia

The people of the Philadelphia church were faithful and much like the people in Smyrna, were willing to suffer for doing what is right and true. But they also had a vision to reach the lost. They were not large and did not have a wealth of resources, but Jesus promised to take care of their enemies for them and to honor them.

Laodicea

The Laodicea church was foolish and arrogant. They depended on money and lacked intimacy with God which kept them from seeing things as they really were.

2 Corinthians 5:10 and 1 Corinthians 3:10-15 talk about the bema seat judgment. This is where Christians will be rewarded for what they did on earth with the things God gave them to steward: time, talent and treasure. Are you ready for Christ's return? Are you right with God, willing to hold nothing back from Him? Are you using what He has given you to the best of your ability with the strength He gives you?

Spend some time talking to Him about all this.

Alpha & Omega

Week 12

Day 5

Alpha and Omega, what a joy to worship a God who is the Beginning and the End. The author of it all. We love Your bigness. We love that thinking about You and Your greatness baffles our minds. You are such a great God and we love You!

Reflecting on the week:

Write down the things that stood out to you and the things the Lord was speaking to you about. Is there a theme? Talk to Him about what next steps He wants you to take and then spend some time writing down and praising Him for Who He is and what He has done.

Read Psalm 136. Write your own Psalm 136 with the things you recorded above.

Afterword

I hope that you have beheld your King and have had the great privilege of seeing Him transform your life through your sacrificial steps of faith. Each of the topics covered in this study are essential for living a missional life, a life lived on purpose for God's glory. My hope is that it will not stop here but that through the enablement of the Holy Spirit, you will continue to take steps of faith, big and small for the purpose of knowing God and making Him known.

A final step of faith in this study that I believe will be helpful to you for living out your purpose is to prayerfully plan out, write out and live out a strategic plan. A strategic plan is a simple plan of action of how you are going to walk out the mission that God has given you. It helps you evaluate the resources God has given you and think through what you will need and the steps you will have to take in order to look back on your life and say it was well invested for God's glory.

I will show you my personal strategic plan as an example. Then will have you practice developing one using Amber's story we read about in Week 10, Day 3. And then you will write your own.

Laura's Personal Ministry Strategic Plan

#2 Situational Analysis: (Your INVEST acronym summed up)
Teaching (speaking and writing), discipling, leading, organizing and raising up and sending out young missionaries for God's glory.

Values:
→ Living and sharing the Spirit-filled life
→ Effectiveness and focus toward purpose
→ Standing up for what's right and true.
→ Risking life for Christ-living with eternal perspective.
→ Daily time with the Lord
→ Day of rest

#3 Critical Mass: (what is required to see my mission and vision fulfilled)
Time spent with the Lord, time spent with college girls-sharing my faith and discipling them, talking about the spirit-filled life often with them, helping them spend time with the Lord and live the G.C.

#1 Direction:
Purpose: *To glorify God, to know God and make Him known.*
Mission: *To make multiplying disciples through the process of evangelism and discipleship.*
Vision: *I desire to see a vast number of college women raised up in Christ and sent out as laborers to make Jesus known, and I long for the day I get to see the spiritual multiplication God brought about as a result.*

#4 Critical Path Steps: (the absolute and essential things I must do to move toward fulfilling my vision and mission)

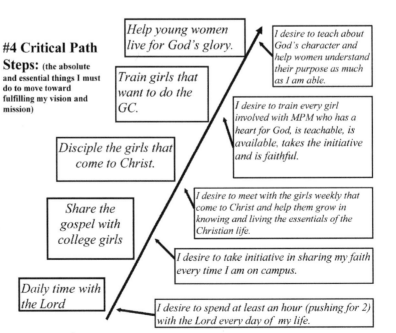

Help young women live for God's glory.

Train girls that want to do the GC.

Disciple the girls that come to Christ.

Share the gospel with college girls

Daily time with the Lord

I desire to teach about God's character and help women understand their purpose as much as I am able.

I desire to train every girl involved with MPM who has a heart for God, is teachable, is available, takes the initiative and is faithful.

I desire to meet with the girls weekly that come to Christ and help them grow in knowing and living the essentials of the Christian life.

I desire to take initiative in sharing my faith every time I am on campus.

I desire to spend at least an hour (pushing for 2) with the Lord every day of my life.

Reread Amber's story on Week 10, Day 3. Below plot what you think her strategic plan could have been.

Amber's Strategic Plan

#2 Situational Analysis: (what were some of her strengths and weaknesses?)

#1 Direction:
Purpose: *To glorify God, to know God and make Him known.*
Mission: *To make multiplying disciples through the process of evangelism and discipleship.*
Vision:

Values:

#4 Critical Path Steps: (the absolute and essential things she did to move toward fulfilling her vision and mission)

#3 Critical Mass: (what is required to see the mission fulfilled)

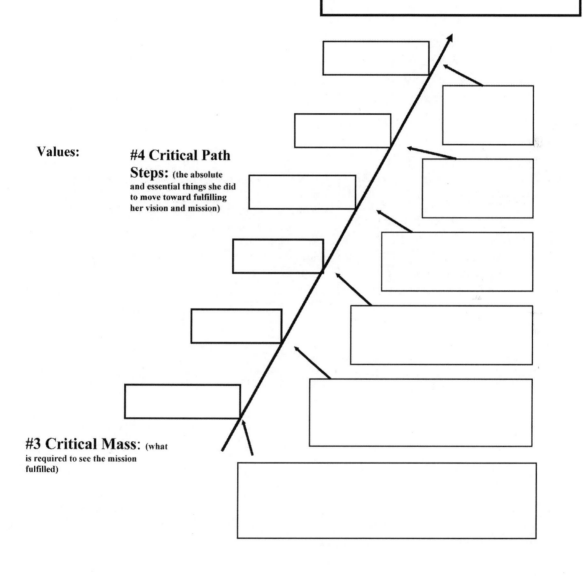

Look back at Week 10, Day 3. Write down what you wrote for your Vision-where your Current Reality, Uniqueness and Mission align.

Write down how you answered the question "How can you use your uniqueness to carry out the mission Jesus gave you of making multiplying disciples through the process of evangelism and discipleship in your sphere of influence?"

Taking these two statements, mesh them together in a sentence describe what this would look like if you could take a picture of it. Write this statement as your Vision in the Direction box below. Then fill in the rest following the numbers. Use the boxes on the right side of the arrow to write down some specific goals for each of your critical path steps.

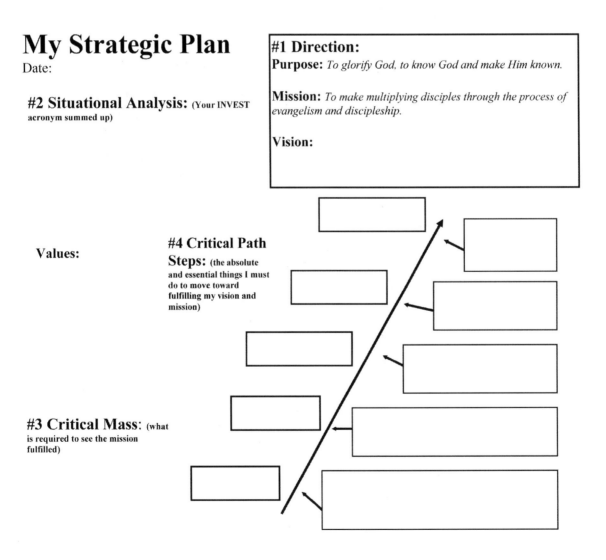

My Strategic Plan
Date:

#2 Situational Analysis: (Your INVEST acronym summed up)

#1 Direction:
Purpose: *To glorify God, to know God and make Him known.*

Mission: *To make multiplying disciples through the process of evangelism and discipleship.*

Vision:

Values:

#4 Critical Path Steps: (the absolute and essential things I must do to move toward fulfilling my vision and mission)

#3 Critical Mass: (what is required to see the mission fulfilled)

Small Group Discussion Questions

Week 1

Pursuing

· What encouraged you the most this week? Why?

· What challenged you the most this week? Why?

· What did God use to speak to you?

· In your prayer life, to what extent do you share your heart with the Lord?

· What fears produce resistance to letting Jesus know your deep longings?

· How did God lead you to respond to Him this week?

· Discuss your thoughts on God saying "No" to something you asked Him for after you vulnerably took your heart to Him.

· In your individual prayer experience, you found a photo and thought of how God had shown Himself in your life through that photo. Please show or describe the photo you chose with the group.

· Spend some time praying together as a group, starting with a significant time of praising Him for who He is, (it may help to praise Him using Scripture), followed by a time of thanking Him for the things and people He has put in your life.

Week 2

Empowering

· What encouraged you the most this week? Why?

· What challenged you the most this week? Why?

· What did God use to speak to you?

· What are your thoughts and feelings about the first story under Ears to Hear under Day 2?

· Do you tend to think you are far worse than you'd imagined, or not that bad?

· Generally, in what types of situations do you tend to depend on the Holy Spirit's help? Why? Why not other situations?

· What specifically keeps you from turning to the Lord in dependence on His ability instead of your own strength? Why?

- Is there a brave enough person in the group to draw out the three circles diagram like the "Spirit-filled Life" video on the website? If not, please watch the video as a group online.

Week 3

Intimate

- What encouraged you the most this week? Why?
- What challenged you the most this week? Why?
- What did God use to speak to you?
- How confident are you in hearing God's voice and why?
- Would you describe your relationship with God as intimate? Why or why not?
- Aside from what you know about God, do you have examples of times you have experienced Him in a personal way? Please share one.
- Discuss the role of God's Word in light of making decisions.
- What do you think are the most common reasons for not spending time in God's Word on a regular basis? Which one(s) do you most relate with?

  Here's what I think would top the list.

  1. Not enough time.

  2. I don't get anything out of it. I don't want to.

  3. Intimidation. I don't know what to read.

     *What did you write down as the lie and truth of each of these?

- If you don't already spend chunks of time in Scripture on a regular basis, what would intrinsically motivate and keep you motivated to feast on God's Word in a regular way? Are there steps you should take toward this?
- How did God reveal Himself to you this week?

Week 4

Holy

- What encouraged you the most this week? Why?
- What challenged you the most this week? Why?
- What did God use to speak to you?
- Why do you think it is a common misunderstanding that God is more holy and just in the Old Testament and not so much in the New Testament?
- What would happen in your life if you didn't believe God really was holy and will always act completely just?

- What would happen if you didn't believe your sin was really that bad and nothing really needed to be done about it?
- Since the time you made the decision to admit your guilt before God and receive His forgiveness, how has your view of God's holiness changed? How has your view of your own inadequacies changed?
- How has reflecting on God's holiness influenced your relationship with God?

Week 5

Gracious

- What encouraged you the most this week? Why?
- What challenged you the most this week? Why?
- What did God use to speak to you?
- This week take the rest of your time together to pray for each person in the group individually. Have them share specific concerns they would like prayer for and then go around the circle, having each person pray for her ending by sharing an identity truth (or a few) with her from page 91-94.

Week 6

El Shaddai

- What encouraged you the most this week? Why?
- What challenged you the most this week? Why?
- What did God use to speak to you?
- Look back and share your answers on page 99 to the questions, "Think of scenarios in the Bible where God spoke; what was the action that followed?" and "What emotions were aroused in you as you thought about this?"
- Look back and share your answers on page 101 to the questions, "What are some fears and hesitations you may have about being called and commissioned?" and "How can you actively trust God with these fears and hesitations?"
- World Christian Roles:
  1. The Goers. The frontline warriors.
  2. The Senders. The financial rope holders.
  3. The Welcomers. Ministers of hospitality-ministering to the world from your own country (international students)
  4. The Mobilizers. The strategic motivators.

  Which of these gets you excited? Why?

- Describe your experience with short term mission's trips. Discuss the value of short-term mission's trips and how they relate to the World Christian Roles. Discuss upcoming mission's opportunities.

Week 7

Revealing

- What encouraged you the most this week? Why?
- What challenged you the most this week? Why?
- What did God use to speak to you?
- Share your Page Jumpers from Day 1.
- This will take some time, but will be well worth it in developing deeper relationships with each other. Share your INVEST answers from Day 2.
- Describe yourself in terms of what it takes to stop you and what it takes to get you going.
- What are the things that are going to keep you from continually taking steps in active faith to pursue your passion for displaying God's character?
- Share what you wrote down for the question, "What are some specific, realistic, measurable, with an end-in-sight goal you can make related to what God has been putting on your heart?"
- Using a 3x5 card, write down the answers to the two questions above for the person on your right and pray for them about these things throughout the next week.

Week 8

Emmanuel

- Take some time to review the chapter.
- What encouraged you the most this week? Why?
- What challenged you the most this week? Why?
- What did God use to speak to you?
- "Impossible situations have a way of giving God a chance to shine." Describe a time when you saw this happen in your life. (You may want to share something you wrote down from the Here Am I section on Day 1.)
- What did you write down for your answers to the questions, "Who have you allowed to be a Samuel in your life who can call you out on sin?" and "Who would you like to give permission to be a Samuel in your life?" on page 130.
- Go through each question of Day 4 together sharing your answers.

Week 9

Victorious

- What encouraged you the most this week? Why?
- What challenged you the most this week? Why?
- What did God use to speak to you?
- What story from Day 1 struck you or encouraged you the most?
- What risks have you taken to display God's heart and passion?
- At age 95, what do you suppose you would have wished you risked more of?
- What fears keep you from action?
- Discuss some of the questions under Eyes to See on Day 2.
- What sound barrier is hardest for you to break? What question could you use to help you break through it?
- Share your answers from the questions on Day 5.

Week 10

Elohim

- What encouraged you the most this week? Why?
- What challenged you the most this week? Why?
- What did God use to speak to you?
- How has your view of suffering been encouraged or challenged?
- How did you answer the question, "How can you use your uniqueness to carry out the mission Jesus gave you of making multiplying disciples through the process of evangelism and discipleship in your sphere of influence?"
- Share some of your answers under Strategizing on Day 3 with each other.
- How has your view of fellowship changed?
- Share the thoughts you wrote down from Day 5 with each other.

Week 11

I AM

- What encouraged you the most this week? Why?
- What challenged you the most this week? Why?
- What did God use to speak to you?
- Share your answers from Day 2 under Eyes to See with each other.

- Share your answers from Day 3 under Eyes to See with each other.

- Describe a few instances you have seen of someone honoring someone else and the effects it had.

- Who in your life has a consistent track record of honoring people? What opportunities do they use to honor people?

- How are you at honoring people? What aspects of it do you find hard? What do you find easy?

- What is something you can start doing this week to help you make honoring others a habit in your life?

- Looking back at Day 4 Ears to Hear, share your thoughts about martyrdom.

- Share your answers from Day 4 under Heart to Understand.

Week 12

Alpha and Omega

- What encouraged you the most this week? Why?

- What challenged you the most this week? Why?

- What did God use to speak to you?

- How has your view of heaven changed after this week's study? How does that affect your emotions and eternal perspective?

- What are some things you look forward to seeing, feeling or doing in heaven?

- Share your answers from Day 3 under Heart to Understand.

- Share your answers from Day 4 under Eyes to See with each other.

- Share your reflections from the week on Day 5.

- Share your Strategic Plan with the group under the Afterward.